CATALOGUE OF
THE RARE ASTRONOMICAL BOOKS
IN THE SAN DIEGO STATE
UNIVERSITY LIBRARY

Isaacus Newton Eq: Aur.

G. Kneller Eques pinx.   J. Smith Fecit et ex. 1712.

CATALOGUE OF THE RARE ASTRONOMICAL BOOKS

IN THE

SAN DIEGO STATE UNIVERSITY LIBRARY

by
Louis A. Kenney

Introduction by
Owen Gingerich

Friends of the
Malcolm A. Love Library
San Diego State University
1988

Also distributed by
University of Washington Press
P.O. Box 50096
Seattle, Washington 98145-5096
ISBN: 0–295–96801–X

FRONTISPIECE: *Sir Isaac Newton (1642–1727)*.
Portrait engraved by John Smith (1652?–1742).
Ernst Zinner Collection of Portraits of Scientists,
San Diego State University Library.

CONTENTS

PREFACE

In late 1966, when San Diego State University was expanding rapidly, that great antiquarian bookseller Jacob Zeitlin (1902–87) asked me if the library might be interested in a private collection on the history of astronomy. The owner, Dr. Ernst Zinner (1886–1970), was one of the great elder scholars of the history of astronomy and had long been a professor of astronomy at the University of Munich and director of the Remeis Astronomical Observatory at Bamberg, West Germany. Dr. Zinner feared the Russians would buy his collection and take it to the Soviet Union. He preferred to see it sold to an American university.

With the help of a contribution from the newly formed Friends of the Malcolm A. Love Library and Jake's masterful coordinating skills, the library purchased the collection from Dr. Zinner. The books, packed in a large wooden crate the size of an upright piano, arrived from his home in Bamberg in February 1967. It contained over five thousand items, more than half of them books; some of its riches remain to be fully catalogued. In a letter that he wrote to me on March 24, 1967, Dr. Zinner said, "It was through great personal effort that I assembled those books. If they are appreciated now in San Diego, I am happy."

Over the next two decades Zeitlin and other rare book dealers added to the collection's strengths by offering rare early astronomical works to the Friends of the Library. These works may be identified by the absence of the words "Zinner Collection" in the annotation. Included among those acquisitions have been several incunabula and a substantial number of sixteenth- and seventeenth-century imprints.

From the time the Zinner Collection arrived, members of the Board of the Friends of the Library and others have expressed the need to make its holdings known. They wanted a beautiful book, one that would please the eye of the bibliophile and be useful to scholars. Although I had thought someone specializing in astronomy or in the history of science should prepare this catalogue, Board members persuaded me to undertake the task.

I express gratitude to all who contributed to the preparation of this book. Special thanks go to Dr. Owen Gingerich for his advice, but most of all for his introductory essay. I acknowledge with thanks Helen Marcy Johnson for her support and unflagging encouragement.

Thanks are also due the members of the Friends of the Library, its board, and Special Collections Librarian Ruth E. Leerhoff. I want to thank Dr. Robert S. Westman, Professor of the History of

Science at the University of California, Los Angeles, who reviewed the manuscript. He recommended adding more biographical information about the authors and other improvements requiring additional research. Finally to be thanked is Clay K. Perkins for the meticulous care he took in reading the galley proof. His genuine interest and scholarly attention to detail strengthened the authoritativeness of this catalogue.

The Friends intend to publish other catalogues of books in the San Diego State University Library including rare herbals and early botanical works, portraits of scientists in the Zinner Collection, the Calvert E. Norland Collection, rare florals in the Wormser Collection, Sir John Hill's works, and orchid books in the Reginald Davis Collection.

Louis A. Kenney
University Librarian Emeritus
San Diego State University

THOUGHTS ON THE ZINNER COLLECTION AT SAN DIEGO STATE UNIVERSITY

Owen Gingerich
Harvard-Smithsonian Center
for Astrophysics

Many years ago, when I was a young instructor at Harvard, a very clever undergraduate occasionally came to baby-sit for us. One evening I asked her why she had chosen Harvard, and she described how impressed she had been, upon first seeing the course catalogue, by all the foreign languages offered. "And," I asked, "how many language classes have you taken?" "None," was her candid reply.

Such is the elusive fabric from which reputation and mystique are born! Few may take advantage of such an opportunity, but just knowing it is there creates a sense of quality and helps put a place on the map. For some of us, what puts San Diego State University on the map is the Zinner Collection in the Malcolm A. Love Library.

Fifteen years ago, when I was preparing the entry on Erasmus Reinhold for what has now become a standard reference tool, the multivolume *Dictionary of Scientific Biography*, I found a reference to the *Weihnachtsbüchlein* of 1908 from Saalfeld, a town in East Germany. This "Little Christmas Book," an ephemeral offering from Reinhold's home town, is not listed in the *National Union Catalog*, nor was it available in the largest library of either West Germany (Munich) or East Germany (Leipzig). Then inspiration struck and I called San Diego. Yes, this scarce item was found there, and a photo copy was promptly on its way to me. Today, users of the *Dictionary of Scientific Biography* not only see a citation to this rare reference, but they also discover where in the world they can find it.

Unique research materials are only one aspect of a resource like the Zinner Collection. Originally formed by Ernst Zinner, an eminent astronomer, bibliographer, and historian of astronomy, the collection contains a highly regarded and well-indexed set of astronomical portraits as well as manuscripts, scarce central European theses, and a special group of rare astronomy books. A continuing acquisitions policy has particularly enhanced this latter category, which in addition to providing unusual research materials also offers inspiration to a diverse group of students, faculty, and friends.

In an age of instant electronic communication, ubiquitous photocopy machines, and bulky Sunday newspapers of more than a hundred pages, we tend to forget the revolutionary impact when paper, movable type, and sticky printer's ink first came together to transform the Western world. The letterpress works of five centuries ago, books printed before 1501, are called "incunabula," literally, the "cradle" of printing. What splendid craftsmanship is represented in that pioneering age! Carefully made rag paper, far better preserved today than most nineteenth- and twentieth-century stock!

Lovingly cut letters and initials hark back to the finest in classical and manuscript traditions.

This is not to say that computer typesetting and photolithography lack craft or that there were no slovenly printers in the fifteenth century. Rather, to achieve quality in our own day requires an awareness of the finest accomplishments of those who laid the foundations for the information world we have inherited.

Few institutions can own a Gutenberg Bible or a Mainz Psalter, but no university library worthy of its name should go without some representative of the heroic age when printing was in its infancy. And what better candidate could be chosen than the first appearance in print of the world's most enduring textbook, that magnificent achievement of classical mathematics, Euclid's *Elements?* In the Zinner Collection it is the prince of half a dozen incunabula. Printed in Venice in 1482 by the finest scientific printer of the incunabulum period, this first edition of Euclid's text reveals an innovative approach to the problem of printing mathematical diagrams. Impressed in the generous margins of Ratdolt's Euclid are numerous geometrical constructions for the theorems and proofs essential to the understanding of the text and cleverly constructed of smaller parts to speed production of the book. This edition is still worth some study, for no one is quite sure how Ratdolt's bag of tricks worked for the assembly of these mathematical figures.

Another key incunabulum in the Zinner Collection is the second longest-lived scientific textbook, Sacro Bosco's *Sphera.* Written by a British astronomer at the University of Paris in the 1200s, it rapidly became the standard text for teaching the geometry of the celestial sphere and its related seasonal movements. Ratdolt's edition of 1485 combines with the Sacro Bosco a newer, more advanced text from the fifteenth-century Viennese professor Georg Peurbach. This edition of the *Theoricae Novae Planetarum* or "New Handbook of the Planets" is distinguished by the first use of multicolor printing, which portrays in red, yellow, and black the crystalline spheres of the various planetary mechanisms.

The Alfonsine Tables of 1492 in the Zinner Collection is not a first edition, but it *is* a copy of the edition the young Copernicus bought while a student at Kraków in the 1490s. The Polish astronomer used these tables heavily as a standard source of information for planetary parameters and for the ancient calendar. His library was not large, but his reference works were almost entirely printed books—without the availability of printed material Copernicus might well have lacked the information he needed for his reform of astronomy.

Likewise, if printing had not preserved Copernicus's heliocentric cosmology with the full supporting tables and mathematics, the scientific revolution might well have been delayed. Copernicus's *De Revolutionibus* was printed twice in the sixteenth century: in 1543 (the year of his death) and again in 1566. This second edition, almost as rare as the first, included both Copernicus's treatise and the hard-to-find *Narratio Prima* of Copernicus's only student, Georg Joachim Rheticus; it is this edition that is found in the Zinner Collection. Since the first edition from a Nürnberg printer was distributed largely in Lutheran territory, this Basel edition supplied England and the Catholic countries: John Flamsteed and Edmund Halley (the first two Astronomers Royal) and Galileo Galilei were among the astronomers who owned and studied it.

Flamsteed is well represented in the Zinner Collection with his three-volume *Historiae Coelestis Britannicae* (London, 1725) and his *Atlas Coelestis* (London, 1753). The first Astronomer Royal's observations originally saw the light of day in a pirated version organized by Edmund Halley in 1712 with the connivance of Isaac Newton. Flamsteed vehemently protested what he considered to be an inadequate presentation of his data, and when political fortunes changed, he captured the undistributed portion of the edition, burned the offending pages, and used the remainder as the basis of his augmented version. Since he had fewer than 250 copies to work with, Flamsteed's three-volume set is comparatively scarce.

No Halley work yet appears in the Zinner Collection, but his comet does. The 1607 apparition of the comet now known as Halley's appears in a detailed foldout in Johann Kepler's *De Cometis Libelli Tres* (Augsburg, 1619). Kepler, emphasizing the apparently ephemeral nature of comets, proposed that they moved through the solar system in a straight line. Though his interpretation proved faulty, his work was one of those consulted by Halley in 1695 when his researches established the periodic nature of this comet—not so ephemeral after all!

Galileo is represented in the Zinner Collection by the first collected edition of his works—the Bologna *Opere* of 1655. This set lacks one of Galileo's most famous works, the *Dialogo*, which was still on the *Index* of prohibited books. Not until 1710 would an Italian publisher have the audacity to reprint it—and then the Naples house adopted a false Florentine imprint. Nevertheless, the Zinner Collection does include the first Latin text of the *Dialogo*, the 1635 Elzevier edition from Strasbourg, which carried the renewed discussion of the Copernican system far beyond the Italian-speaking zone.

The 1632 first edition of the *Dialogo* is not particularly rare and is surely a major desideratum for this astronomical collection. When it is someday acquired, students will be able to compare the interesting differences in the treatment of the frontispieces between the Italian and Latin versions. In both engravings three figures stand in earnest discussion of the Copernican and Aristotelian cosmologies. In the first edition the figure representing Copernicus looks for all the world like Galileo himself, whereas the Protestant scholars who sponsored the Latin edition replaced that image with a standard portrait of Copernicus.

Besides the classics of Copernicus, Galileo, and Kepler, there are several fine scientific showpieces in the Zinner Collection. Tycho Brahe's stunningly illustrated *Mechanica* (Nürnberg, 1602) was designed to show off his repertoire of astronomical devices. Shown in woodblocks and engravings are Tycho's great mural quadrant, his celestial globe, the plan of the Uraniborg observatory, plus a score of other newly perfected sextants, quadrants, and spheres. His related *Astronomiae Instauratae Progymnasmata* (Prague, 1602) was intended to convince the nobility at Prague that its author had constructed the most extraordinary uranographic instruments the world had ever seen. Johann Bayer's *Uranometria* (Augsburg, 1603) not only standardized modern stellar nomenclature by assigning Greek letters to the stars, but in its artistic figures it remains the classic astronomical atlas of all times. Nevertheless, the atlas of Johannes Hevelius, the *Uranographia* (Gdánsk, 1687), also in the Zinner Collection, surpasses Bayer in accuracy and in the beauty of its splendid engravings.

All of these remarkable books make unusual and inspirational teaching tools, both for conveying the history of printing and communication and for establishing a genuine contact with the bygone intellectual leaders in the history of astronomy. These treasures of the Zinner Collection help to make real the often abstract contributions of scientists from times past. But in many instances the books are also direct tools for historical or even modern astronomical research. For example, a few years ago Flamsteed's *Historiae Coelestis Britannicae* provided an unexpected insight into contemporary astronomy when in it was discovered what may be a unique observation from 1680 of a supernova in Cassiopeia.

For many years I have been searching for copies of Copernicus's book in libraries throughout the world (including the Zinner Collection) to examine the marginalia sometimes inserted by early readers who studied with pen in hand. These sixteenth- and seventeenth-century notes have yielded new insights into the way Copernicus's doctrine was treated in its earliest years. Although the San Diego Copernicus does not have interesting marginal notes, several other volumes in the collection do offer enticing annotations worthy of further examination. The volume of Ptolemy's collected works from 1551 bears the marks of intensive study by an unidentified Renaissance astronomer. And the Leovitius *Ephemeridum* (Augsburg, 1557), a volume fatter than a Webster's unabridged dictionary, is marked in the catalogue as having "extensive marginalia." The next time I'm in San Diego, I aim to head straight to the Zinner Collection in the Malcolm A. Love Library in order to have a closer look at these two precious volumes with their unique testimonials to sixteenth-century readers.

Meanwhile, I hope that students, faculty, and friends of San Diego State University take advantage of this wonderful link with their intellectual heritage, but even if they never come to look at the books, I hope they will still have a feeling of pride just knowing that a world-class collection is at their doorstep.

REFERENCES

DSB   *Dictionary of Scientific Biography*. New York: Scribner, 1970–80

Goff   Goff, Frederick F. *Incunabula in American Libraries*. Millwood, N.Y.: Kraus Reprint, 1973. [© 1964]

Houzeau   Houzeau, J. C. *Vade-Mecum de astronomie*. Bruxelles: F. Hayez, 1882.

Iselin   Iselin, Jacob Christoph. *Neu-vermehrtes historisch-geographisches allgemeines Lexicon*. 3d ed., 6 vols. Basel: J. Brandmüller, 1742–44.

Lalande   Lalande, Jérôme. *Bibliographie astronomique*. Amsterdam: J. C. Gieben, 1970 (reimpression of 1803 edition).

NUC   *National Union Catalog*. Chicago: American Library Association, 1968.

Poggendorff   Poggendorff, Johann C. *Biographisch-literarisches Handwörterbuch für Mathematik, Astronomie, Physik mit Geophysik, Chemie, Kristallographie und verwandte Wissensgebiete*. Leipzig: J. A. Barth, 1863–1986.

Zinner   Zinner, Ernst. *Geschichte und Bibliographie der astronomischen Literatur in Deutschland zur Zeit der Renaissance*. 2d ed. Stuttgart: A. Hiersemann, 1964.

NATIONAL UNION CATALOG
LOCATION SYMBOLS

AzU	University of Arizona, Tucson		InU	Indiana University, Bloomington
CLL	Los Angeles County Law Library		KU	University of Kansas, Lawrence
CLSU	University of Southern California, Los Angeles		KU-M	University of Kansas Medical Center, Kansas City
CLU;CLU-C	University of California, Los Angeles		KyLx.	Lexington (Kentucky) Public Library
CSdS	San Diego State University		KyU	University of Kentucky, Lexington
CSmH	Henry E. Huntington Library, San Marino		LNT	Tulane University, New Orleans
CSt	Stanford University		LU	Louisiana State University, Baton Rouge
CU	University of California, Berkeley		MeB	Bowdoin College, Brunswick, Maine
CU-S	University of California, San Diego		MdAN	U.S. Naval Academy, Annapolis, Maryland
CaBVaU	University of British Columbia, Vancouver		MdBJ	Johns Hopkins University
CoCC	Colorado College, Colorado Springs		MdBP	Peabody Institute, Baltimore
CoU	University of Colorado, Boulder		MA	Amherst College, Amherst, Massachusetts
CtNowa	Burndy Library, Norwalk, Connecticut		MB	Boston Public Library
CtU	University of Connecticut, Storrs		MBAt	Boston Athenaeum
CtY	Yale University		MBCo;MBM	Countway Library of Medicine, Boston
CtY-M	Yale University Medical School		MBdaf	U.S. Air Force Cambridge Research Center, Bedford, Massachusetts
DAU	American University, Washington, D.C.			
DCU	Catholic University of America, Washington, D.C.		MBMu	Museum of Fine Arts, Boston
DFo	Folger Shakespeare Library, Washington, D.C.		MCM	Massachusetts Institute of Technology, Cambridge
DLC; P-4	Library of Congress; Priority 4 Collection		MH	Harvard University, Cambridge
DNLM	National Library of Medicine, Bethesda, Maryland		MH-A	Harvard Univeristy, Arnold Arboretum
DN-Ob	U.S. Naval Observatory, Washington, D.C.		MH-AH	Harvard University, Andover Theological Library
DSI	Smithsonian Institution, Washington, D.C.		MNS	Smith College, Northampton, Massachusetts
FU	University of Florida, Gainesville		MSaE	Essex Institute, Salem, Massachusetts
GEU	Emory University, Atlanta		MWA	American Antiquarian Society, Worcester, Massachusetts
IaU	University of Iowa, Iowa City			
ICJ	John Crerar Library, Chicago		MWelC	Wellesley College, Wellesley, Massachusetts
ICN	Newberry Library, Chicago		MWiW	Williams College, Williamstown, Massachusetts
ICU	University of Chicago		MWiW-C	Williams College, Chapin Library, Williamstown
IEN	Northwestern University, Evanston, Illinois		MiD	Detroit Public Library
IU	University of Illinois, Urbana		MiU	University of Michigan, Ann Arbor

MnU	University of Minnesota, Minneapolis
MoSW	Washington University, Saint Louis
Nh	New Hampshire State Library, Concord
NhD	Dartmouth College, Hanover, New Hampshire
NjN	New Brunswick (New Jersey) Public Library
NjNbS	New Brunswick (New Jersey) Theological Seminary
NjP	Princeton University
NjR	Rutgers University, New Brunswick
N	New York State Library, Albany
NBuG	Grosvenor Reference Division, Buffalo and Erie County Library, Buffalo, New York
NCH	Hamilton College, Clinton, New York
NCorniC	Corning Glass Works Library, Corning, New York
NIC	Cornell University, Ithaca
NN	New York Public Library
NNC	Columbia University
NNE	Engineering Societies Library, New York City
NNH	Hispanic Society of America, New York City
NNNAM	New York Academy of Medicine, New York City
NNU-W	Washington Square Library, New York City
NNUT	Union Theological Society Library, New York City
NPV	Vassar College, Poughkeepsie, New York
NRU	University of Rochester, Rochester, New York
NWM	U.S. Military Academy, West Point, New York
NcD	Duke University, Durham, North Carolina
NcD-MC	Duke University Medical College, Durham
NcGU	University of North Carolina, Greensboro
NcRS	North Carolina State University, Raleigh
NcU	University of North Carolina, Chapel Hill
OCl	Cleveland (Ohio) Public Library
OClCS	Case Western Reserve University, Cleveland, Ohio
OCU	University of Cincinnati
ODW	Wright State University, Dayton, Ohio
OGaK	Kenyon College, Gambier, Ohio
OO	Oberlin College, Oberlin, Ohio
OU	Ohio State University, Columbus
OkU	University of Oklahoma, Norman
OrPR	Reed College, Portland, Oregon
OrU	University of Oregon, Eugene
PBa	Academy of the New Church, Bryn Athyn, Pennsylvania
PBm	Bryn Mawr College, Bryn Mawr, Pennsylvania
PBL	Lehigh University, Bethlehem, Pennsylvania
PHi	Historical Society of Pennsylvania, Philadelphia
PHC	Haverford College, Haverford, Pennsylvania
PKsL	Longwood Gardens, Kennett Square, Pennsylvania
PMA	Allegheny College, Meadville, Pennsylvania
PP	Free Library, Philadelphia
PPAN	Academy of Natural Sciences, Philadelphia
PPAmP	American Philosophical Society, Philadelphia
PPC	College of Physicians, Philadelphia
PPF; PPFrankI	Franklin Institute, Philadelphia
PPiD	Duquesne University, Pittsburgh
PPL	Library Company of Philadelphia
PPL-R	Library Company of Philadelphia, Ridgeway Branch
PPLT	Lutheran Theological Seminary, Philadelphia
PPT	Temple University, Philadelphia
PPULC	Union Library Catalogue, Philadelphia
PSC	Swarthmore College, Swarthmore, Pennsylvania
PU	University of Pennsylvania, Philadelphia
RPB	Brown University, Providence, Rhode Island
RPJCB	John Carter Brown Library, Providence
ScU	University of South Carolina, Columbia
TU	University of Tennessee, Knoxville
TxDaM-P	Southern Methodist University, Dallas, Texas
TxU	University of Texas, Austin
UU	University of Utah, Salt Lake City
ViLxW	Washington and Lee University, Lexington, Virginia
ViNeM	Mariners' Museum, Newport News, Virginia
ViRA	Richmond (Virginia) Academy of Medicine
ViU	University of Virginia, Charlottesville
ViW	College of William and Mary, Williamsburg, Virginia
WU	University of Wisconsin, Madison

GOFF LOCATION SYMBOLS

AELow	Albert E. Lownes, Providence, Rhode Island
AmBML	Annmary Brown Memorial Library, Brown University, Providence, Rhode Island
BMawrCL	Bryn Mawr College, Bryn Mawr, Pennsylvania
BMedL	Boston Medical Library
BPJ	Biblioteca Público del Estado de Jalisco, Guadalajara, Mexico
BPubL	Boston Public Library
BrUL	Brown University, Providence, Rhode Island
BurL	Burndy Library, Norwalk, Connecticut
ChL	Chapin Library, Williams College, Williamstown, Massachusetts
ColUL	Columbia University, New York City
CPhL	College of Physicians, Philadelphia
CUAL	Catholic University of America, Washington, D.C.
FolgSL	Folger Shakespeare Library, Washington, D.C.
HamCL	Hamilton College, Clinton, New York
HarvCL	Harvard University, Cambridge, Massachusetts
HDC	Homor D. Crotty, San Marino, California
HDH	Harrison D. Horblit, New York City
HEHL	Henry E. Huntington Library, San Marino, California
HNCL	Holy Name College, Washington, D.C.
IS	Irving Sporn, M.D., Portland, Maine
JCBL	John Carter Brown Library, Brown University, Providence, Rhode Island
JCreL	John Crerar Library, Chicago
LC	Library of Congress, Washington, D.C.
LeUL(H)	Lehigh University, Bethlehem, Pennsylvania
LIHSL	Long Island Historical Society, Brooklyn, New York
McGUL	McGill University, Montreal

MFArtL	Museum of Fine Arts, Boston
MMu(P)L	Metropolitan Museum of Art, New York City
NavObL	U.S. Naval Observatory, Washington, D.C.
NewL	Newberry Library, Chicago
NLM	National Library of Medicine, Bethesda, Maryland
NYHisSL	New-York Historical Society, New York City
NYPL	New York Public Library, New York City
OFE	Mrs. Otto F. Ege, Cleveland, Ohio
OhStUL	Ohio State University, Columbus
PML	Pierpont Morgan Library, New York City
RSS	Reinhard S. Speck, M.D., Daly City, California
SoMethUL	Southern Methodist University, Dallas, Texas
StanUL	Stanford University, Palo Alto, California
TGM	Thomas Gresham Machen, Baltimore, Maryland
UCalBL	University of California, Berkeley
UCalLA(B)L	University of California, Los Angeles
UCalS(M)L	University of California, San Francisco
UESocL	Engineering Societies Library, New York City
UIllL	University of Illinois, Urbana
UKanL	University of Kansas, Lawrence
UMichL	University of Michigan, Ann Arbor
UMin(B)L	University of Minnesota, Minneapolis
UNCaL	University of North Carolina, Chapel Hill
UOkL	University of Oklahoma, Norman
UTexL	University of Texas, Austin
UVa(Mc)L	University of Virginia, Charlottesville
WArtGL	Walters Art Gallery, Baltimore, Maryland
WDM	William D. Morgan, Saint Paul, Minnesota
YUL	Yale University, New Haven
YU(M)L	Yale University Medical School, New Haven

Of the 211 items in this catalogue 88 came in the original Ernst Zinner Collection. Of the eight incunabula dated from 1471 to 1492, two were in that original collection: Albertus Magnus, 1491 (item 2); and Sacro Bosco, 1485 (item 156).

There are 59 sixteenth-century and 91 seventeenth-century imprints. The remaining works printed after 1700 were selected for inclusion because of their significance in the history of astronomy.

San Diego State University Library has issued checklists of books on several aspects of astronomy in the Zinner Collection since 1969. No complete catalogue of its holdings has been published.

Among the 158 pre-1700 imprints 44 different cities and 117 different printer-publishers are represented. Venice has the largest number of imprints with 25 and the most printers with 17. London follows with 14 imprints and Augsburg with 10. The most unusual place of publication is probably Kraków (item 175).

Authors' names: The names and dates of authors are as complete as research could make them. The Library of Congress form of authors' names is usually preferred.

Titles: Long titles have been shortened.

Imprints: In imprints (place, publisher, and date) the name of the city is given in a modern form.

Pagination: Stating the pagination of books, especially those printed before 1700, poses problems. To resolve most of them and to keep pagination statements simple, only the total number of leaves is given for the older works.

Size: The size of the book is given in centimeters. If a single size is given, it is the height. If two dimensions are given, the height is first, followed by the width. Illustrations are the same size as the originals except where the word reduced appears in the caption.

Title pages: Many title pages have been reproduced. They are the quintessential products of the art of the early printers. A majority of books printed during the first fifty years after the invention of printing had no title pages. Like the manuscript books before them, the title and authorship of the first printed books usually appeared at the top of the first page of the text. Often that line was printed in red. The first separate title page in a printed book had already appeared at Mainz in 1463, but complete title pages only became common between 1525 and 1550. Many printers decorated them with lavish designs to make them aesthetically pleasing.

Disputations: Academic disputations are entered under the name of the faculty moderator, the one designated "preses," followed by the name of the respondent.

vſq3 ad obitū. Neq3 ei iudicarent aſtrologi p̄ natiuitates:niſi q3 hoꝛa impꝛegnatiois vix pōt certificari: vñ inquit ptolomeꝰ hoꝛa natiuitatis eſſe ſm videre:quare ergo vxoꝛes regi vel p̄ncipis aut magnatis exiſtente eo in optimis ꝯditionibꝰ nō eligemus viro hoꝛa ſuſapiēdi ex a liberū:ſi creatoꝛ vniuerſi generatōis annuerit vt ſc3 eueniant nato bona que ex ſerie liberoꝛ natiuitatū aſtrologus futura, p̄nunctiat:ꜣre iterū non eligimꝰ hoꝛa farmaciā exhibendo ſi ꝯſtituerimꝰ quid aſcendens ꞇ ſcatoꝛes ex ſignis ruminātibus et precipue in capꝛicoꝛno, ꝓuocāt vomitū et cū b ſi ſciuerimꝰ: q2 opoꝛtet eas pꝛoiici ab aſpectu vtruſq3 infoꝛtune ſaturni videlicet et martis eo q3 Saturnus reſtringit medicinā, Mars vo reducit vſq3 ad ſanguinē:et cū ſciuerimus q3 luna exīte cū ioue operatiōis purgatoꝛij minuit anguſtia ruſum in magiſterio Cirurgie quare non cauebo facere inciſionē luna exīte in ſigno ſcatiōne bſite ſup illo mēbꝛu3 Tunc eni eſt membꝛū valde reumaticū ꞇ doloꝛ reuma ꝓuocat Et audeo me dicere vidiſſe quaſi infinita accītia eueniſſe: vidi hoiem imperitū parīt medicīe ꞇ aſtroꝛ qui p periculo ſquinātie minuit ſibi de bꝛachioluna exīte in geminis ꜣ habet ſcatione ſuper bꝛachia ꞇ abſq3 vlla manifeſta egritudine excepta modica bꝛachij inflatōne moꝛtuus eſt die ſeptia . Sciui quoq3 quendā pacientē fiſtulā:iuxta caput longatōis fuiſſe inciſum: luna exīte in Scoꝛpione:q̄ ſcat ſup ptes illas a quodā miſero cirurgico qui erat ignarus vtriuſq3 magiſterij: medicīe ſc3 et aſtroꝛ:ꞇ abſq3 vere inciſione aut alia cauſa rōnali inter manꝰ eū tenentiū inuentus eſt moꝛtu? ipſa hoꝛa:ꜣn nō videt ab aliq̄ cauſa interficiente ſubito accidiſſe:vt ſunt opilatōes ventriculoꝛu3 cerebꝛi aut leſione ſpiritualiū: ſeu defectu ſpiritualiū q3 ſi inuenit inter electiones aliqd apparens friuolū:vt eſt indumēta noua inducere:luna in leone ꞇc. attendi debet q3 pto. cū eſſet vir tante auctoꝛitatis non dixit hoc niſi ſcaret maioꝛa:ꞇ ꝓpter b inuit q3 ſigna fixa ꞇtilia ſunt ad res quaꝛ ſtabilitatē volumꝰ ſicut ꞇ doꝛmus que dicunt anguli:ſigna vo mobilia ſicut ꞇ res eadens ab angulis ad res cito mutabiles:ꜣn receſſio cito mutatur ꞇ non ecōuerſo. Cetex tale q3 intelligit de p̄ma inductōe alicuius nati: vt ſuenſes tredecima differentia ſcdi capituli vt patet libꝛo d̄ electionibus hali p̄mo.   Capitulum. XVI.

Arte vero que est de ima

p̄ ginibꝰ aſtronomici nō defendo aliꝰ:ꝓpt affinitatē quā h3 cū necromāticis:quā ſupius in eoꝛ captis dcm b eas.ſ. nanciſci vtutē a figura celeſti iuxta verbū pto. noio: qd ibi tactū ē ſc3 q3 imagines ꜣ ibi ſūt ꞇc. Et niſi q2 nihil phibꝛ eā defendere ſin q3 poſſunt negari defendi. Eſto itaq3 exēpli gꝛa:q3 cum pꝛedict ꝯditōibꝰ ſūdaꝛ imago deſtructōis ſcoꝛpionū ab illo loco quādiu fuerit b imago ibi ſuata. Nō videꝛ igitur inſcriptio eſſe caracterū:ſi in doꝛſo eiꝰ ſculpaꝛ b nomē deſtructio. Siꝛ nec ſi in fronte eiꝰſcribaꝛ b nomē Scoꝛpio:qd eſt nomē ſpēi fugāde ꞇ in pectoꝛe nomē aſcendēti ꞇ nomē eiꝰ dñi ꜣ eſt mars:ꞇ nomē lune ſicut in imaginibꝰ ad amoꝛē ꞇ b nomē amoꝛ ſcribaꝛ i vel treſmanu ſiniſtra ꜣs igiꝛ cultꝰ exhibeꝛ ei ſiquis i medio loco:a ꜣ ipam ſpecie fugare voluerit fuerit imago ſculpta capite deoꝛſum ꞇ ſurſum pedibꝰ eleuatis:nō cōmendo eas ſed non videꝛ q3 abſq3 ratione debeant iniquitatem alioꝛū poꝛtare.
    C libꝛis vo necromāticis ſine iudicio melioꝛis ſnie videꝛ magis q3 debeāt ſuari b deſtrui. Tempꝰ eñi ꝓpe eſt iā foꝛte:qd ꝓpt quaſdā cauſas ꜣs mō taceo:eas ſalte occaſionaꝛ pderit inſpexiſſe nihilominꝰ ab eoꝛ vſu caueāt
    Unt pterea quidā libꝛi experimē   (ſibi inſpectoꝛes. tales:quoꝛ noia cū necromācia ſunt ꝓtumelia:vt ſunt geomācia p̄romanciaꞇ aromācia:ꜣ ad veꝛ nō mereꝛ dici raro ſcie b garromancia Sane ydromācia extis aſaliū cōmededis inſpiciēdiſq̄s libꝛis:ꞇ pyromācia in figura ignis:ꜣ cō ſumiꝛ holocauſtū:, pculdubio ydolatrie ſpēꝛ nō excludit i geo mācia nihil taliū inuenio b, pſidit in ſarno ꞇ vſio hoꝛe:ꜣ ei, p radice ponūꝛ:gaudeꝛq3 numeꝛ rōne fulciri:ꞇ mlti ſunt ꜣ ei teſtimoniū phibēt nō ſicut de arenācia:friuola ē ei licet ſir p rōne pſumat ſe iactitare: de Ciromācia vo volo determiatōꝛ mē tione faceꝛ pcipue ad pñs:q2 foꝛte ps eſt phiſonomie ꜣre collecta videꝛ ex ſcatōibꝰ magiſterij aſtroꝛ ſup coꝛpꝰ ꞇ aias:dū moꝛes ai ꝓuincit:ex exterioꝛi ſigno coꝛpis: nō q2 vnū ſit cā alteriꝰ ſ q2 vioꝛ ab eodē cauſata: p ꜣ deꝰ ſit bñdictꝰ i ſecꝲa ſecꝲoꝛ amē

Explicit liber Alberti magni epī Ratiſponen. de duabus ſa pientijs aut de recapitulatiōe omnium libꝛoꝛum aſtronomie.

---

2. Albertus Magnus, *De Duabus Sapientijs* [Concerning the two wisdoms] (1491?)
colophon and verso of the preceding page (reduced)

ASTRONOMIA
Teutsch.

[handwritten notes: Jumpt. Stephani M. — Frantner c.w. M.C.]

Himmels Lauff/
Wirckung vnnd Natürliche
Influentz der Planeten vnnd Gestirn/
Auß grund der Astronomei/ nach jeder Zeit/ Jar/ Tag vnnd
Stunden Constellation. In Natiuiteten/zur Artznei/wolfart/vñ allem leben der Menschen zuwissen von nöten.Mit sampt Astronomischer vñ Ma-
thematischer Instrument/als Astrolabien/Quadranten/Compaßt/Sonn
vhren/vnd Nocturnal/Künstlicher zurichtung vnd nützli-
chem gebrauch. Alles Innhalt bey-
gelegten Registers.

Cum Gratia & Priuilegio Imperiali.

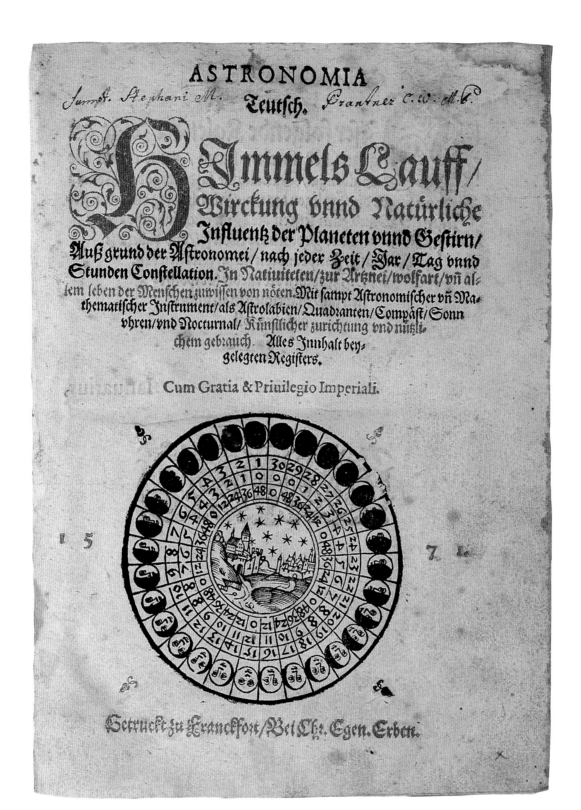

1 5   7 1.

Getruckt zu Franckfort/Bei Chr. Egen. Erben.

9. *Astronomia Teutsch* [German astronomy] (1571) title page

التقويم سنة ٤٠٩

Sive

EPHEMERIDES
PERSARUM

PER

TOTUM ANNUM,

JUXTA EPOCHAS CELE-
BRIORES ORIENTIS,

ALEXANDREAM,

CHRISTI, DIOCLETIANI,

HEGIRÆ, JESDEGIR-
DICAM ET GELALÆAM,

Unà cum Motibus VII. Planetarum, eorumque Syzy-
giis, tàm Lunaribus quàm mutuis, Manfionibus ☽. Horo-
fcopis ☊. atque Longit. Dierum tabulis.

Philologis, Chronologis, Aftro-
nomis utilisfimæ,

è Libello

ARABICE, PERSICE ATQVE
TURCICE M^Sto.

Prædâ Militis Germani ex Hungariâ;

Nunc Latinè verfæ

ET V. COMMENTARIORUM
LIBRIS ILLUSTRATÆ

à

MATTHIA FRIDERICO BECKIO,

Proftant AUGUSTÆ Vindelicorum,
Apud LAUR. KRONIGERUM & THEOPH. GOEBELII Hæred.
Typis JAC. KOPMAIERI, Reipubl. Typogr. An. M. DC. XCV.
& M. DC. XCVI. excufa.

14. Beck, *Ephemerides Persarum* [Ephemerides of the Persians]
(1695−96) title page (reduced)

SPHAERA MVNDI.
SEV
COSMOGRAPHIA.

Demonſtratiua, ac facili Methodo tradita:

IN QVA TOTIVS MVNDI FABRICA,
VNA CVM NOVIS, TYCHONIS, KEPLERI, GALILAEI,
aliorumq; Aſtronomorum adinuentis continetur.

ACCESSERE

I. *Breuis introductio ad Geographiam.*
II. *Apparatus ad Mathematicarum ſtudium.*
III. *Echometria, ideſt Geometrica traditio de Echo.*

Authore Ioſepho Blancano Bononienſi è Societate IESV,
Mathematicarum in Gymnaſio Parmenſi profeſſore.

Ad Illuſtriſſimum, ac Nobiliſſimum
PETRVM FRANCISCVM MALASPINAM
AEDIFICIORVM MARCHIONEM.

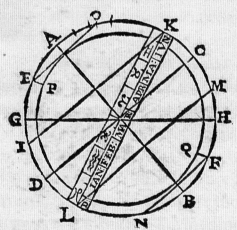

BONONIÆ, Typis Sebaſtiani Bonomij. *Superiorum Permiſſu.*
Sumptibus Hieronymi Tamburini. 1620.

16. Biancani, *Sphaera Mundi* [The sphere of the world] (1620) title page

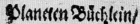

Planeten Büchlein/

Wie mann eines Jeden

Menschen Art/ Natur/ vñ Complexion/
nach dem er vnder eim Planeten vnd Zeichen geborn
ist/ erkennen sol. Item der siben Planeten Natur/ vnd Eigen-
schafften/ Vnd was man in ein jedes Planeten stund/thun/oder
meiden sol/sehr nützlich zu wissen. Durch

Peter Creutziger/in zeiten deß Hochberümpten Astronomi
M. Johan Liechtenbergers Discipels.

Getruckt zu Franck   furt am Mayn.

ANNO. M. D.   LXX.

41. Creutzer, *Planeten Büchlein* [Little planet book] (1570) title page

21

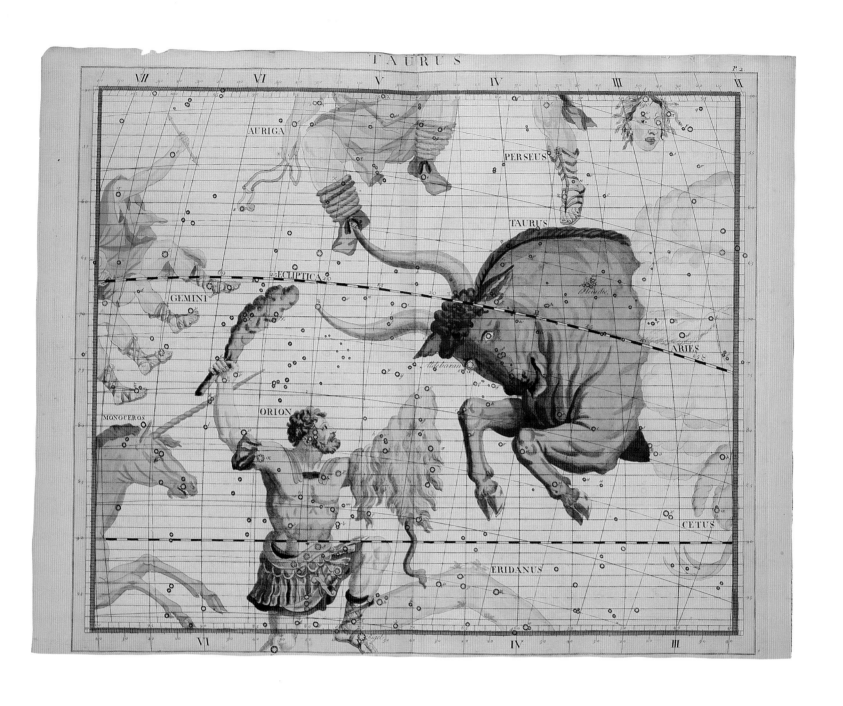

58. Flamsteed, *Atlas Coelestis* [Celestial atlas] (1753) plate number 26 (reduced)

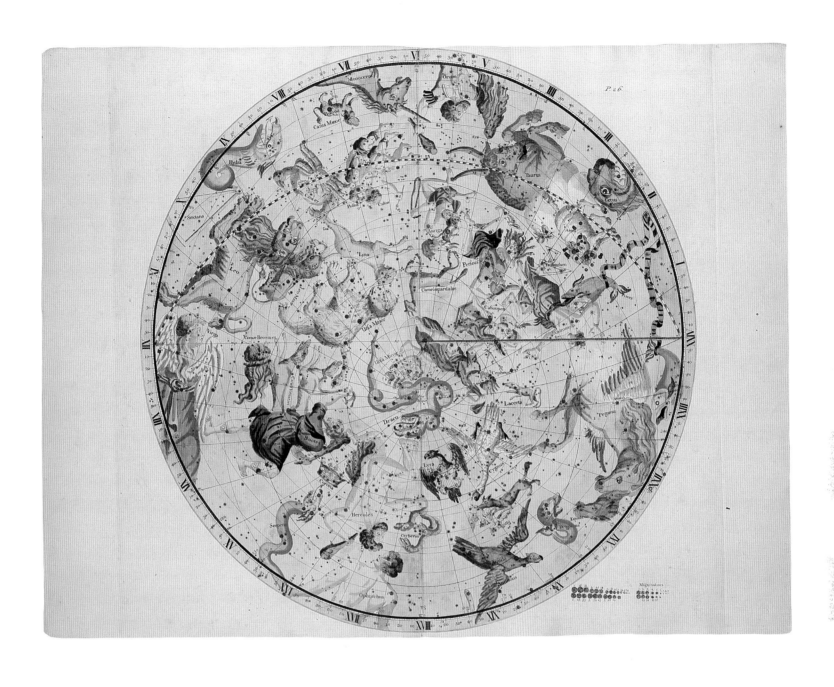

58. Flamsteed, *Atlas Coelestis* (1753) plate number 2 (reduced)

ENTRETIENS
SUR
LA PLURALITÉ
DES
MONDES.

Par M. DE FONTENELLE
De l'Academie Françoise, de celle des Sciences
& de celle des Inscriptions.

Nouvelle Edition augmentée d'un Septiéme
Entretien & de diverses piéces de Mr.
de Fontenelle.

A AMSTERDAM,
Aux dépens d'ETIENNE ROGER Marchand,
Libraire, chez qui l'on trouve un affortiment
Général de Musique.

M. DCCXIX.

60. Fontenelle, *Entretiens sur la pluralité des mondes*
[Communications concerning the plurality of the worlds] (1719) title page

78. *Das grosse Planeten Buch* [The great planet book] (1644) title page

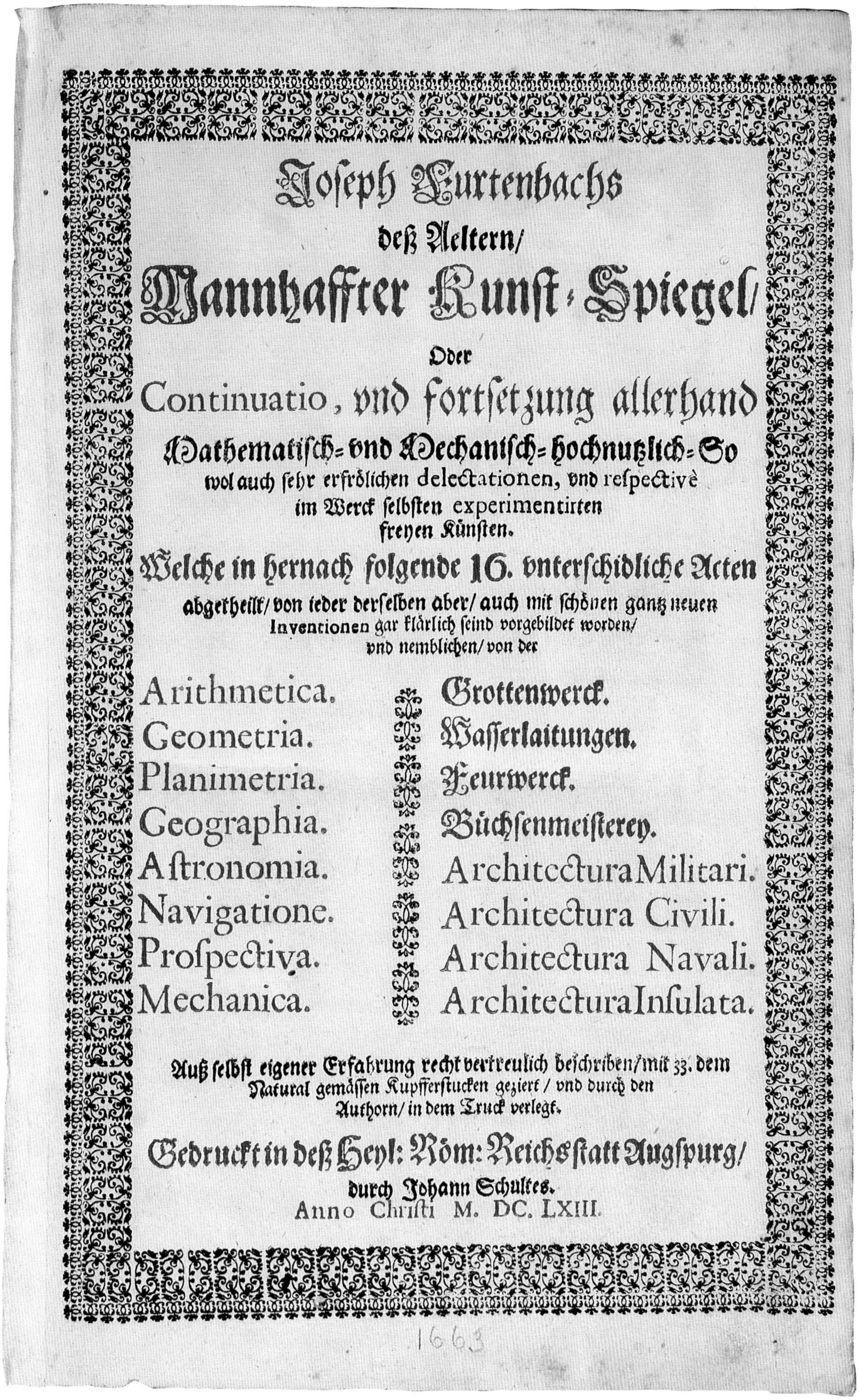

Joseph Furtenbachs

deß Aeltern/

Mannhaffter Kunst-Spiegel/

Oder

Continuatio, vnd fortsetzung allerhand

Mathematisch= vnd Mechanisch=hochnutzlich=So
wol auch sehr erfrölichen delectationen, vnd respectivè
im Werck selbsten experimentirten
freyen Künsten.

Welche in hernach folgende 16. vnterschidliche Acten
abgetheilt/ von ieder derselben aber/ auch mit schönen gantz neuen
Inventionen gar klärlich seind vorgebildet worden/
vnd nemblichen/ von der

Arithmetica.	Grottenwerck.
Geometria.	Wasserlaitungen.
Planimetria.	Feurwerck.
Geographia.	Büchsenmeisterey.
Astronomia.	Architectura Militari.
Navigatione.	Architectura Civili.
Prospectiva.	Architectura Navali.
Mechanica.	Architectura Insulata.

Auß selbst eigener Erfahrung recht vertreulich beschriben/mit 33. dem
Natural gemässen Kupfferstucken geziert / vnd durch den
Authorn/ in dem Truck verlegt.

Gedruckt in deß Heyl: Röm: Reichsstatt Augspurg/
durch Johann Schultes.
Anno Christi M. DC. LXIII.

1663

64. Furtenbach, *Dess Aeltern Mannhaffter Kunst-Spiegel*
[Concerning the ancient strong optical mirror] (1663) title page (reduced)

URANIA:

OR,

A Compleat VIEW of the HEAVENS;

CONTAINING THE

ANTIENT *and* MODERN

ASTRONOMY,

In Form of a DICTIONARY:

Illuftrated with a great Number of Figures,

COMPRISING

All the CONSTELLATIONS, with the STARS laid down according to their exact Situations and Magnitudes, from repeated and accurate OBSERVATIONS.

IN WHICH,

Befide Explanations of all the Terms ufed in that SCIENCE, by the early as well as late AUTHORS, and in the *Arabian*, as well as the *Egyptian* and *Grecian* ASTRONOMY, the Science is traced from its Origin to the prefent Period, and the Improvements made, from Time to Time, are laid down in a plain and familiar Manner.

The SUN, STARS, PLANETS, and COMETS are defcribed; and their THEORY explained according to the received Opinions of the prefent Time; the feveral Syftems of the Univerfe are delivered; and the CONSTELLATIONS are defcribed at large, with the Number, Magnitude, and Situation of the STARS that compofe them; their ORIGIN explained according to the *Egyptian* Hieroglyphics, and the *Grecian* Fable; and a very particular Enquiry is made into the Hiftory of thofe mentioned in the Sacred Writings, and in the Old Poets and Hiftorians.

A WORK intended for general USE, intelligible to all Capacities, and calculated for ENTERTAINMENT as well as INSTRUCTION.

By JOHN HILL, *M. D.*

MEMBER of the ROYAL ACADEMY OF SCIENCES, *Bourdeaux*, &c.

LONDON:

Printed for T. GARDNER, at *Cowley's Head*, in the *Strand*; and Sold by all the Bookfellers in *Great Britain* and *Ireland*.

M, DCC, LIV.

84. Hill, *Urania* (1754) title page

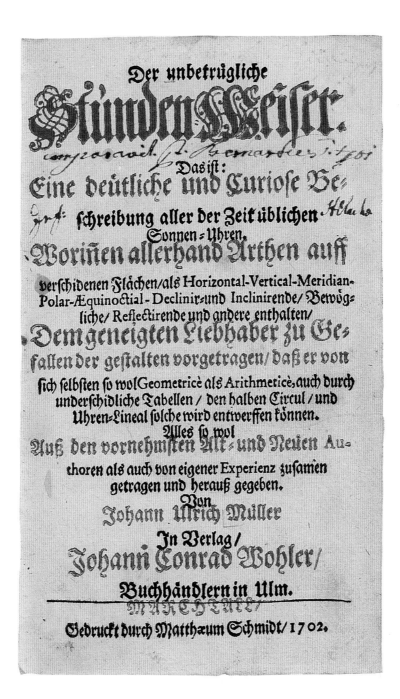

Der unbetrügliche

Stünden-Weiser.

Das ist:

Eine deütliche und Curiose Beschreibung aller der Zeit üblichen
Sonnen-Uhren,

Worinnen allerhand Arthen auff

verschidenen Flächen/als Horizontal-Vertical-Meridian-
Polar-Æquinoctial-Declinir-und Inclinirende/Bewög-
liche/Reflectirende und andere enthalten/

Dem geneigten Liebhaber zu Ge-
fallen der gestalten vorgetragen/daß er von

sich selbsten so wol Geometricè als Arithmeticè, auch durch
underschidliche Tabellen/den halben Circul/und
Uhren-Lineal solche wird entwerffen können.

Alles so wol
Auß den vornehmsten Alt-und Neüen Au-
thoren als auch von eigener Experienz zusamen
getragen und herauß gegeben.

Von
Johann Ulrich Müller

In Verlag/
Johann Conrad Wohler/

Buchhändlern in Ulm.

Gedruckt durch Matthæum Schmidt/1702.

127. Müller, *Der unbetrügliche Stünden-Weiser* [The unerring timekeeper] (1702) title page (reduced)

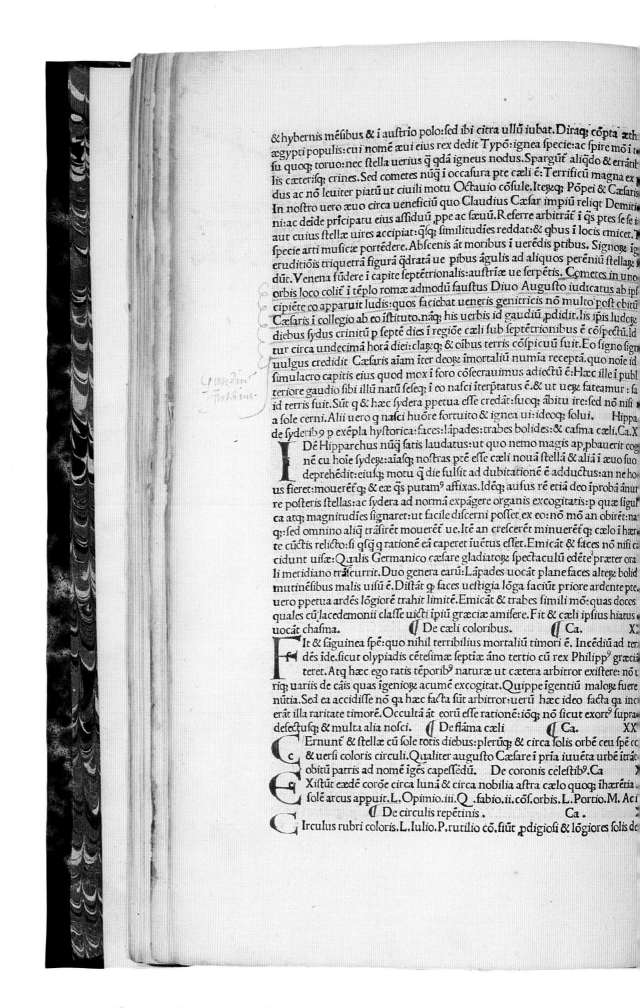

& hybernis mésibus & i auftrio polo:fed ibi citra ullũ iubat.Diraq; cõpta æth
ægypti populis:cui nomé æui eius rex dedit Typõ:ignea fpecie:ac fpire mõ i t
fu quoq; toruo:nec ftella uerius q̃ q̃dã igneus nodus.Spargũt aliq̃do & errãtb
lis cæterifq; crines.Sed cometes nũq̃ i occafura pte cæli é:Terrificũ magna ex
dus ac nõ leuiter piatũ ut ciuili motu Octauio cõfule.Iteq̃q; Põpei & Cæfaris
In noftro uero æuo circa ueneficiũ quo Claudius Cæfar impiũ reliqt Domiti
ni:ac deide pṙicipatu eius affiduũ ppe ac fæuũ.Referre arbitrãt i q̃s ptes fe fe i
aut cuius ftellæ uires accipiat:q̃fq; fimilitudies reddat:& qbus i locis emicet.
fpecie arti muficæ portédere.Abfcenis ãt moribus i uerédis ṗtibus. Signoṙ ig
eruditiõis triquetrã figurã q̃drata ue ṗibus ãgulis ad aliquos peréniũ ftellaṙ
dũt.Venena fũdere i capite feptétrionalis:auftriæ ue ferpétis. Cometes in uno
orbis loco colit i téplo romæ admodũ fauftus Diuo Augufto iudicatus ab ipf
cipiéte eo apparuit ludis:quos faciebat ueneris genitricis nõ multo poft obitũ
Cæfaris i collegio ab eo iftituto.naq; his uerbis id gaudiũ ṗdidit.Iis ipis ludoṙ
diebus fydus crinitũ p fepté dies i regiõe cæli fub feptétrionibus é cõfpectũ.Id
tur circa undecimã horã diei:claṙq; & oibus terris cõfpicuũ fuit.Eo figno figṅ
uulgus credidit Cæfaris aiam iter deoṙ imortaliũ numia receptã.quo noie id
fimulacro capitis eius quod mox i foro cõfecrauimus adiectũ é:Hæc ille i publ
teriore gaudio fibi illũ natũ fefeq; i eo nafci iterṗtatus é.& ut ueṙ fateamur : fa
id terris fuit.Sũt q̃ & hæc fydera ṗpetua effe credãt:fuoq; ãbitu ire:fed nõ nifi
a fole cerni.Alii uero q nafci huõre fortuito & ignea ui:ideoq; folui. Hippa
de fyderibᵍ p exépla hyftorica:faces:lãpades:trabes bolides:& cafma cæli.Ca.X

I Dé Hipparchus nũq̃ fatis laudatus:ut quo nemo magis ap̃pbauerit cog
né cu hoie fyderṙ:aiafq; noftras pté effe cæli noua ftellã & alia i æuo fuo
deprehédit:eiufq; motu q̃ die fulfit ad dubitationé é adductus:an ne ho
us fieret:mouereté q; & eæ q̃s putamᵍ affixas.Idéq; aufus ré etiã deo iprobã ãnũ
re pofteris ftellas:ac fydera ad normã expãgere organis excogitatis:p q̃æ figuḷ
ca atq; magnitudies fignaret:ut facile difcerni poffet.ex eo:nõ mõ an obirét:na
q;:fed omnino aliq̃ trãfirét mouereté ue.Ité an crefcerét minuereté q; cælo i hæ
te cũctis relicto:fi q̃fq; q ratione eã caperet iuétus effet.Emicãt & faces nõ nifi c
cidunt uifæ:Qualis Germanico cæfare gladiatoṙ fpectaculũ edéte præter ora
li meridiano trãfcurrit.Duo genera earũ:Lãpades uocãt plane faces alteṙ bolid
mutinéfibus malis uifũ é.Diftãt q̃ faces ueftigia lõga faciũt priore ardente pte.
uero ṗpetua ardés lõgioré trahit limité.Emicãt & trabes fimili mõ:quas docē
quales cũ lacedemonii claffe uicti ipiũ græciæ amifere.Fit & cæli ipfius hiatus
uocãt chafma.   ¶ De cæli coloribus.   ¶ Ca.   XX

F It & faguinea fpé:quo nihil terribilius mortaliũ timori é. Incédiũ ad ter
dés ide.ficut olypiadis cétefimæ feptiæ ãno tertio cũ rex Philippᵍ græciã
teret.Atq; hæc ego ratis téporibᵍ naturæ ut cætera arbitror exiftere: nõ u
riq; uariis de cãis quas igenioṙ acumé excogitat.Quippe igentiũ maloṙ fuere
nũtia.Sed ea accidiffe nõ qa hæc facta fũt arbitror:ueru hæc ideo facta qa inc
erãt illa raritate timoré.Occultã ãt eorũ effe rationé:ioq; nõ ficut exorᵍ fupra
defectufq; & multa alia nofci. ¶ De flãma cæli   ¶ Ca.   XX

C Ernunt & ftellæ cũ fole totis diebus:pleruq; & circa folis orbé ceu fpé
& uerfi coloris circuli.Qualiter augufto Cæfare i pria iuuéta urbé itrã
obitũ patris ad nomé igés capeffédũ.   De coronis celeftibᵍ.Ca   X
Xiftũt eædé coróe circa lunã & circa nobilia aftra cælo quoq; ihærétia
folé arcus appuit.L.Opimio.iii.Q.fabio.ii.cõf.orbis.L.Portio.M.Aci
          ¶ De circulis repétinis .   Ca .   XX
C Irculus rubri coloris.L.Iulio.P.rutilio cõ.fiũt ṗdigiofi & lõgiores folis dē

143. Plinius, *Naturalis Historiae* [Natural history] (1483)
lines concerning comets underscored by some previous owner (reduced)

qualis ociſo dictatore. Cæſare & antoniano bello totius pene anni pallore continuo.

¶ Plures ſoles. ¶ Ca. XXXI.

ET rurſus plures ſoles cernūt:nec ſupra ipm nec iſra ſe:ſed ex obliquo nūq̃ iux
ta:nec cõtra terrã:nec noctu.ſed aut oriéte aut occidéte.Semel i meridie cõſpec
ti i boſphoro pdūt:q̃ a matutio tp̃e durauerūt i occaſū.Trinos ſoles ãtiq̃ ſæpius uide
re.Sicut Sp.Poſtumio.Q .Minutio:Q .Martio.M.Portio.M.Antonio.P.Dolobella
&.M.Lepido.L.Plãco cõſ.& noſtra ætas uidit Diuo Claudio pricipe conſulatu eius
Cornelio Orfito collega.Plures ſimul q̃ tres uiſi ad hoc æui nunq̃ produnt.

¶ Plures lunæ. ¶ Ca. XXXII.

LVnæ quoq̃ trinæ:ut Cn.Domitio.C.F.L.Annio cõ.apparuere : quos pleriq̃
appellauerūt ſoles nocturnos ¶ Die q̃ lux nocte. ¶ Ca. XXXIII.

LVmen de cælo noctu uiſū eſt.C.Cecilio.Cn.Papyrio conſ.& ſæpe alias ut diei
ſpecies noctu luceret. ¶ Clypei ardentes. ¶ Ca. XXXIIII.

CLypeus ardés ab occaſu ad ortū ſintillãs trãſcurrit ſolis occaſū.L.Valerio.Cn.
Mario conſ. ¶ Oſtentum cæli. ¶ Ca. XXXV.

SIntillã e ſtella cadere:& augeri terræ appropinquãte: ac poſtq̃ i lunæ magni
tudiné facta ſit illuxiſſe ceu nubilo die.Dein cū i cælū ſe recipit:lãpadé factã
ſemel unq̃ pditur.Cn.Octauio.C.Scribonio conſ.Vidit hoc Licinius Syllanus pcõ
ſul cū comitatu ſuo. ¶ De diſcurſu ſtellarū. ¶ Ca. XXXVI.

FIeri uidét & diſcurſus ſtellaȝ nūq̃ temere ut nõ ex ea pte truces uéti coriãt :&
ex iis tūc pcellæ i mari terriſq̃. De ſtellis caſtorit ¶ Ca. XXXVII.

VIdi i nocturnis militū uigiliis ihærere pilis p uallo fulguȝ effigies:ex & áténis
nauigãtiū aliiſq̃ nauiū ptibus ceu uocali quodã ſono iſiſtūt ut uolucres ſedé
ex ſede mutãtes.Graues cū ſolitariæ uenere:mergéteſq̃ nauigia:& ſi i carinæ ima de
ciderint exurétes.Geminæ aūt ſalutares:& pſperi curſus pnūtiæ.q̃rū aduétu ſuga
ri dirã illã ac minacé appellatãq̃ Helenã ſerūt.Et o id Polluci & Caſtori id numé aſ
ſignãt:eoſq̃ i mari deos iuocãt.Hoium quoq̃ capita ueſptinis horis magno pſagio cir
cūfulgét.Oia icerta rõe & i naturæ maieſtate abdita. ¶ De aere. XXXXVIII.

HActenus de mūdo ipſo ſyderibuſq̃.Nūc reliq̃ celi memorabilia.Nãq̃ & hoc cæ
lū appellauere maiores:qd̃ alio noïe aëra:oë qd̃ iani ſimile uitalé hunc ſpiritū
fudit.Infra lunã hæc ſedes:multoq̃ iſerior.Vt aïaduerto ppemodū cõſtare:iſinitū ex
ſupiore natura aëris & terreni halit9 miſcés utraq̃ ſorte cõfūdit.Hic nubila:tonitrua
& alia fulmina.Hic grãdies:& pruinæ:imbres:pcellæ:turbies.Hic pluria mortaliū ma
la:& reȝ naturæ pugna ſecū.Terrena i cælū tédétia dprimit ſydeȝ uis.Eadéq̃ q̃ ſpõ
te nõ ſubeãt ad ſe trahūt.Decidūt ibres.Nebulæ ſubeūt.Siccãt amnes.Ruūt grãdines
Torrét radii:& terrã i mediū undiq̃ ipellūt.Iidé i fracti reſiliūt:& q̃ potuere auferunt
ſecū.Vapor ex alto cadit:rurſūq̃ i altū redit.Véti igruūt ianes.Iidéq̃ cū rapina reme
ant.Tot aïaliū hauſtus ſpiritū e ſublimi trahit.At ille cõtra nitit:Telluſq̃ ut iani cæ
lo ſpiritū iſūdit.Sic ultro citro cõmeãre natura ut torméto aliquo mūdi celeritate diſ
cordia accédat:nec ſtare pugnæ licet:ſed aſſidue rapta cū uoluit.Et circa terrã imé
ſo reȝ cãs globo tédit:ſubide p nubes cælū aliud obtexés.Vétoȝ hoc regnū.Itaq̃ pci
pua eoȝ natura ibi:& ferme reliq̃s cõplexa cãs:quoniã & tonitruū & fulminū iactus
hoȝ uiolétiæ pleriq̃ aſſignãt.Quin & io lapidibus pluere iterim cp̃ uéto ſint rapti:&
multa ſimiliter.Quã ob ré plura ſimul dicéda ſt. De æſtatis tépeſtatib9.C.XXXIX.

TEmpeſtatū rerūq̃ q̃ſdã ſtatas eé cãs:q̃ſdã uero fortuitas:aut adhuc rõis icõptæ
maifeſtū é.Quis.n.æſtates & hyemes qq̃ i tpribus9 ãnua uice itelligūt ſyderū mo
tu fieri dubitet?Ergo ut ſolis natura tépãdo itelligit ãno:ſic reliquoȝ quoq̃ ſydeȝ p
pria é qbuſq̃ uis:& ad ſuã cuiq̃ naturã fertilis.Alia ſt i liquoré ſoluti hūoris foecūda
alia cõcreti i pruias:aut coacti i niues:at glaciati i grãdies.Alia flat9 tp̃is:alia uaporis

clinat ut patebit. S3 epicyclus ei9motu duplici mouet̃ fc3 i lon/
gũ & in latũ. In longitudinẽ quidẽ ficut epicycli fupiorũ femp
t̃ in decẽnouem menfib9folarib9fere femel reuoluit̃.unde fo/
lem in hoc ficut fupiores nõ refpicit.Terminorũ expofitiones
p oĩa fũt hic ficut in trib9fupiorib9.   DE MERCVRIO.

Ercuri9habet orbes qnc3 & epicyclũ.quo3 extre/
mi duo fũt eccẽtrici f̃m qd. fupficies nãc3 cõuexa
fupremi & cõcaua infimi mũdo cõcentricẽ fũt.cõ/
caua aũt fupremi & cõuexa infimi eccẽtricẽ mũdo
fibiipfis t̃n cõcentricẽ. & centrũ earũ t̃m a centro
ẽquantis quantũ centrũ ẽquantis a centro mundi diftat.Et ipfũ
THEORICA ORBIVM MERCVRII.

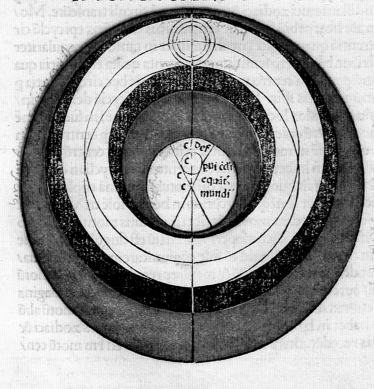

156. Sacro Bosco, *Sphaera Mundi* [The sphere of the world] (1485)
diagram showing the orbit of Mercury, printed in two colors; marginalia

30

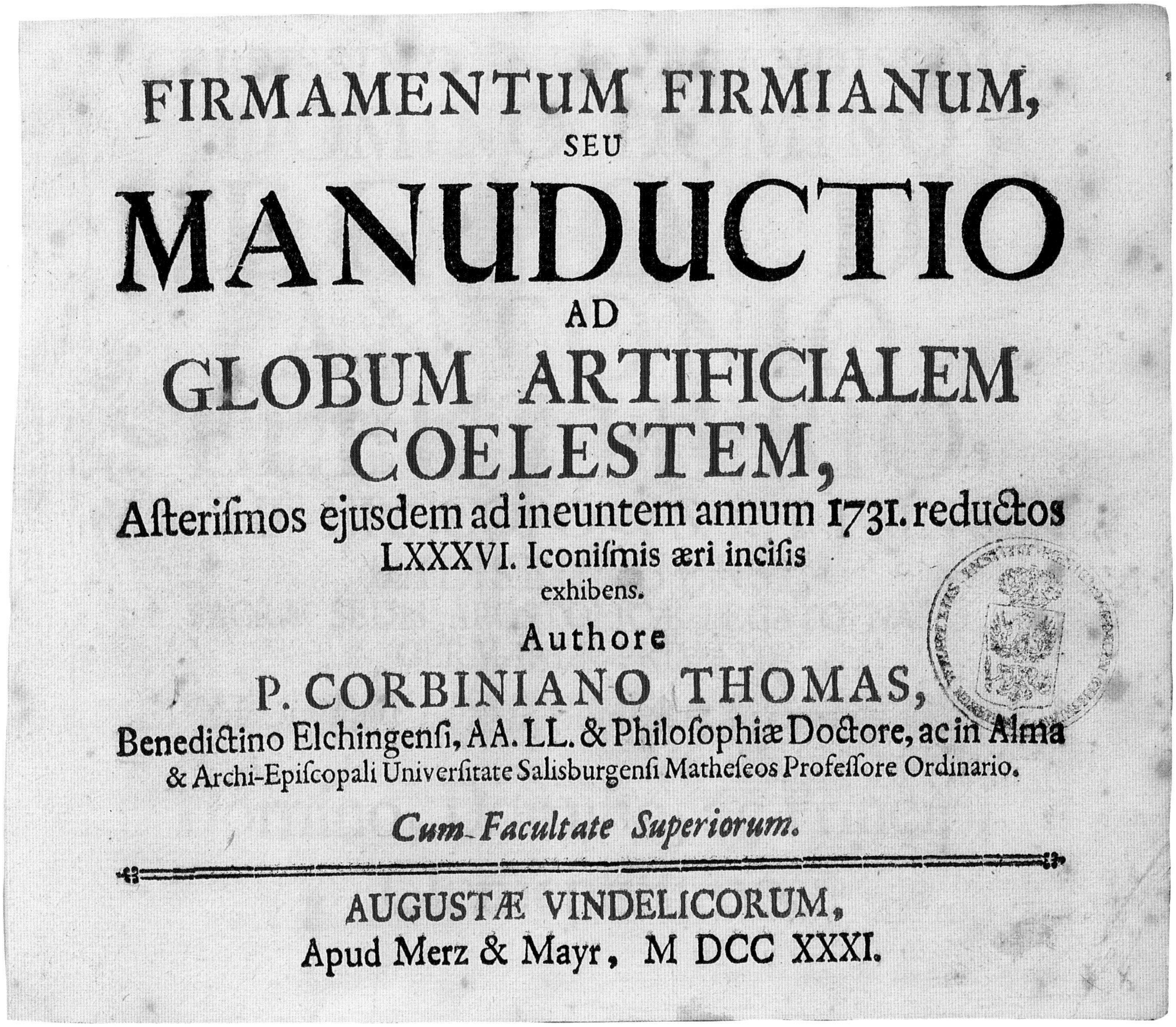

FIRMAMENTUM FIRMIANUM,

SEU

MANUDUCTIO

AD

GLOBUM ARTIFICIALEM
COELESTEM,

Afterifmos ejusdem ad ineuntem annum 1731. reductos
LXXXVI. Iconifmis æri incifis
exhibens.

Authore

P. CORBINIANO THOMAS,

Benedictino Elchingenfi, AA. LL. & Philofophiæ Doctore, ac in Alma
& Archi-Epifcopali Univerfitate Salisburgenfi Matheseos Profeffore Ordinario.

Cum Facultate Superiorum.

AUGUSTÆ VINDELICORUM,
Apud Merz & Mayr, M DCC XXXI.

186. Thomas, *Firmamentum Firmianum* [Orb of the fixed stars] (1731) title page

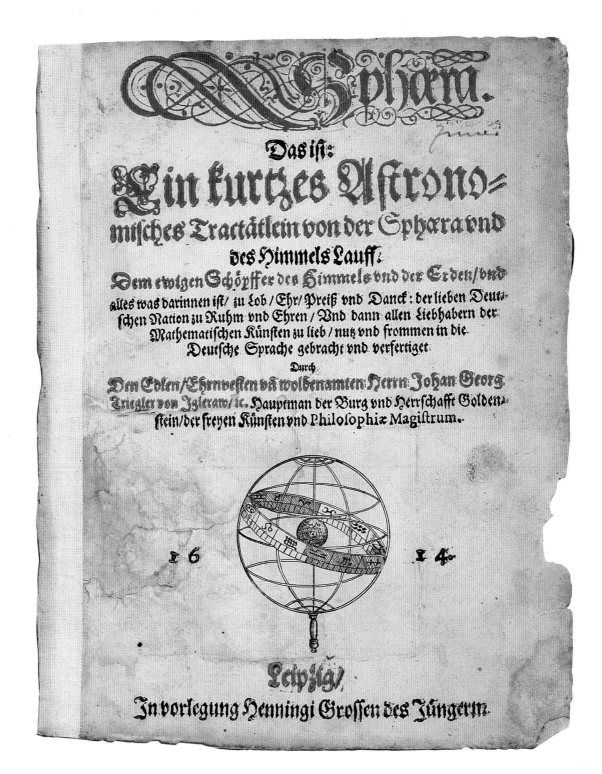

Sphæra.

Das ist:

Ein kurtzes Astrono-

misches Tractätlein von der Sphæra und
des Himmels Lauff:

Dem ewigen Schöpffer des Himmels und der Erden/und
alles was darinnen ist/ zu Lob/Ehr/Preiß und Danck: der lieben Deut-
schen Nation zu Ruhm und Ehren/ Und dann allen Liebhabern der
Mathematischen Künsten zu lieb/nutz und frommen in die
Deutsche Sprache gebracht und verfertiget.

Durch

Den Edlen/Ehrnvesten vñ wolbenamten Herrn Johan Georg
Triegler von Iglaraw/ꝛc. Hauptman der Burg und Herrschafft Golden-
stein/der freyen Künsten und Philosophiæ Magistrum.

1 6   1 4.

Leipzig/

In verlegung Henningi Grossen des Jüngern.

187. Triegler, *Sphaera. Das ist ein kurtzes Astronomisches Tractätlein*
[Sphere. That is a short astronomical treatise] (1614) title page

32

CATALOGUE OF
THE RARE
ASTRONOMICAL
BOOKS
IN THE
SAN DIEGO STATE
UNIVERSITY
LIBRARY

1 *Ablainung und Widerlegung der Astrologiae,* und
Iudiciariae, und Aberglaubischen Calendermacher

Augsburg: Andrea Erffurt, 1654

20 cm. 48 leaves.

Quotes the ancients and recent astronomers.
"Nicolaus Copernicus setzt die Sonne in das Mittel
dess Kraiss der Welt; vermaint die Erde werde
bewegt...." (Nicolas Copernicus places the sun at the
center of a circle of the universe; claims the earth
moves....) [p. 26].

Included with this work, paged separately:
*Der ander Theil. Ein Verzaichnuss der Kayser, Königen, und
fürtrefflichen Männer, welche die Sternkunst geübt und
gezieret haben.*

Zinner Collection

NUC: NIC

2 ALBERTUS MAGNUS, SAINT, BISHOP OF
RATISBON, 1193?–1280

*De Duabus Sapientijs et de Recapitulatione Omnium
Librorum Astronomiae*

Nürnberg: K. Hochfeder, ca.1491

21 cm. Quarto. 12 leaves. Marginalia throughout, sixteenth-century hand.

Author was a medieval German philosopher and
theologian. He quotes Aristotle, Ptolemy, Arab writers, and others. He presents the Ptolemaic system.

Zinner Collection

Zinner, 539

NUC: CtY; DLC; ICN; MBCo; MH

Goff: BMedL; HarvCL; HEHL; LC; NewL; YUL

3 ALFONSO X, EL SABIO, KING OF CASTILE AND
LEÓN, 1221–84

Tabule Astronomice

Venice: Johannes Hamman, 1492

21 cm. Quarto. 114 leaves. Second edition. Illustrations,
woodcut initials and other initial letters in blue. Modern
calf binding, gilt on spine.

Famed Alfonsine astronomical tables used to predict
the motion of the planets and stars. This is the last incunabulum edition and appears to be as rare as the
first edition of 1483.

Houzeau, 1962; Lalande, p. 19

NUC: CtY; DLC; ICN; IU; MBM; MH; NCH; TxU

Goff: BMedL; BPubL; BurL; HamCL; HarvCL; HDH;
HEHL; LC; LC(T); LeUL(H); LIHSL; NavObL; NewL;
NLM; NYPL; UMichL; UOkL; UTexL; WDM

4 AMICO, GIOVANNI BATTISTA, 1512–38

*...De Motibus Corporum Coelestiū iuxta Principia
Peripatetica sine Eccentricis & Epicyclis*

Venice: J. Patavino & V. Roffinello, 1536

22 cm. 27 leaves. Decorated woodcut initial and twenty
diagrams. This work is bound with Fracastoro, G.,
Homocentrica, 1538 (item 61).

Very little is known about Amico. He was born at
Cosenza, studied at the University of Padua, and was
killed there due to the invidiousness of his doctrine.
Departing from Ptolemaic theory he believed the
stars moved homocentrically and less epicyclically.

NUC: ICJ; MH

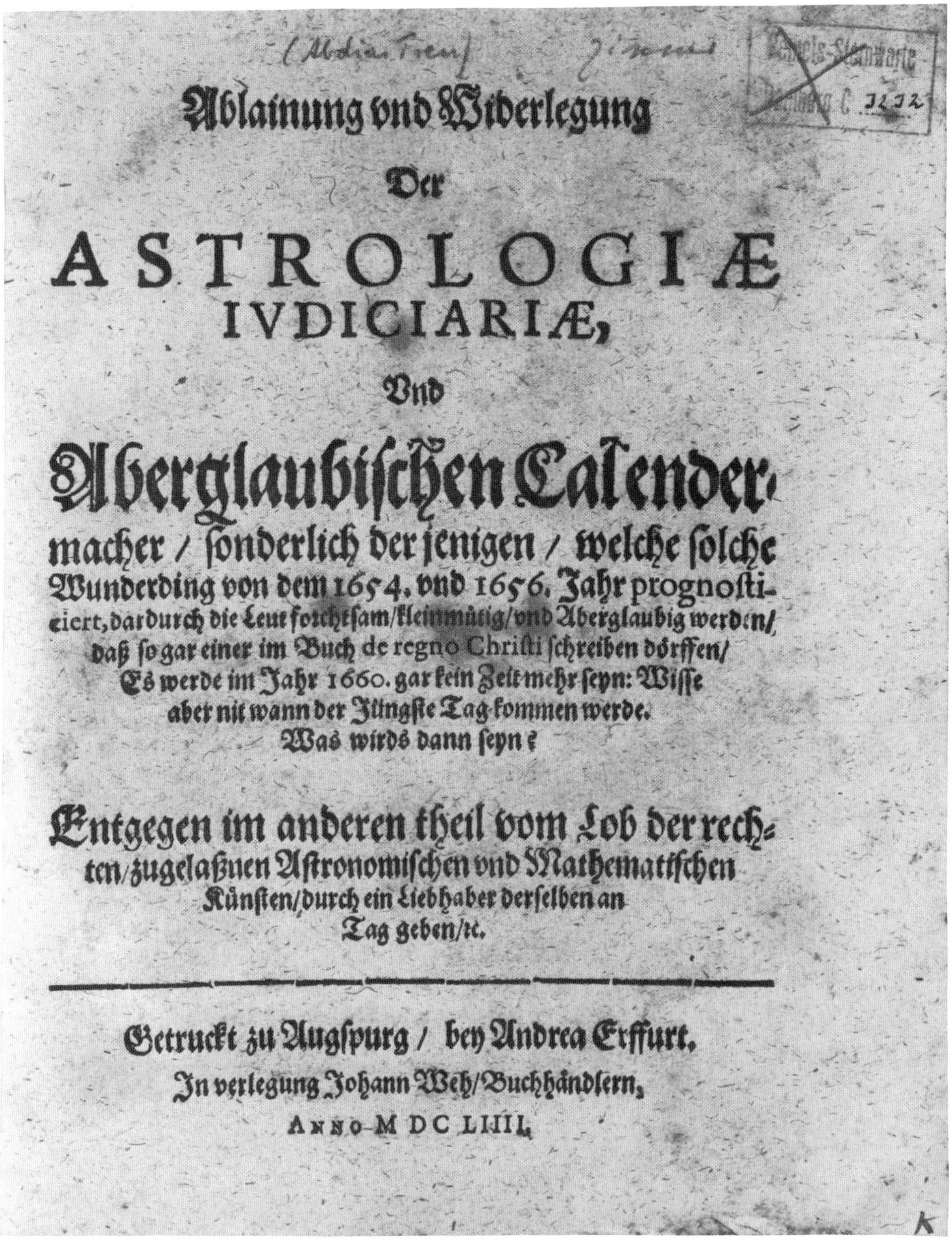

Ablainung vnd Widerlegung

Der

ASTROLOGIÆ
IVDICIARIÆ,

Vnd

Aberglaubischen Calender-

macher / sonderlich der jenigen / welche solche
Wunderding von dem 1654. vnd 1656. Jahr prognosti-
ciert, dardurch die Leut forchtsam/kleinmütig/vnd Aberglaubig werden/
daß so gar einer im Buch de regno Christi schreiben dörffen/
Es werde im Jahr 1660. gar kein Zeit mehr seyn: Wisse
aber nit wann der Jüngste Tag kommen werde.
Was wirds dann seyn?

Entgegen im anderen theil vom Lob der rech-

ten/zugelaßnen Astronomischen vnd Mathematischen
Künsten/durch ein Liebhaber derselben an
Tag geben/rc.

———————————————————————

Getruckt zu Augspurg / bey Andrea Erffurt.
In verlegung Johann Weh/Buchhändlern,
ANNO M DC LIIII.

1. *Ablainung und Widerlegung* [Report and review] (1654) title page

Incipit liber Alberti magni de duabus sapientijs
et de recapitulatione omnium librorū astronomie.

OCcasione quorundam li

brorū/apud quos nō eſt radix ſcientie:qui cum ſint
vere ſapientie inimici:hoc eſt dñi noſtri ieſu chriſti:
qui eſt imago patris et ſapientia p quē fecit z ſecula:fidei ama
toribus katholice ſunt merito ſuſpecti:placuit quibuſdam ma
gnis viris/vt libros quoſdã alioz forte innoxios accuſarent:
qm̄ em̄ plures antedictorū libroz nigromanciā palliāt pfeſſio
ne aſtronomie mentientes libros notabiles de eadem fecere et
apud bonos et graues abhoiabiles reddiderunt. Quare qui
dam zelator fidei et philoſophie vtriuſcz frater ſcilicet in ordi
ne ſuo applicuit animum:vt faceret commemorationem vtro
rumcz librorum exponens initium materiam titulos et conti
nentias ſinguloz in generali et qui fuerūt eorū auctores:vt ſ.
liciti ab illicitis ſepararēt:et aggreſſus eſt/vt diceret nutu dei.

Capitulum primum.

DVe ſunt magne ſapien

tie z vtracz nomine aſtronomie cenſet: quax pri
ma eſt in ſcientia figure celi pmi et equalitate mo
tus eiº ſuper polos equatoris dici/z celoz ſup eo
poſitoz qui ſunt oppoſiti ſup polos alios extra primos et ipſi
ſunt celi ſtellarū fixarū et errantiū:quarū figura eſt velud figu
ra ſperaz inuice cōtinentiū. An ſcia quocz deſcriptionū circu
lorum in eis:quoruidā eque diſtātiū equatori:et quorundā cō
centricoz eidē ſm̄ declinationē ab ipo. Et alioz egreſſe cuſpi
dis:et quorundā concentricoz ſup ſperas egreſſorū:et alioruz
ſilr oim concētricoz ſup cuſpidē equatoris ad quātitatē egreſ/
ſionis cuſpidū egreſſoris. Et in egritate vniuſcuiuſcz eorum et
elongatiōe a terra. Et qualiter mouent planete motu orbium
deferentiū z motu corporū in orbibus. Et quid accidat eis ex
variatione ſitus:vt ſunt piectiones radioz inuiſibiles z eclip
ſes ſolis et lune. Ceterorūcz planetarū adinuice:et eſſe corū in
circulo ſue augis vt ſunt eleuatō depreſſio motus latitudis re
flectionis et inflectionis et in circulo breui: vt ſunt ſtatio dire

a ı

2. Albertus Magnus, *De Duabus Sapientijs* [Concerning the two wisdoms] (ca. 1491) incipit

37

Exhortatoria in impressionē tabularū Astronomicarū Alfonsi Regis.

Augustinus Morauus Olomucensis Johanni Lucilio Santritter Heilbronnensi S.P.D.

Quū temporum nostrorum conditionē mecum ipse reputo Johannes Luciū Amice suauissime:eamcz ex priscorū illorū imagine diligentius expendo atcz pertracto.gloriari sepe non mediocriter soleo: id me potissimū etatis incidisse: in quo post defectos pene optimarū disciplinarū fructus: is demū studiorum ardor succreuerit: vt ą longa vetustatis negligentia deperierant: iam redeant iterū:ac rediuiuo quodam spiritu in meliorē propemodū frugem excitenf atcz repullulent.Quis enī vehemētius non indoluerat:fecūdissima illa ingenia: locupletissima studia:illas inquā omniū virtutū faces ita a splendore z dignitate concidere potuisse vncz: vt eorū aliquādiu vix vestigia quedā inuenirenf.Nō Philosophia:non Oratoria:non Poetica:non Mathematica vsquā supererat ą feda barbaries ita sumerserit oīa:vt a clade illa longe calamitosissima:egre nobis ad id vscz eui respirare sit vatū.Uerum enimuero:quo magis illa tempora luctuosa fuere:quibus omnis studior honos conciderat:eo plus his nostris gratulandū Amice suauissime existimo: quibus preclara ingenia ad pristinum iterum calorem reuiuiscunt: Quin etiam si vllus apud inferos sensus inuenif: gaudere etiam manes ipsos existimem:cz eorum labores:exercitia:vigilie:vna cum eis iā fere sepulte in lucē denuo prodeant: ac multipharia disperse in vnū veluti corpus congregenf iterum atcz subsidant. Id quū in omni disciplinarū genere incredibili imprimis celeritate confectū sit: vtpote vbi ad cōmunē causam in vnū fere omnes conspirarūt:preter ceteros tn Georgius Purbachiº:et Johannes ille de Regio mōte:viri germani:latinecz ac grece lingue iuxta eruditi: Sideralis sibi negocij parte eouscz tutati sunt: vt cum ceteri non nisi alias pertractata disquirerent:hi sibi z incognita z intentata prius:proprio vt aiunt Marte desumūt. Quū enī multos varioscz errores validius detriumphassent: ad ea etiā animū adijcere tentarūt:ą vetez plericz aut difficultate deterriti:aut laborū pertesi itacta omnino pterierāt.Nō si vl Pitagoras ille ąa primus grecis(vt Aristoxenº scribit)pondera z mensurādi rationē inuexit: Si Anaximāder Milesius: quia primus Celestia signa Conuersionescz solares: Horoscopia et Equinoctia adnotarit.Si.L.denicz Sulpicius apud Latinos:Thales Milesius apud Grecos quia defectus Solis z Lune primi prodiderunt: sūmo honore sūmacz veneratione habiti:miris laudibus efferunf:Quid tandē his iure tribuerim:qui ea que antea tancz i Apollis quodā sacello a cōmuni hominū cōtuitu abscōdebanf:ita nobis prodiderūt: vt omnibus iamiamcz manifesta esse valeant z cognita.Sed quorsum ista inquies efflagitabā abs te cōtinuo conui

A   2

3. Alfonso X, *Tabule Astronomice* [Astronomical tables] (1492) incipit

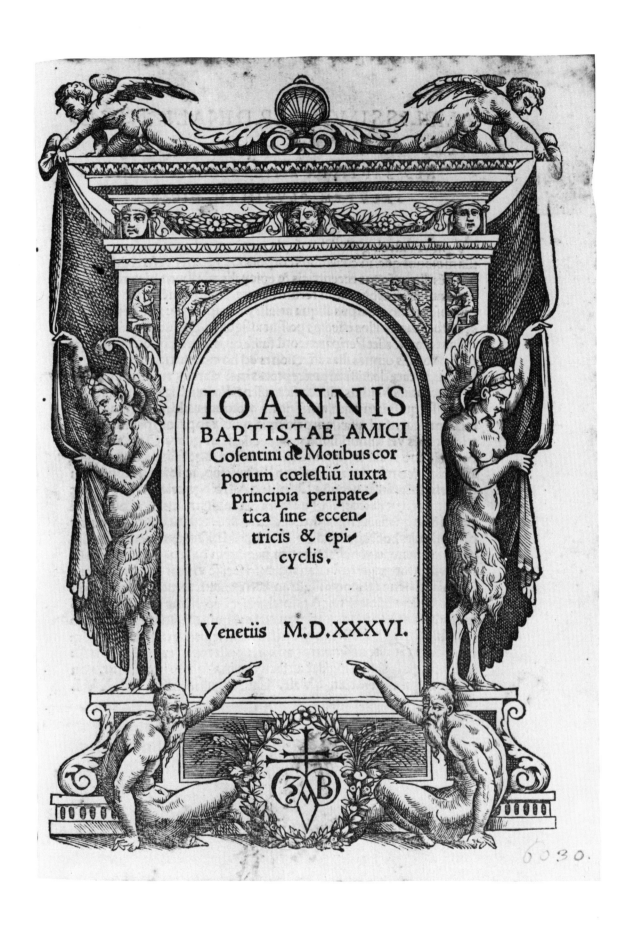

IOANNIS
BAPTISTAE AMICI
Cosentini de Motibus cor
porum cœlestiū iuxta
principia peripate
tica sine eccen
tricis & epi
cyclis.

Venetiis M.D.XXXVI.

4. Amico, *De Motibus Corporum Coelestiū* [Concerning the movements
of the heavenly bodies] (1536) title page

5 AMMAN, CAESARIUS, 1727–92

Quadrans Astronomicus

Augsburg: Eberhard Klett, 1770

21 cm. 91 pages. Two folding plates. Printers' devices. Provenance, title page: "Stephane ex Dono Ras Celleb; Mauritio Prantner... D: Franz Seraph: Sallinger."

Amman, a Jesuit professor of mathematics and Hebrew at the University of Ingolstadt, was born at Innsbruck. He was appointed director of the astronomical observatory at Dillingen. Besides the book listed here he was the author of *De Lumine et Visione, de Determinatio Systematis Planetarum Exercitatio Mathematica* (Ingolstadt, 1770) [*Poggendorff*, v. 1, p. 38].

Zinner Collection

Lalande, p. 517

NUC: NN; NNC

6 APIANUS, PETRUS, 1495–1552

Cosmographiae Introductio cum quibusdam Geometriae ac Astronomiae

Venice: F. Bindo, 1537

16 cm. 32 leaves. Woodcut diagram on title page, twenty-eight woodcuts in text, printer's device on recto of last leaf. Bound with Sacro Bosco, J. *Liber de Sphaera*, 1541 (item 161).

Born Peter Bienewitz at Leisnig, Germany, Petrus Apianus was a pioneer in astronomical and geographical instrumentation. Apianus is the Latin translation

of part of his family name, Biene, which means "bee" in German. He studied mathematics and astronomy at Leipzig and Vienna and established a reputation as an outstanding mathematician after the publication of his first work *Typus Orbis Universalis* (Vienna, 1520). He was appointed professor of mathematics at Ingolstadt in 1524; he remained there until his death except for visiting professorships that he held at Leipzig, Vienna, Tübingen, Padua, and Ferrara.

He was consulted by the great sixteenth-century Hapsburg ruler, the Holy Roman Emperor Charles V, who raised him to the nobility through bestowing knighthood upon him.

Apianus's first major work, *Cosmographia seu Descriptio Totius Orbis* (1524), was based on Ptolemy. In its later form, as modified by Gemma Frisius (item 72), his *Cosmographia* was one of the most popular texts of the sixteenth century.

His second major work, a large folio volume *Astronomicum Caesareum* (represented by a 1967 facsimile in the San Diego State University Library), contains twenty-one ingenious volvelles printed in color. These imaginative mechanical devices provided data on the position and movement of celestial bodies (*DSB*, v. 1, pp. 178–9).

Apianus was also famous for his comprehensive paleontological work *Inscriptiones Sacrosanctae Vetustatis* (Ingolstadt, 1534). There is a copy in the San Diego State University Library.

Houzeau, 2393; Lalande lists nineteen editions, but not this one.

NUC: DLC; ICN; MH; NN; NNH; RPJCB

7 ARCHENHOLD, FRIEDRICH SIMON, 1861–1939, editor

Alte Kometen-Einblattdrucke

Berlin: Treptow-Sternwarte, 1900?

58 × 44 cm. 25 plates. Unbound in portfolio. Reprints of broadsides reporting comets sighted in the fifteenth through seventeenth centuries.

Zinner Collection

NUC: CU; ICU

title page (reduced)

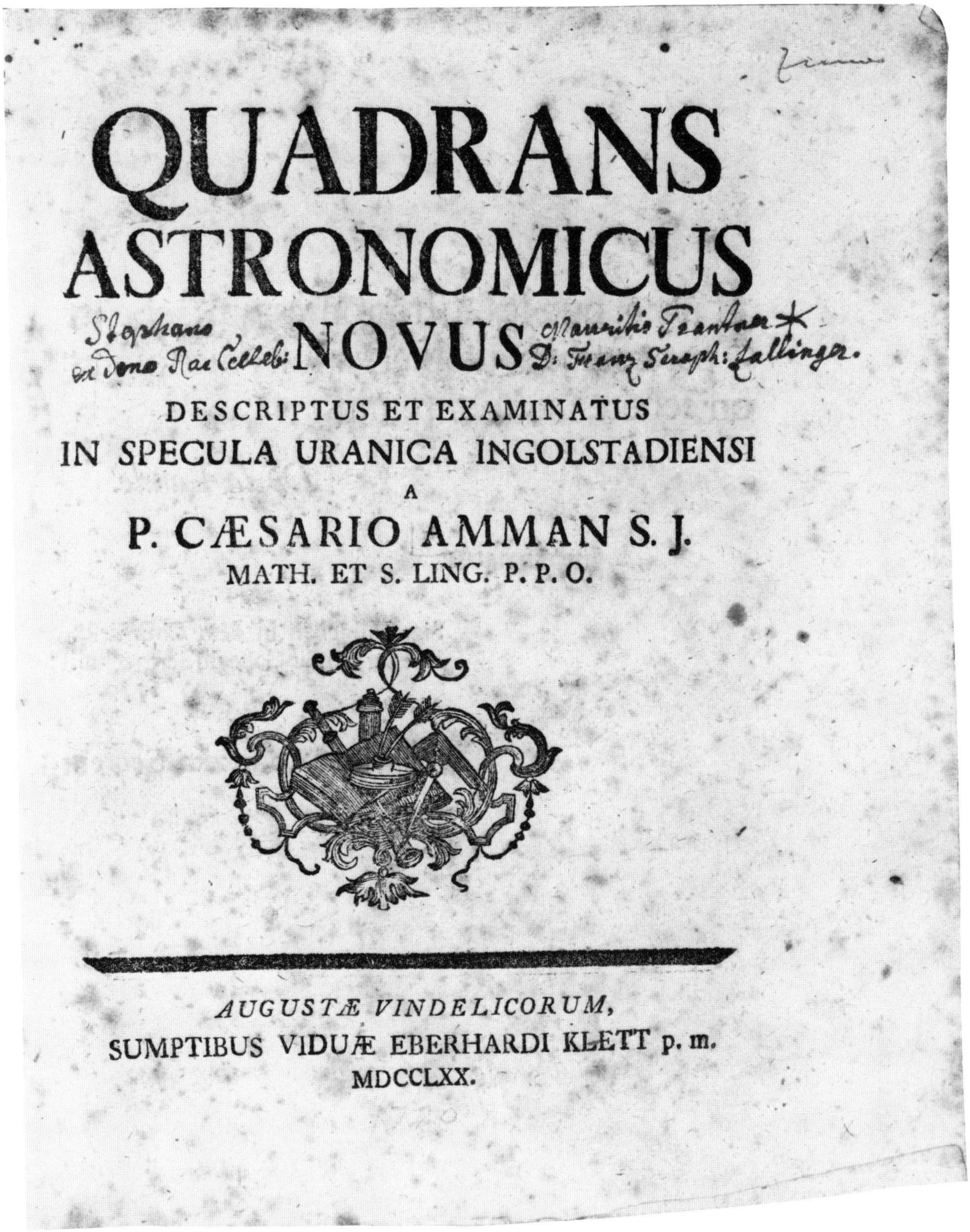

QUADRANS ASTRONOMICUS

Stephano ex dono Rae Cellebi NOVUS *Mauritio Trantaa D. Franz Seraph: Fallinger*

DESCRIPTUS ET EXAMINATUS
IN SPECULA URANICA INGOLSTADIENSI
A
P. CÆSARIO AMMAN S. J.
MATH. ET S. LING. P. P. O.

AUGUSTÆ VINDELICORUM,
SUMPTIBUS VIDUÆ EBERHARDI KLETT p. m.
MDCCLXX.

5. Amman, *Quadrans Astronomicus* [The astronomical quadrant] (1770) title page

Figura huius diuiſionis tibi hic
ab oculos poſita eſt.

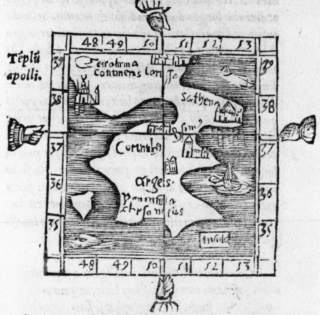

DE VSV TABVLARVM PTOLE.

& qualiter vniuſcuiuſq; regionis, loci aut oppidi
ſitus in illis ſit inueniendus. Cap. XVIII.

INueſtigaturus itaq; alicuius oppidi ſitum in tabulis
Ptolemæi Elicias in primis gradus longitudinis &
latitudinis ex abaco regionum, prouinciarum, & oppiſ

6. Apianus, *Cosmographiae Introductio* [Introduction to cosmography] (1537)

Diſer Comet, ſo ein geſchweiffter Stern, von wenig Haaren, das Haüpt wünderbar
hell, mit einem ſehr langen Schweiff, erſchien eine Stünd nach der Soñen Untergang.
ſehende nach Nidergang, ſchnell im Laüff Mercurialiſcher Natür, ünter dem
Geſtirn deß Löwen, correſpondirende mit der erſten Geſtalt der Jungfraüen. Er
ſtrecket ſich 700 Welſcher Meilen weit. Aſtrologiſch davon zü ürtheilen, be
deütet ſolcher groſſe Unfrüchtbarkeit, Mangel Getreids, Schnee, groſſe ünd ſchäd
liche Regen, ünd (welches Gott verhüte) einige Peſtilenz. Venus iſt in dem
Perigeo ihres Epicicli; dahero zü müthmaſſen, daß ſolcher der Chriſtenheit
Glück, ünd dem Türckiſchen Reich Niderlag, ünd deſſelben
Untergang bedeüte

7. Archenhold, *Alte Kometen-Einblattdrucke* [Old prints of comets] (1900?)
Reproduction from collection of old prints of comets. [Illustration of the comet
visible above Naples March 4, 1702] (reduced)

8 ARCHIMEDES, 287?–212 B.C.

Opera Non Nulla a Federico Commandino Urbinate

Venice: Paulus Manutius, 1558

32 cm. Folio. 126 leaves. Two parts in one volume. Contemporary limp vellum. Aldine device on title pages and verso of last leaf. Numerous woodcut text diagrams and decorated initial letters. Extensive marginalia and corrections to text.

From the library of Ladislao Reti (1901–73), whom Bern Dibner judged "the foremost authority on the technological work of Leonardo da Vinci." Born in Fiume in what is now Yugoslavia, Dr. Reti took degrees in chemical engineering at the universities of Vienna and Bologna. A linguist, he was fluent in German as well as Italian and Hungarian. He also knew Spanish, Portuguese, English, and French.

Aldine Press printer's device

Dr. Reti's most significant work was the transcription, editing, and translation into Spanish, French, and English of the long-lost *Codex Madrid* of Leonardo. He also assembled a fine library of fifteenth- and sixteenth-century books in the history of science.

Houzeau, 752

NUC: CSt; CoCC; CtY, DFo; ICJ; ICU; IU; MH; MiU; NIC; NN; NNC; NNNAM; NNU-W; NjP; OkU; PPAN; PPFrankI; PPULC; WU

9 *Astronomia Teutsch. Himmels Lauff*

Frankfurt am Main: Chr. Egenoffs Erben, 1571

20 cm. 116 leaves. Illustrations, tables, title printed in red and black. Signature on title page. Decorated initials, 146 superb woodcuts. Bound in eighteenth-century three-quarter calf, red spine label, gold lettering and decoration.

Zinner Collection

Zinner, 2540

NUC: no copy

10 *Astronomica Veterum Scripta*

Heidelberg: Officina Sanctandreana, 1589

16 cm. 238 leaves. Woodcut illustrations. Title vignette. Text in Latin and Greek.

Zinner, 3356

NUC: CtY; DFo; IEN; MBAt; MH; MiU; NcD; NBuG; NCH; NNC; OkU; PPLT; PPULC; PU; RPB; ViLxW

11 BALDE, JAKOB, 1604–68

De Eclipsi Solari

Munich: Lucas Straub, 1662

14 cm. 119 leaves. Three copper-engraved plates, decorated initials, contemporary limp vellum binding.

Zinner Collection

NUC: IU; NjP; NNC; WU

12 BAUMANN, HEINRICH, 1634–69, preses; Respondens, EMANUEL HAMMER

Q.B.V.D. Disputatio Physica de Stellis

Wittenberg: J. Haken, 1666

20 cm. 16 leaves.

Heinrich Baumann was born at Torgau, in the vicinity of Leipzig, where his father was an archdeacon. He studied at Wittenberg and became director and professor at the gymnasium at Coburg. He wrote mostly on theological subjects (*Iselin*, v. 1, p. 825).

Zinner Collection

NUC: no copy

ARCHIMEDIS
CIRCVLI DIMENSIO.

PROPOSITIO I.

QVILIBET circulus æqualis est triangulo rectangulo : cuius quidem semidiameter uni laterum, quæ circa rectũ angulũ sunt, ambitus uero basi eius est æqualis.

Sit a b c d circulus, ut ponitur. Dico eum æqualem esse triangulo e . si enim fieri potest, sit primum maior circulus : & ipsi inscribatur quadratum a c : secenturq́; circunferentiæ bifariam : & sint portiones iam minores excessu, quo circulus ipsum triangulum excedit. erit figura rectilinea adhuc triangulo maior. Sumatur centrum n ; & perpendicularis n x. minor est igitur n x trianguli latere . est autem & ambitus rectilineæ figuræ reliquo latere minor ; quoniam & minor est circuli ambitu . quare figura rectilinea minor est triangulo e : quod est absurdum .

Sit deinde , si fieri potest , circulus minor triangulo e : & circumscribatur quadratum : circũferentiisq́; bifariam sectis , per ea puncta contingentes lineæ ducãtur. erit angulus o a r rectus. & idcirco linea o r maior , quàm r m ; quòd r m ipsi r a sit æqualis. triangulum igitur r o p maius est , quàm dimidium figuræ o f a m. itaque sumantur portiones , ipsi p f a similes ; quæ quidem minores sint eo , quo triangulum e excedit circulum a b c d. erit figura circumscripta adhuc triangulo e minor : quod item est absurdum , cum sit maior : nam ipsa quidem n a æqualis est trianguli catheto : ambitus uero maior est basi eiusdem . ex quibus sequitur circulum triangulo e æqualem esse.

PROPOSITIO II.

Circulus ad quadratũ diametri eam proportionẽ habet , quàm XI ad XIIII.

Sit circulus, cuius diameter a b : & circumscribatur quadratũ c g : & ipsius c d dupla sit d e : sit autem e f, septima eiusdẽ c d. Quo-

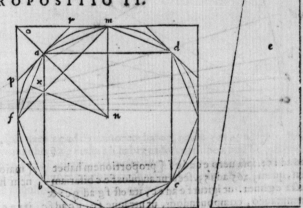

ständigen werden/so ferz du nur ein wenig verstand vnnd ingenium
brauchen wilt. Besihe die zwo figuren.

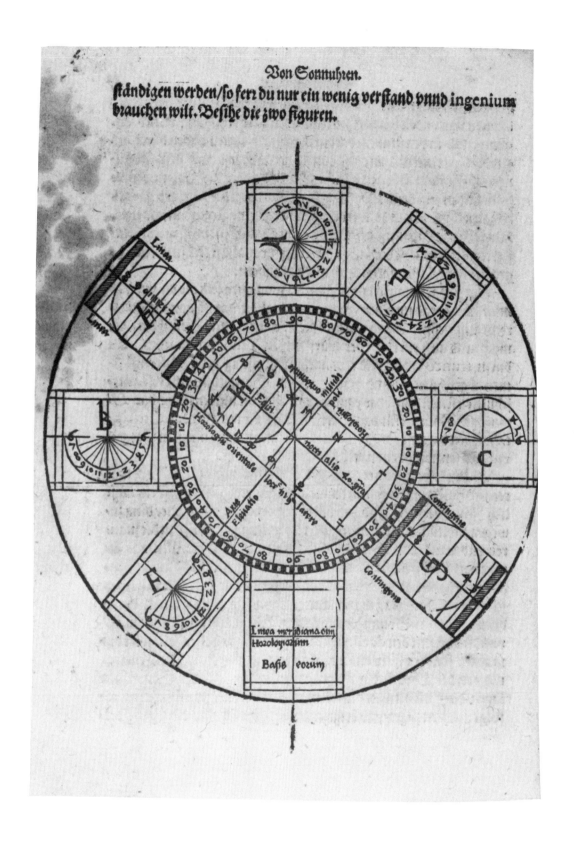

9. *Astronomia Teutsch* [German astronomy] (1571) concerning sundials

ASTRONOMICA
VETERVM SCRIPTA
ISAGOGICA GRÆCA
& Latina.

Auct. Græci,

PROCLI SPHÆRA.
ARATI SOLENSIS
Phænomena, & Prognostica,
LEONTIVS ME-
CHANICVS de constru-
ctione Arateæ Sphæræ.

His tribus adiuncta est inter-
pretatio Latina, in qua
verbum de verbo expressum
est.

Latini.

ARATEA Phænomena
cum poetica interpretatione
M. T. CICERONIS,
FESTI RVFI Auieni
GERMANICI CÆS.
cū cōmentariis incerti auct.
VETERVM Poetarum
Fragmenta Astronomica.
C. IVLI HYGINI
Poeticon Astronomicon.

OPVS non Astronomiæ solum, sed & Poeseos
studiosis apprime vtile.

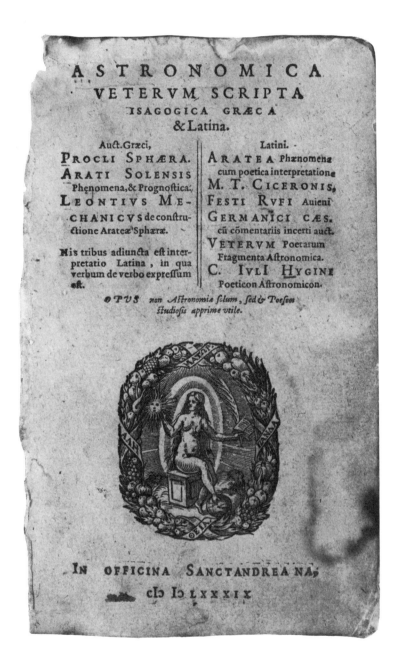

IN OFFICINA SANCTANDREANA,
cIɔ Iɔ LXXXIX

10. *Astronomica Veterum Scripta* [Greek and Latin
astronomical writings] (1589) title page

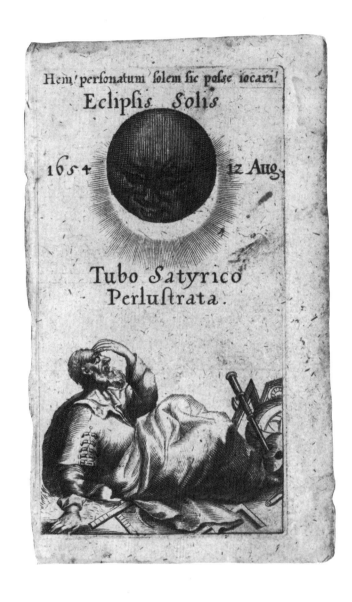

11. Balde, *De Eclipsi Solari* [Concerning eclipses
of the sun] (1662) frontispiece

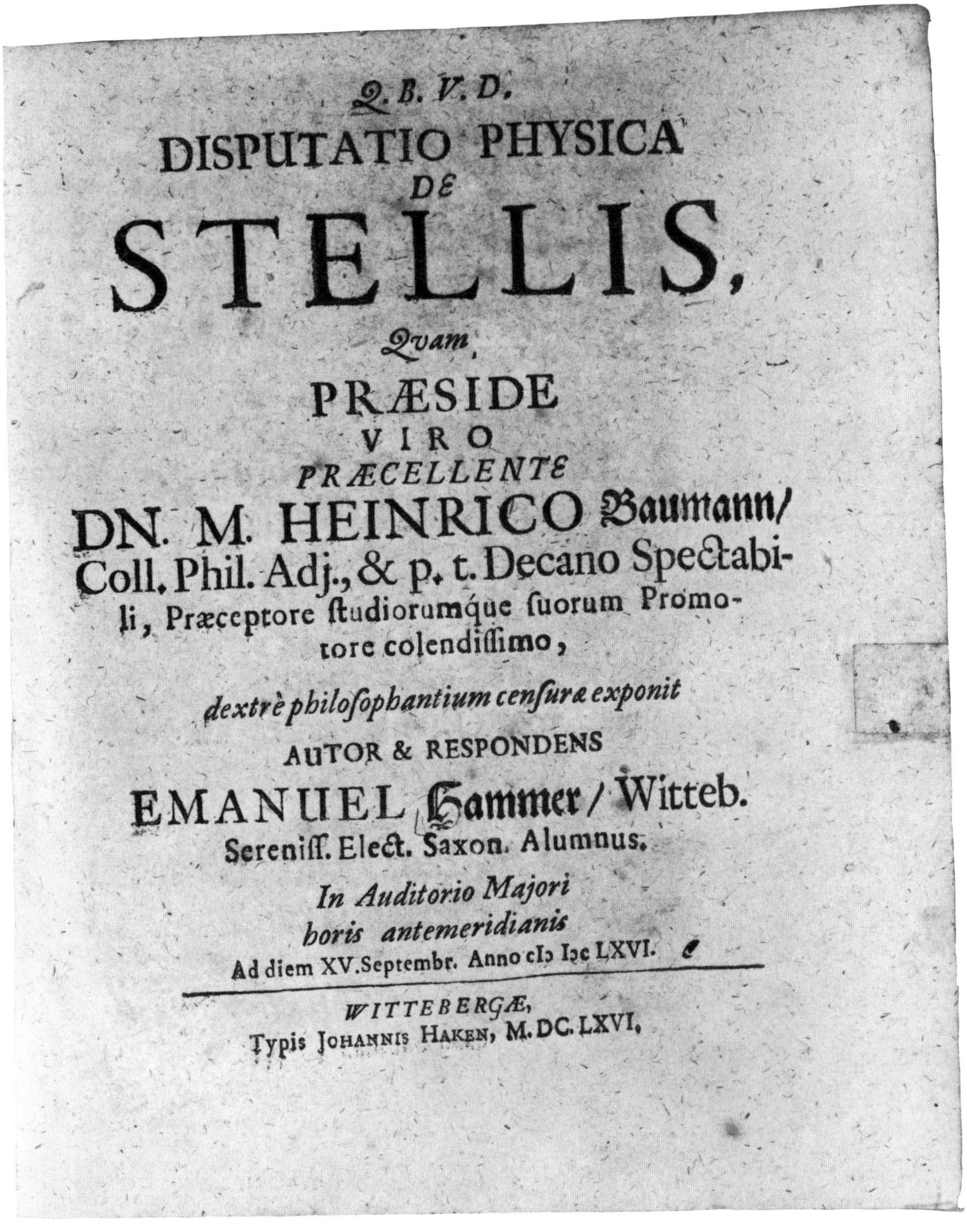

Q. B. V. D.

DISPUTATIO PHYSICA
DE
STELLIS,

Qvam,

PRÆSIDE
VIRO
PRÆCELLENTE
DN. M. HEINRICO Baumann/
Coll. Phil. Adj., & p. t. Decano Spectabi-
li, Præceptore studiorumque suorum Promo-
tore colendissimo,

dextrè philosophantium censura exponit

AUTOR & RESPONDENS

EMANUEL Hammer / Witteb.
Sereniss. Elect. Saxon. Alumnus.

In Auditorio Majori
horis antemeridianis
Ad diem XV. Septembr. Anno cIↃ IↃc LXVI.

WITTEBERGÆ,
Typis Johannis Haken, M. DC. LXVI.

12. Baumann, *Disputatio Physica de Stellis* [Physical disputation concerning the stars] (1666)
title page of an academic disputation

13 BAYER, JOHANN, 1572–1625

Uranometria

Augsburg: Christopher Mangus, 1603

36 cm. Folio. 106 leaves. With fine engraved title border and fifty-one double-page engraved plates. Text on verso of the plates and three preliminary leaves. Printer's device on the colophon. Contemporary limp vellum with the author and title written in ink on the spine.

First edition of this first complete star atlas, a fundamental work in that branch of astronomy the author called "uranometry," the science of measuring the distances and magnitudes of the heavenly bodies. The copperplates were beautifully engraved by Alexander Mair.

Johann Bayer, municipal advocate in Augsburg and German astronomer, was the first to reform the ancient method of distinguishing stars as contained in Ptolemy's *Syntaxis*. He introduced the method of assigning to each star in a constellation one of the twenty-four letters of the Greek alphabet. For constellations with more than two-dozen stars, he resorted to the Latin alphabet. He placed these Greek and Latin letters on his star charts. Thus, just a few years before the invention of the telescope enormously increased the number of visible stars, Bayer produced a stellar nomenclature that astronomers still use.

Another copy in the Zinner Collection has the fifty-one folding plates without text, but with an additional leaf on the recto of which are two manuscript diagrams, one showing the Copernican heliocentric planetary system, the other a Tychonian system.

Lalande, p. 139; Zinner, 3951

NUC: DCU; DN-Ob; MH; MNS; NjP; NN; RPB

14 BECK, MATTHIAS FRIEDRICH, 1649–1701

...Ephemerides Persarum per Totum Annum

Augsburg: Laur. Kroniger, 1695–96

33 cm. Folio. 74 leaves. Portrait, diagrams, tables. Title in red and black. Decorated initials. Bound in leather over boards, gold fore edges. First edition.

Zinner Collection

NUC: CSdS

15 *Betrachtung und Bedencken über den...Cometen*

Jena?: n.p., 1681

21 cm. 16 leaves. Folding plate.

Description and explanation of the comet of 1680–81, which had also been observed by Newton, Flamsteed, Bernoulli, and others. The anonymous writer thinks this comet particularly awe-inspiring.

NUC: NNC

16 BIANCANI, GIUSEPPE, 1566–1624

Sphaera Mundi, seu Cosmographia Demonstrativa

Bologna: S. Bonomi, S. Tamburini, 1620

23 cm. 235 leaves. Illustrations, one folding plate, and one volvelle. Title page in red and black with astronomical vignette. Numerous woodcut diagrams in text. Bound in old calf, gilt arms of J. A. deThou and his second wife stamped within double gilt fillets on covers, title in gilt on spine. Armorial bookplate on front pastedown.

First edition discussing the recent telescopic discoveries and current theories of Kepler and Galileo.

Biancani, an important Jesuit mathematician and astronomer, was a student of Christopher Clavius and a follower of Tycho Brahe. He presents his own theory of the earth's tendency toward perfect roundness, wherein natural forces operate to plane mountains and fill valleys so that ultimately a smooth-surfaced earth will be completely covered by the ocean as it was primevally. Interestingly, one of the many woodcuts in the text is the first illustration of a thermometer (see p. 111).

Lalande, p. 179

NUC: Ct-M; MH; MiU; WU

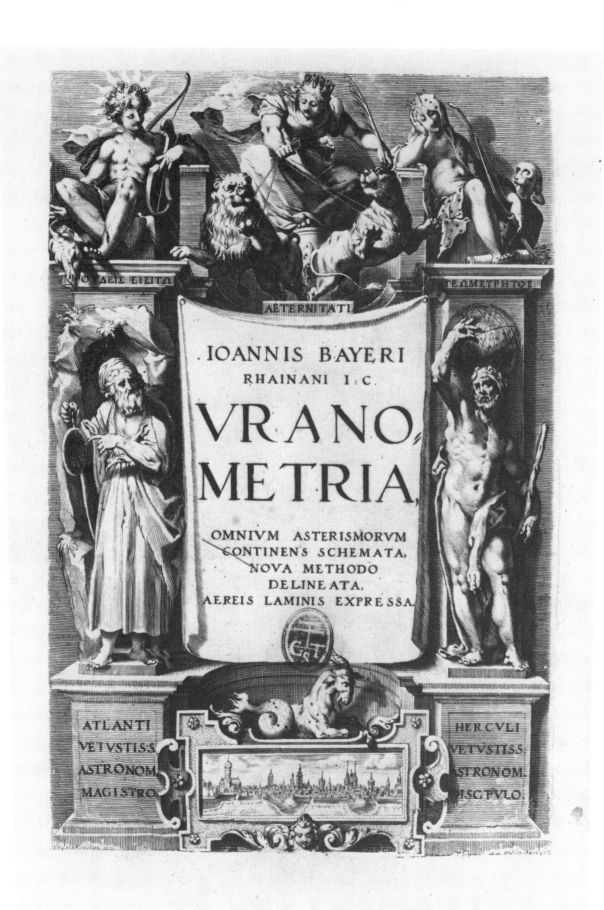

13. Bayer, *Uranometria* [Measuring the distances to the planets] (1603) title page (reduced)

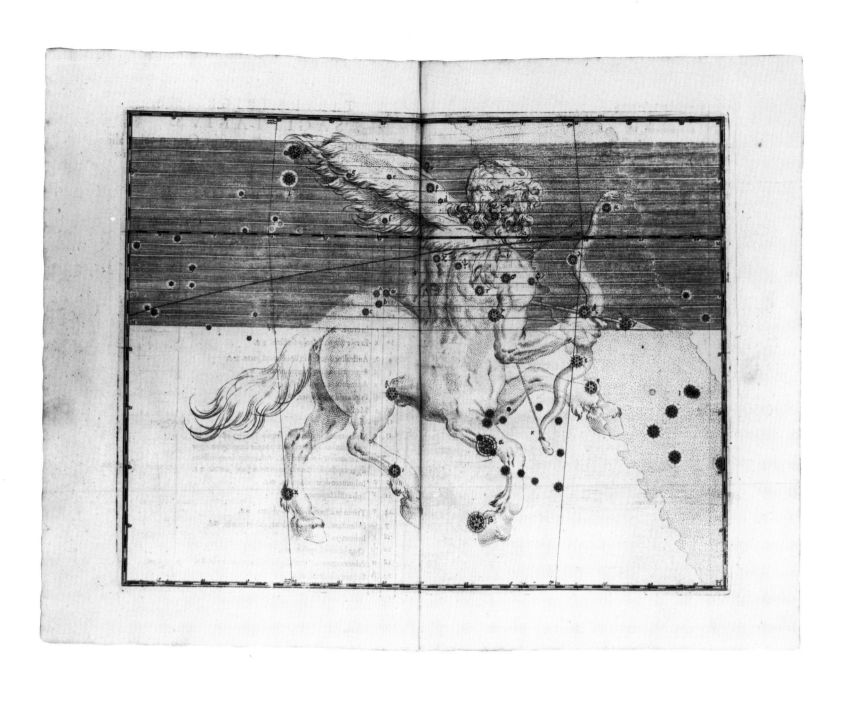

13. Bayer, *Uranometria* (1603) a constellation (reduced)

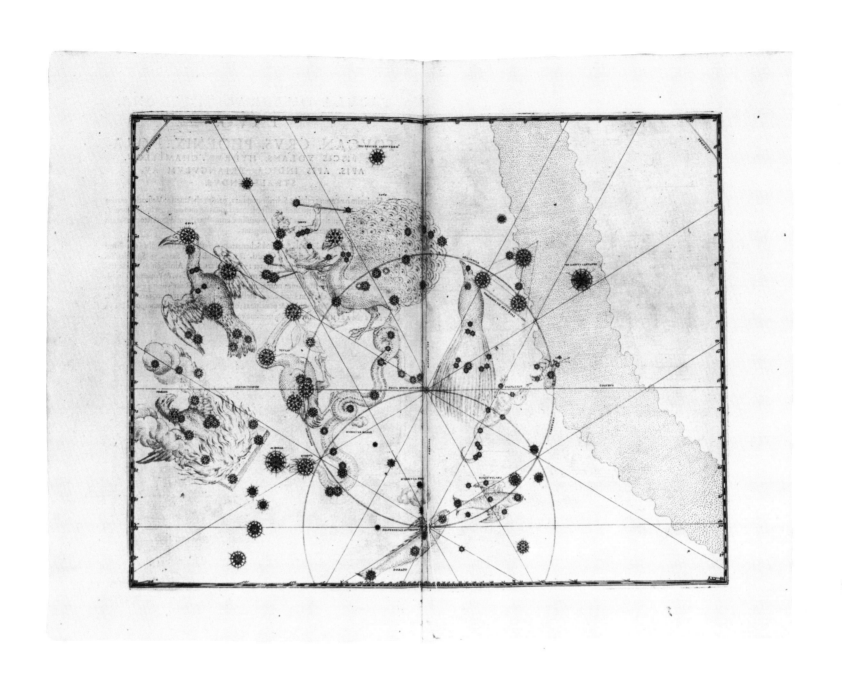

13. Bayer, *Uranometria* (1603) a constellation (reduced)

Greek inscription: Ο ΑΓ(ιος) ΓΕΩΡΓΙΟC

Melchior Haffner *sc:*

14. Beck, *Ephemerides Persarum* [Ephemerides of the Persians] (1695–96)
The Greek inscription reads "Saint George"; the engraver was Melchior Haffner (detail)

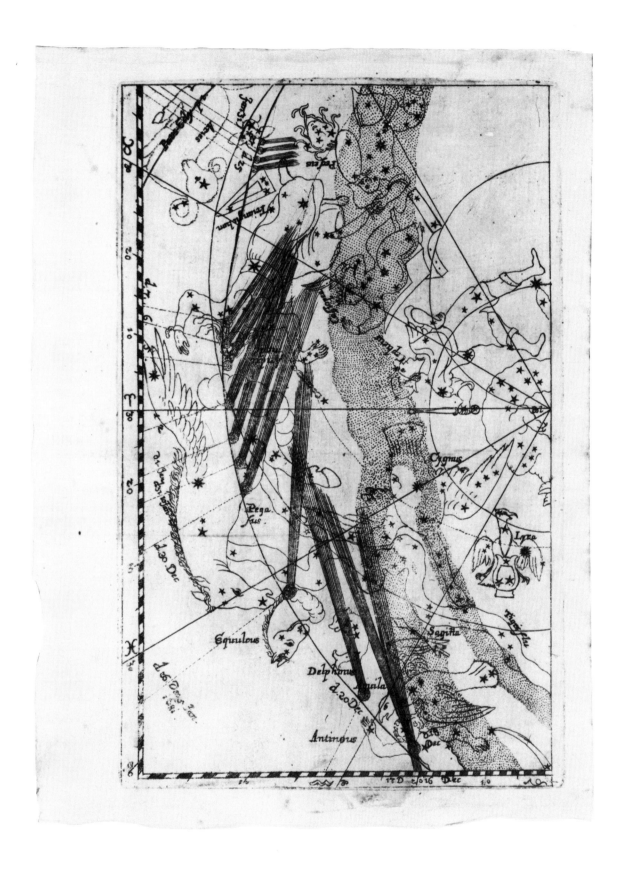

15. *Betrachtung und Bedencken über den…Cometen* [Contemplation and reflection concerning the comet] (1681) folding plate showing the comet's path (reduced)

17 BION, NICOLAS, 1652?–1733

Dritte Eröffnung der neuen Mathematische Werck-Schule

Nürnberg: Peter C. Monath, 1741

22 cm. 432 pages. Twenty folding copper-engraved plates. Title page in red and black with vignette. Bound with item 19. The first edition appeared at Paris in 1699. The sixth and last edition was published there in 1751.

Bion was a French engineer at Paris and a seller of globes and spheres. Through his astronomical instruments he sought to join theory to practice, for which he was accorded the title Engineer to the King. He was the author of three books on mathematical and astronomical instruments.

   This work and the titles cited in items 18 and 19 were translated from the French into German and edited by Johann Gabriel Doppelmayr (1671–1750), who was an astronomer and mathematician. He attended the universities of Altdorf (1696) and Halle. In 1704 he was appointed professor of mathematics at the Aegidien Gymnasium at Nürnberg. His many writings, not noted for originality, included a major work *Atlas Novus Coelestis* (Nürnberg, 1742), a collection of diagrams, star charts and a selenographic map (*DSB*, v. 4, pp. 166–7). Star maps I–VI (unbound) are in the Zinner Collection.

Zinner Collection. Another copy in Amelang Collection, San Diego State University Library.

Lalande, p. 336

NUC: no copy

18 BION, NICOLAS, 1652?–1733

Neu-eröffnete Mathematische Werck-Schule

Nürnberg: Peter C. Monath, 1741

22 cm. 224 leaves. The title page in red and black, copper-engraved frontispiece, and twenty-eight folding plates. Fourth edition.

Zinner Collection. Another copy in Amelang Collection.

Lalande, p. 336

NUC: CSdS; MH; NN; NNC

19 BION, NICOLAS, 1652?–1733

Weitere Eröffnung der neuen Mathematische Werck-Schule

Nürnberg: Peter C. Monath, 1727

22 cm. 48 pages. Illustrations. Bound with his *Dritte Eröffnung der neuen Mathematische Werck-Schule*, Nürnberg, 1741 (item 17).

Amelang Collection. A copy of 1741 edition also in Zinner Collection.

Lalande, p. 336

NUC: CSdS

20 BLUNDEVILLE, THOMAS, fl. 1561

...His Exercises, Containing Eight Treatises

London: J. Windet, 1597

20 cm. 398 leaves. Second edition, corrected and augmented by the author. Bound in modern morocco. Profusely illustrated. Printer's device. Decorated initial letters, borders, headpieces, and tailpieces throughout. Tables, charts, diagrams, folding plates, and three volvelles. Ex Libris Henry C. Taylor and Harrison D. Horblit. The book has four parts, each with its own title page and printer's vignette. Signatures on two title pages, some inked out. Legible on main title page: "John North(?) Colby(?) his Booke, 1626." Other provenance, title page *A Briefe Description of the Tables* (leaf 47) "Le Strange Browne, (?) his Booke December the first 1624."

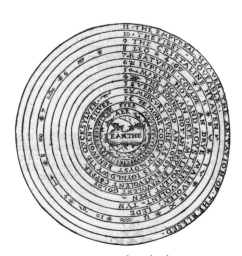

a geocentric celestial sphere

Popular sixteenth-century mathematical textbook contains chapters on Blagrave's astrolabe, Molyneux's globes, Hood's cross-staff, and Gemma Frisius's quadratum nauticum. There are also accounts of the voyages of Drake, Cavendish and other explorers. America is mentioned several times and references to the compass reflect Blundeville's knowledge of variations in the earth's magnetic field.

NUC: CtY; ICN; MH; MWiW; NIC; RPJCB; ViNeM

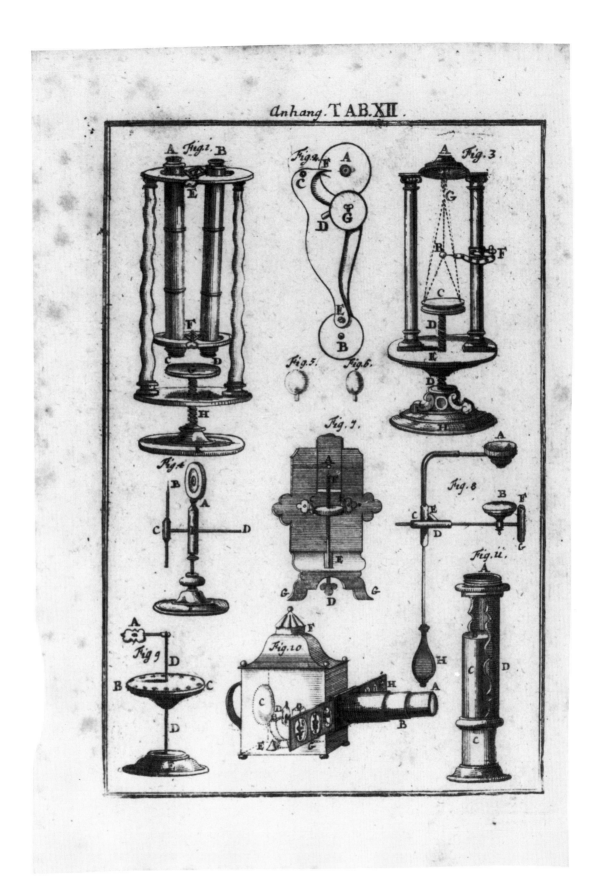

17. Bion, *Dritte Eröffnung der neuen Mathematische Werck-Schule*
[Third opening of the new mathematical work school] (1741)

18. Bion, *Neu-ëroffnete Mathematische Werck-Schule* [Newly opened mathematical work school] (1741)
frontispiece "fundamental instruction on how mathematical instruments are fabricated and used"

A plaine Treatise of the first

principles of Cosmographie, and spe-
cially of the Spheare, representing the shape
of the whole world:
Together with all the chiefest and most neces-
sarie vses thereof, written by M. *Blundevill* of
Newton Flotman, *Anno Dom.* 1594.

The heauens declare the glory of God, and the
firmament sheweth his handy worke. Psal. 19.

LONDON
Printed by *Iohn Windet.* 1597.

20. Blundeville, *His Exercises* (1597) title page of one of the treatises

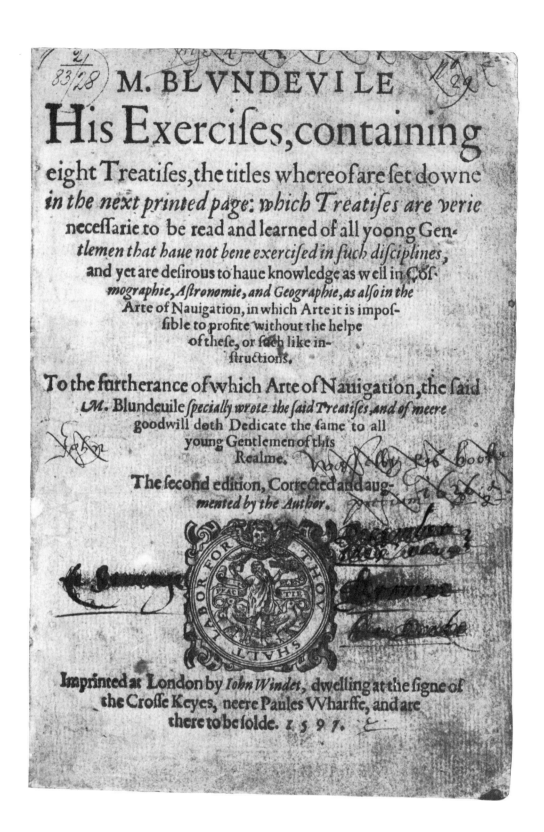

M. BLVNDEVILE

His Exercises, containing

eight Treatises, the titles whereof are set downe
in the next printed page: which Treatises are verie
neceſſarie to be read and learned of all yoong Gentlemen that haue not bene exercised in ſuch diſciplines,
and yet are deſirous to haue knowledge as well in Coſ-
mographie, Aſtronomie, and Geographie, as alſo in the
Arte of Nauigation, in which Arte it is impoſ-
ſible to profite without the helpe
of theſe, or ſuch like in-
ſtructions.

To the furtherance of which Arte of Nauigation, the ſaid
M. Blundeuile ſpecially wrote the ſaid Treatiſes, and of meere
goodwill doth Dedicate the ſame to all
young Gentlemen of this
Realme.

The ſecond edition, Corrected and augmented by the Author.

Imprinted at London by *Iohn Windet*, dwelling at the ſigne of
the Croſſe Keyes, neere Paules Wharſſe, and are
there to be ſolde. 1 5 9 7.

20. Blundeville, *His Exercises* (1597) title page

The shape or figure of the Rectifier of the North Star.

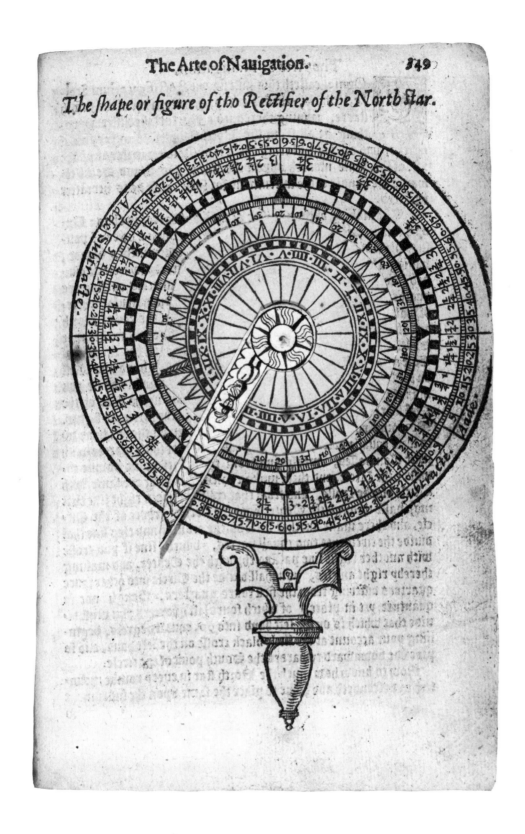

20. Blundeville, *His Exercises* (1597) a volvelle "rectifier of the North Star"

21 BODE, JOHANN ELERT, 1747–1826

Allgemeine Beschreibung und Nachweisung der Gestirne

Berlin: Beym Verfasser, 1801

44 × 27 cm. Paginated 1–32, 1–96. Bound in gold-decorated morocco. Title and text in German and French. Ninety-five pages of constellation tables. First and only edition. The star atlas accompanying this work is item 24, *Uranographia*.

Bode was appointed royal astronomer in Berlin and was a member of the Berlin Academy for nearly forty years. He taught astronomy and published important astronomical tables, two sky atlases, and other works on astronomy.

Zinner Collection

NUC: CtY; DLC; MH; MdBP; NjP; NN; NNC

22 BODE, JOHANN ELERT, 1747–1826

Deutliche Abhandlung

Hamburg: Dietrich A. Harmsen, 1769

18 cm. 48 pages. Second edition. Two folding plates, one colored. Bound with Wiedeburg, J., *Astronomisches Bedenken*, 1744 (item 207).

Zinner Collection

Lalande, p. 512

NUC: DN-Ob; NN; NNC

23 BODE, JOHANN ELERT, 1747–1826

Erläuterung der Sternkunde

Berlin: C. F. Himburg, 1793

22 cm. Two volumes. Second edition. Illustrations, nineteen folding copperplates.

Lalande, p. 627

NUC: CSdS; NNC; OkU; WU

24 BODE, JOHANN ELERT, 1747–1826

Uranographia sive Astrorum Descriptio

Berlin: Apud Autorem, 1801

67 × 103 cm. Twenty engraved unbound star charts in portfolio. First and only edition.

Bode's two sky atlases were for a long time indispensable tools for astronomers. His *Vorstellung der Gestirne*, which, according to the example set by John Flamsteed's atlas (item 58), contained more than 5,000 stars. His later *Uranographia* 1801 surpassed all its predecessors by listing over 17,000 stars and containing, for the first time, the nebulae, star clusters, and double stars discovered by William Herschel (*DSB*, v. 2, pp. 220–21).

NUC: CtY; DN-Ob; MdBP; NCH; NN; NNC; PPAmP; RPB

ALLGEMEINE

BESCHREIBUNG UND NACHWEISUNG

DER

GESTIRNE

NEBST

VERZEICHNISS

DER

GERADEN AUFSTEIGUNG UND ABWEICHUNG VON 17240 STERNEN,
DOPPELSTERNEN, NEBELFLECKEN UND STERNHAUFEN.

VON

J. E. BODE,

KÖNIGL. ASTRONOM, MITGLIED DER AKADEMIEN UND SOCIETÄTEN DER WISSENSCHAFTEN ZU BERLIN, LONDON, PETERSBURG, STOCKHOLM
UND UTRECHT, WIE AUCH DER BERLINSCHEN GESELLSCHAFT NATURFORSCHENDER FREUNDE.

(ZU DESSEN URANOGRAPHIE GEHÖRIG.)

BERLIN 1801.
BEYM VERFASSER.

DESCRIPTION

ET

CONNOISSANCE GÉNÉRALE

DES

CONSTELLATIONS

AVEC

UN CATALOGUE DE L'ASCENSION DROITE ET DE LA DÉCLINAISON
DE 17240 ÉTOILES, DOUBLES, NÉBULEUSES ET AMAS D'ÉTOILES.

PAR

J. E. BODE,

ASTRONOME ROYAL, MEMBRE DES ACADÉMIES ET SOCIÉTÉS DES SCIENCES DE BERLIN, LONDRES, ST. PÉTERSBOURG, STOCKHOLM
ET UTRECHT, ET DE LA SOCIÉTÉ DES SCRUTATEURS DE LA NATURE A BERLIN.

(POUR SERVIR DE SUITE A SON URANOGRAPHIE.)

A BERLIN,
CHEZ L'AUTEUR.
1801.

21. Bode, *Allgemeine Beschreibung und Nachweisung der Gestirne* [General description
and information on the stars] (1801) title page (reduced)

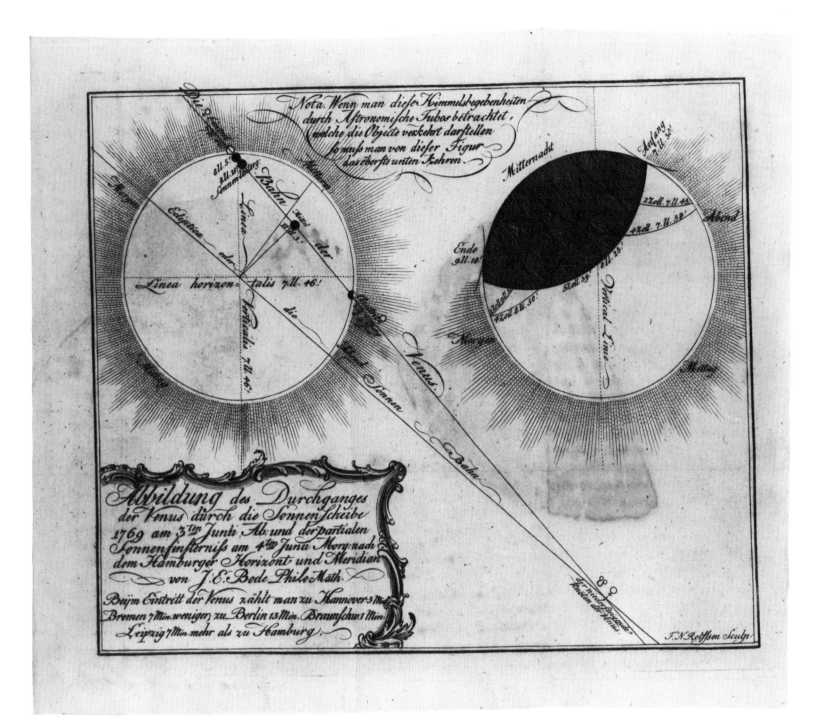

22. Bode, *Deutliche Abhandlung* [Clear discussion] (1769)
illustration of the passage of Venus

24. Bode, *Uranographia* [Uranography] (1801) fine engraved map of constellations (reduced)

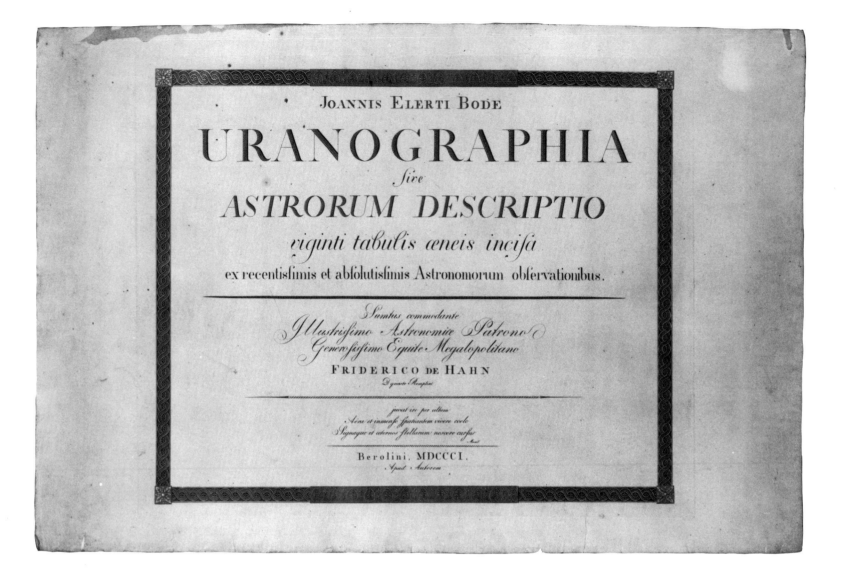

JOANNIS ELERTI BODE

URANOGRAPHIA

sive

ASTRORUM DESCRIPTIO

viginti tabulis æneis incisa

ex recentissimis et absolutissimis Astronomorum observationibus.

Sumtus commodante

Illustrissimo Astronomiæ Patrono

Generosissimo Equite Megalopolitano

FRIDERICO DE HAHN

De quarto Receptus

juvat ire per altum

Aere et immenso spatiantem vivere cœlo

Signaque et æternos stellarum noscere cursus

Berolini, MDCCCI.

Apud Auctorem

24. Bode, *Uranographia* (1801) title page (reduced)

25 BONATTI, GUIDO, ca. 1210–97?

Decem Tractatus Astronomie

Augsburg: Erhard Ratdolt, 1491

22.5 cm. 407 leaves. First edition of a beautifully printed incunabulum. Bound in modern brown calf.

This work relies heavily on the writings of the Arab astrologers as well as those of Ptolemy and writers of the classical period.

Bonatti was born within the first twenty years of the thirteenth century and died ca. 1297. He was the author of several astronomical works. In 1260 he held the title "Astrologus Communis Florentiae de Forolivio" (Astrologer of the Florentine community Forli).

Lalande, p. 19; Zinner, 424

NUC: DLC; NN; OkU; RPB

Goff: BMedL; BrUL; BurL; ColUL; HarvCL; HDC; HDH; HEHL; HNCL; LC; NYPL; UCalS(M)L; UIllL; UOkL

26 BOREL, PIERRE, 1620–89

De Vero Telescopii Inventore

The Hague: Adrian Vlacq, (1655–56)

21 cm. 98 leaves. Three parts in one volume. Illustrations, engraved portraits, folding plate, and numerous woodcuts. Vellum over boards. Added title page for Part three: *Observationum Microscopicarum Centuria*, 1656.

a telescope

First edition of the earliest authority incorrectly assigning the invention of the telescope to Zacharias Jansen rather than to Hans Lipperhey. Borel gives a full account of the construction of telescopes and information on how to grind lenses. Part three contains microscopical observations illustrated with small woodcuts of insects and other objects observed. Provenance, title page: "Levignon M. Par"; colophon: "D.D. De la Maltiere Socius." This book is also notable for having at the foot of page 63 Huygens's announcement of his discovery of the rings of Saturn in the form of an anagram, disguised in this way to secure priority.

Houzeau, 3200; Lalande, p. 241

NUC: CtY; DFo; DN-Ob; DNLM; ICJ; KU-M; MB; MH; MdAN; NIC; NNC; PPULC; PU-F; RPJCB

27 BORELLI, GIOVANNI ALFONSO, 1608–79

Euclide rinnovato

Bologna: Gio. B. Ferroni, 1663

18 cm. 171 leaves. Numerous engraved diagrams, vignettes, decorated endpieces. Contemporary vellum. Signature on title page. Page 307 misnumbered 507, page 217 misnumbered 117.

This Italian translation of his Latin edition of 1658 is one of Borelli's major works. He was a brilliant astronomer, mathematician, teacher, and a friend of Galileo and Malpighi. In 1655 he established his own small observatory near Florence and published his findings. He was highly respected by his contemporaries.

NUC: NIC

In noie dñi amen. Incipit liber introductorius ad iudicia stellarum: z est non solu introductorius ad iudicia: sed est iudicioru astronomie: editus a guidone bonato de forlinio de prouincia romandiole italie: z collegit in eo ex dictis philosophoru ea que visa sunt sibi fore vtilia ad introducendum volentes intendere iudicijs astrozum z ea que videbant competere volentibus iudicare scm significationes stellarum z ad alia quedam ipsis iudicijs pertinentia.

In nomine dñi nostri ihesu xpi, miseratozis z pij veri dei z veri hominis cui nõ est par nec cõsimilis nec esse posset eiusq beatissime matris marie semper virginis gloriose ac beati valeriani martyris capitanei atqz gubernatoris z defensozis cõmunis forliuij qui cum patre simul atqz spusctõ in vnitate essentie atqz trinitate personaru a fidelibus oratur nec nõ z glorificat trinus z vnus: nec est alius deus preter ipsum qui celum z terra cuz omnibus que in eis sunt fecit atqz firmauit cunctaqz in hoim vtilitate produxit: ornauitqz celu stellis tãqz lucernis illuminantib9 vt suis virtutib9 cuncta inferiora disponerent atqz regerent hoibusqz ducatu prout eis cõcessum est similiter exhiberent: preposuitqz rationales cuctis alijs aiantibus vt oia eis seruirent ipsoqz prroganter sentire atqz intelligere fecit: ipsis etia corporum supcelestiu motus atqz ipsorum significata manifestauit: z extendit eis cclu sicut pellem vt possent in eo z per euz cõicante z reuelante diuina sapientia non solu preterita vel presentia cognoscere sed etiam futura cauerent prescirent z nunciare valerent. Ego igif guido bonatus de forlinio cu aliquid in astronomie studuissem z multa opera nostrox predecessoru inspexissem q licet honorandi sunt plurimuqz a nobis reuerendi tamen quidam eox breuiloquiu amantes quãuis dicerent se locuturos introducendis fuit eorum intentio loqui prouectis jn alijs scientijs licet in astronomia z maxime iu iudicijs introducendi forent z rudes. volui componere hoc opus atqz compilare ex dictis antiquozum qui mihi visi sunt incessisse itinere veritatis vtiliora que in ipsis reperta sunt z in hoc opere ponere ad hoc vt tam illis qui non sunt multu in alijs introducti scientijs qz in astronomia vtile foret z ipi leuiter licet forte non multum breuiter venire possent ad optatu finem iudicioru rogans sapientiam atqz diuinã benignitatem licet processerim in diebus qz mihi gratiã cum integritate corporis vita comitante prestare dignef ita qz opus inceptu ad dei honorẽ possim pficere z oim aliox studere volentiu z pcipuc tui bonati nepotis mei vtilitatẽ. Et qm opus erit longu atqz prolixum z longa z difficilia multumqz implicita non possunt paruo numero verborum vndiqz ad plenu enodari ad maiorem prolixitatez vitandam non intendo ponere disputationes nec multas probationes licet forte aliq

a 2

25. Bonatti, *Decem Tractatus Astronomie* [Ten astronomical treatises] (1491) incipit

℃ Incipit secunda pars de his que accidunt planetis in semetipsis
  τ quid accidit vni ab altero.
℃ Capitulum primū de his q̄ accidunt planetis in semetipsis.

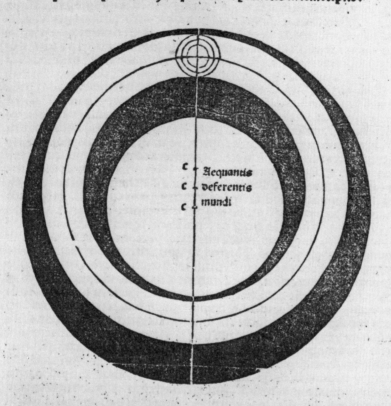

    C · Aequantis
    C · deferentis
    C · mundi

 N ista secunda parte tercij tractatus dicendum est de qui/
buisdam accidentibus que accidunt planetis in semetipsis τ
ad inuicem: τ loquar tibi vt iam introducto τ non vt intro.
ducendo. Et dicam tibi primo fm vestigia philosophorum
de his q̄ accidunt planetis in semetipsis. Et sunt ista de illis
accidentibⁿ sez quando planeta est ascendēs in circulo.augi
sue:τ quando est descendens in eodem circulo:τ quando est
nec ascendens in ipso nec descendēs. ℃ Et dixit alchabiciⁿ
significatio eoꝛ que accidunt planetis in semetipsis est vt sit planeta ascen/
dens in circulo sue augis minoꝛ lumine τ magnitudine atꝗ cursu. Nam cum
planeta fuerit in remotioꝛi parte sui eccentrici a terra in qua est eius aux ipfe

25. Bonatti, *Decem Tractatus Astronomie* (1491) diagram

DE VERO
TELESCOPII
INVENTORE,

Cum brevi omnium

CONSPICILIORUM
HISTORIA.

Ubi de Eorum Confectione, ac Vfu, feu
de Effectibus agitur, novaque quædam
circa ea proponuntur.

Le uiguon Accesfit etiam *Vll. Par.*

CENTVRIA OBSERVATIONVM
MICROCOSPICARUM.

AUTHORE

PETRO BORELLO, *Regis Chriftia-*
niffimi Confiliario, & Medico Ordinario.

HAGÆ-COMITUM,
Ex Typographia Adriani Vlacq.
M. DC. LV.

---

26. Borel, *De Vero Telescopii Inventore* [Concerning the true inventor
of the telescope] (1655–56) title page

HANS LIPPERHEY,

secundus Conspiciliorum inventor .

26. Borel, *De Vero Telescopii Inventore* (1655–56) portrait of Hans Lipperhey

ZACHARIAS IANSEN
sive Ioannides primus Conspiciliorum inventor.

26. Borel, *De Vero Telescopii Inventore* (1655–56) portrait of Zacharias Jansen

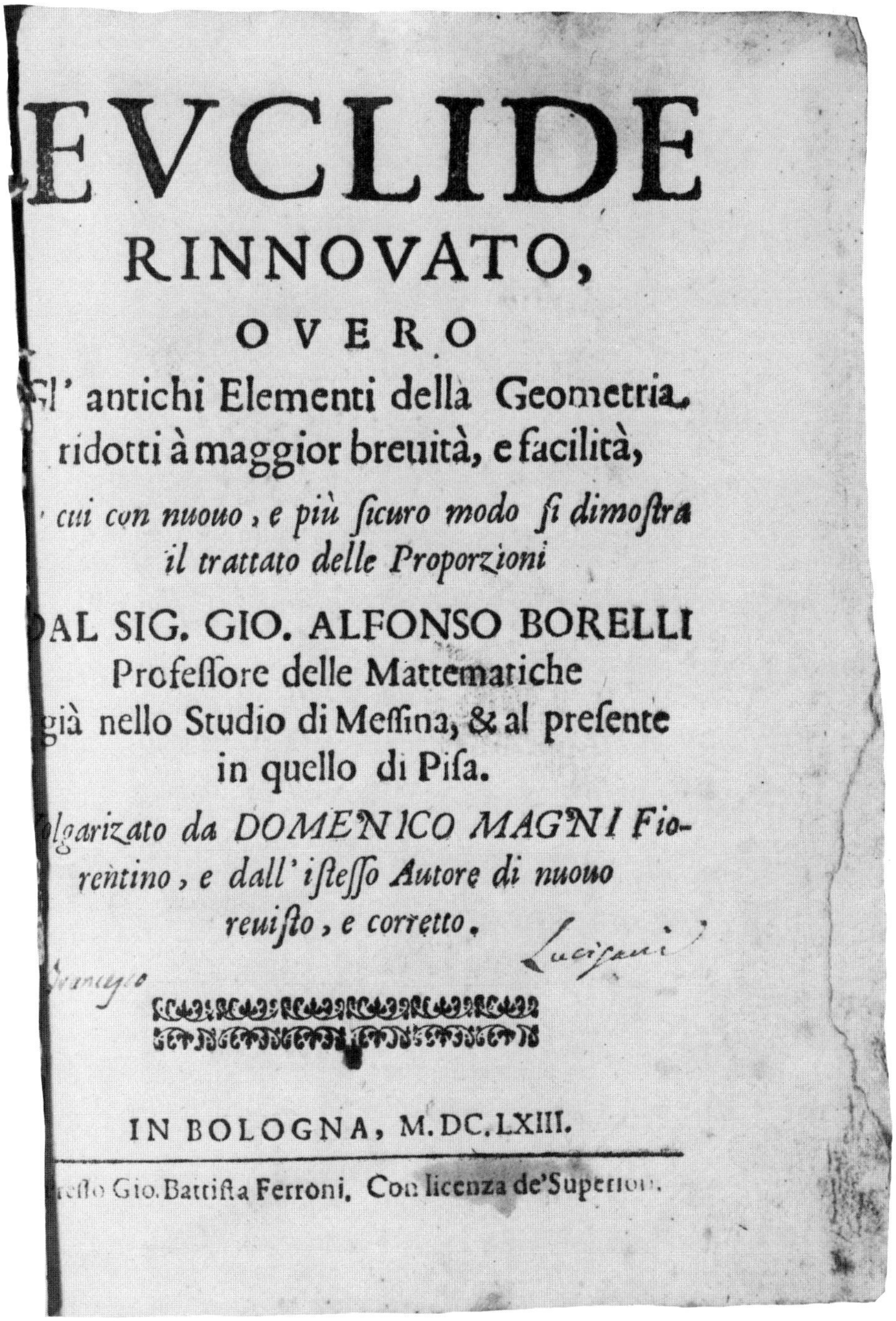

EVCLIDE
RINNOVATO,
OVERO

Gl' antichi Elementi della Geometria,
ridotti à maggior breuità, e facilità,

*cui con nuouo, e più ficuro modo fi dimoſtra
il trattato delle Proporzioni*

DAL SIG. GIO. ALFONSO BORELLI
Profeſſore delle Mattematiche
già nello Studio di Meſſina, & al preſente
in quello di Piſa.

Volgarizato da *DOMENICO MAGNI* Fiorentino, e dall' iſteſſo Autore di nuouo
reuiſto, e corretto.

Lucifani

Vangelo

~~~~~~~~~~~~~~~~~~~~~~~~~~~~~~~~~~~~~~

IN BOLOGNA, M.DC.LXIII.

preſſo Gio. Battiſta Ferroni. Con licenza de'Superiori.

27. Borelli, *Euclide rinnovato* [Euclid restored] (1663) title page

28 BRAHE, TYCHO, 1546–1601

Astronomiae Instauratae Mechanica

Nürnberg: Levin Hulse, 1602

32 cm. 54 leaves. Illustrations, maps, plans. Fine engraved portrait of Brahe on title page. Title and text pages printed within ruled border. Thirty woodcuts, most full page in size. Fine historiated initial letters, large woodcut tailpieces. Bound in original vellum. Printer L. Hulse is also author of *Theoria et Praxis* (item 87).

This work contains illustrations of Brahe's instruments and observatories. It is the reprint of Brahe's most important work first issued at Wandsbeck near Hamburg in a limited edition of about forty copies in 1598. NUC lists only three copies of that first edition in American libraries.

In this famous book Brahe described his fine instruments, which were either his own inventions or considerably improved versions of older ones.

Brahe's accurate observations of the positions of the sun, moon, stars, and planets provided the basis for refinements of the Copernican doctrine. His work led to Kepler's reformation of astronomy. Kepler was his most famous pupil.

He was of a noble family, independently wealthy. In his personal library in 1560 were Sacro Bosco, *Sphaera* (represented by items 156–65); Peter Apian, *Cosmographiae* (item 6); Gemma Frisius, *Apian's Cosmographia* (item 72); and Regiomontanus, *Tabulae Directionum*. He also had a medical handbook and an herbal.

He turned his attention to observational astronomy at the time of the solar eclipse in 1560. In March 1562 his father sent him to Leipzig to study law, which he did, but at the same time pursued his first love, astronomy. Here he used these books: Stadius, *Ephemeris* (item 178); the *Alphonsine Tables* (item 3); the *Prutenic Tables*; Carelli, *Ephemerides 1557* (item 33).

In 1566 Brahe matriculated at the University of Rostock where on December 29, in an unfortunate duel with another Danish nobleman, part of his nose was cut off. He replaced it with a metal shape made of gold, silver, and copper. In 1569 at Augsburg Brahe met the astronomer Cyprian Leovitius (items 105–8). On his way home to Denmark in 1570 he stopped at Ingolstadt where he met Philip Apian, son of Peter.

In September 1574, in the first lecture of his course for young noblemen at the University of Copenhagen, Brahe spoke of the skill of Copernicus, whose system, although not in accord with physical principles, was mathematically admirable (*DSB*, v. 2, pp. 401ff).

Brahe built an astronomical observatory on the Danish island Hven. He also established there a paper mill and a printing press for the publication of his writings. He proclaimed that a theory can only be established through observations and the best observations must be secured by means of the best possible instruments.

Lalande, p. 138

NUC: CLU; CtY; DEo; DN-Ob; IaU; ICJ; InU; MH; MiU; MWIW-C; NN; NNC; NNE; OGaK; PBL; PPF; PPULC; TxU

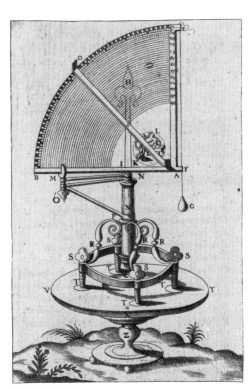

quadrant

29 BRAHE, TYCHO, 1546–1601

Historia Coelestis

Augsburg: Simon Utzschneider, 1666

34 cm. 564 leaves. Thick folio volume. Numerous fine full-page engraved plates including a Brahe portrait. Bound in hand-tooled contemporary pigskin over boards.

First edition of Brahe's vast astronomical observations. Contains a catalogue and tables of the fixed and movable stars along with Brahe's own observations for the years 1582–92 and 1594–1601.

NUC: CU; CtU; DN-Ob; MB; MH; NN; NNC; PBL; PPL; PPULC; ScU

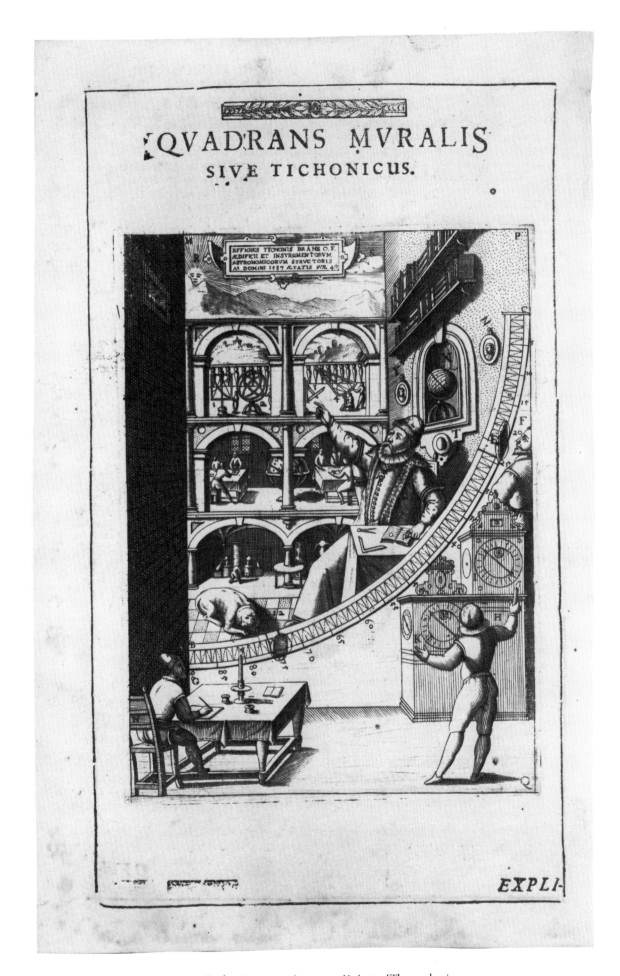

28. Brahe, *Astronomiae Instauratae Mechanica* [The mechanics
of astronomical installations] (1602) view of a wall quadrant
and Tycho Brahe at his observatory (reduced)

28. Brahe, *Astronomiae Instauratae Mechanica* (1602) portrait of Tycho Brahe (reduced)

29. Brahe, *Historia Coelestis* [History of the heavens] (1666)
portrait of Tycho Brahe (reduced)

29. Brahe, *Historia Coelestis* (1666) view of Brahe's observatory on the Danish island Hven (reduced)

QVADRANS MVRALIS TYCHONICVS.

I Nipfo plano *Meridiei* locatus, ut & appulfum Solis ac fiderum denotet, transverfa rima, & altitudinem ab Horizonte, ex Dioptra cum levatur aut demittitur. Ex quo vides quam accurata debuerit fuiffe elaboratio, *Bra-beanorum artificum* ut fine adminiculo Regulæ *Quadrantem gubernantis* fola limbi accurata elimatione, altitudines oftenderet.

Nos ifthic quæ in Quadrantis Area picturis expreffa erant, omifimus, & Lector ipfo Commentariorum percurfu videbit, non minus accura-tas fuiffe animadverfiones, per quadrantes cæteros qui fequuntur, quàm per iftam tantæ magnitudinis & vaftitatis.

QVA-

29. Brahe, *Historia Coelestis* (1666) a Tychonian wall quadrant (reduced)

29. Brahe, *Historia Coelestis* (1666) double-page depiction of Knowledge ruling the world (reduced)

30 BRESSIEU, MAURICE, d. ca. 1608

Metrices Astronomicae

Paris: Aegidius Gorbinus, 1581

33 cm. 67 leaves. First edition. Numerous geometric diagrams. Bound in contemporary limp vellum. Mathematical tables printed in red and black.

Bressieu, native of Grenoble, was professor of mathematics at the Collège Royale, Paris, in the second half of the sixteenth century. He was first to use the term "radius" in place of "sinus totus." "His trigonometry published under the title *Metrices Astronomicae* was very good for its time...." He relied on Ptolemy and Euclid and made references to Regiomontanus and Copernicus. (*DSB*, v. 8, p. 27; Montucla, J. *Histoire des mathématiques*, v. 1, p. 577).

Lalande, p. 112

NUC: MiU

31 BURGES, BARTHOLOMEW

A Short Account of the Solar System

Boston: B. Edes & Son, 1789

17 cm. 10 leaves. Bound in contemporary plain blue paper wrappers. Uncut. Provenance, title page: "Dan[ie]l E. Updike." Large folding plate in portfolio (facsimile). Second edition, corrected.

Early American astronomical work. This second edition is rarer than the first issued the same year. Burges's short account includes Edmund Halley's (erroneous) identification of the comets of 1532 and 1666 and their expected return in 1789.

NUC: CtY; MB; MH; MWA; N; PHi; PPULC; RPJCB

32 BÜTTNER, DANIEL, 1642–96, preses; Respondens, GEORGIUS ERNESTUS CRAVELIUS

Astrologia, sive Disputatio Physica de Stellis

Hamburg: G. Rebenlini, 1682

19 cm. 26 pages.

Zinner Collection

NUC: no copy

33 CARELLI, GIOVANNI BATTISTI, fl. 16th century

Ephemerides... ad Annos XIX Incipientes ab Anno Christi MDLXXVII usque ad Annum MDLXXXV

Venice: Ex Officina Erasmiana, Vincent Valgrisi, 1557

24 cm. 364 leaves. Tables. Bound in modern full leather, gold tooled.

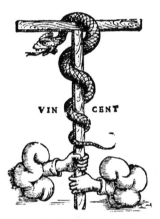

printer's device from the title page

Little is known about Carelli. He was an Italian astronomer and astrologer born at Piacenza. He was at Venice in the mid-sixteenth century.

"Tycho Brahe used the 1557 Ephemerides of Giovanni Battisti Carellus" (*DSB*, v. 2, p. 401).

Lalande, p. 81

NUC: CSdS

MAVRICII BRESSII

GRATIANOPOLITANI REGII
ET RAMEI MATHEMATICARVM
LVTETIÆ PROFESSORIS METRICES
Aſtronomicæ libri quatuor.

HÆC MAXIMAM PARTEM NOVA EST RERVM
Aſtronomicarum & Geographicarum per plana ſphæricáque triangula
dimenſionis ratio, veterique impendio expeditior
& compendioſior.

AD POMPONIVM BELLEVREVM SACRI CON-
SISTORII CONSILIARIVM, REGIS-
QVE LEGATVM.

PARISIIS,
Apud Ægidium Gorbinum, ſub inſigne Spei, è regione
gymnaſij Cameracenſis.
M. D. LXXXI.
CVM PRIVILEGIO REGIS.

30. Bressieu, *Metrices Astronomicae* [Astronomical measurements] (1581) title page (reduced)

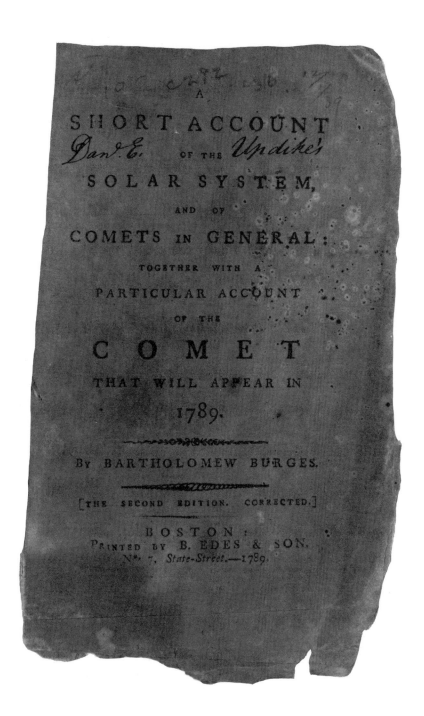

31. Burges, *A Short Account of the Solar System* (1789) title page
of a rare early American astronomical work

ASTROLOGIA
sive
DISPUTATIO PHYSICA
DE
STELLIS,

Quam
ADSPIRANTE S. SANCTA TRINITATE,
In illustri Hamburgensium Athenæo,
PRÆSIDE
DN. DANIELE BÜTTNERO,
J. U. Licentiato & Practico celeberrimo,
quondam ejusdem Facultatis in Academia Elector. Hieran.
jam vero in hoc illustri Athenæo Liberæ Imper. Reipubl.
Hamburg, Professore Publ. Dignissimo, & p. t.
RECTORE gravissimo,
Domino, Fautore & Promotore suo summopere
colendo, honorando,
Publicæ & placidæ Eruditorum Disquisitioni submittit
GEORGIUS ERNESTUS CRAUELIUS,
Osterodensis Saxo.
In Auditorio Philosophorum
Die XXII. April. horis â IX. matutinis,
A. O. R. M. DC. LXXXII.

HAMBURGI,
LITERIS Georgii Rebenlini Senat. Gymnas. & Schol. Typograph.

32. Büttner, *Astrologia, sive Disputatio Physica de Stellis* [Astrology and physical disputation
concerning the stars] (1682) academic disputation title page

EPHEMERIDES
IO. BAPTISTAE
Carelli Placentini,
AD ANNOS XIX.

INCIPIENTES AB ANNO CHRISTI M D LVII.

VSQVE AD ANNVM M D LXXV.

MERIDIANO INCLITAE VRBIS VENETIARVM

DILIGENTISSIME' SVPPVTATAE.

Canones eiusdem mira facilitate omnia Ephemeridibus opportuna declarantes; Vnà cum Iſagogico tractatu Aſtrologiæ ſtudioſis valdè neceſſario.

Cum Pont. Max. ac Illuſtriſſ. Senatus Veneti, Gratia & Priuilegio.

VIN CENT

VENETIIS,
Ex Officina Eraſmiana, Vincentij Valgriſij,
M D LVII.

33. Carelli, *Ephemerides* (1557) title page

34 CECCO D'ASCOLI, 1269–1327

L'acerba

Milano: J.A. Scinzenzeler, 1521

20.5 cm. 76 leaves. Woodcut illustrations throughout, old vellum binding. Bookplate of Ladislao Reti. Provenance, title page: "Pietro Paulo Sala Pittore et chirurgo"; last page: "Petrus Paulus Sala Possidet." The first printed edition appeared at Venice in 1476.

Cecco d'Ascoli was born at or near Ascoli Piceno. His name in the vernacular was Francesco degli Stabili and "Cecco" is a diminutive of Francesco. He was an astrologer and poet.

woodcut vignettes

Cecco was professor of astrology at the University of Bologna where he was first accused of heresy in 1324. He fled to Florence, becoming astrologer to Duke Charles of Calabria. Having (1) already

aroused the suspicion of the church, (2) disagreed strongly with Dante on astrological opinions, and (3) earned the enmity of a leading physician, Dino del Garbo, he was tried again at Florence and burned at the stake 16 September 1327.

His Latin works (commentaries on Sacro Bosco and Alcabizio) are compilations. His more famous encyclopedic poem—*L'acerba*, which was written in the vernacular—contained a polemic against Dante. Except for its attack on Dante and Cecco's tragic death, the *Acerba* would scarcely be remembered (*Poggendorff*, v. 1, pt. 1, p. 410; *Enciclopedia italiana* v. 32, p. 433).

NUC: no copy

35 CELSIUS, ANDERS, 1701–44, preses; Respondens, ANDREAS TULENIUS

Dissertatio Astronomico de Constellatione Arietis

Stockholm: J. L. Horrn, 1740?

18 cm. 31 leaves. Vignette on title page, historiated initials, illustration, tables. Provenance, title page: "Geo. Bånge."

Zinner Collection

NUC: CSdS

36 CENSORINUS, fl. Rome: first half, 3rd century A.D.

De Die Natali. Henric. Lindenbrogius recensuit...

Leiden: Ioannis Maire, 1642

17 cm. 152 leaves. Vignette on title page and coat of arms on verso. One folding plate. Contemporary vellum binding.

Written in A.D. 238, the first part deals with human procreation and pregnancy, the influences of the stars, and music. The second part treats on the divisions of time, sun, moon, stars, year, month, day, and so on. The last part contains short discourses on astronomy, geometry, music, and metrics. The chapter on geometry that treats Euclid's *Elements* differs greatly from other known translations of Euclid. The chapters on metrics contain the oldest known information on Roman metrics (*DSB*, v. 3, p. 175).

Zinner Collection

Houzeau, 525

NUC: CSdS; CtY; DFo; ICU; IU; MH; PPC; PPL; PPULC; PU; WU

Per lo uoler che ciecha la ragione
Se giungie cō la man nó uol uncina
Ma se resurgie la communitate
Tempra man a folle & a mulino
O tu che intorno tua belleza miri
Che si la sciocha gloria timbarda
Se tu hai intellecto come nó sospiri
Guarti a piedi e aueloci passi
Che fai uerso la morte che ti guarda
Et comel tempo che tralucēdo passi
Or pensa dōqua che nel mondo tristo
Si lassa cō solpiri lhumauo aquisto

ꝏDe la natura de le Grughe.

Capitulo. xxii.

Grughe

Anno le Grughe ordine e signore
Et quella che conducie spesso crida
Corregie & amaestra lor tenore
Se quasta raucha laltra in cio soccide
Et quando dorme questa che lor guida
La guardia pone chalcun non le prende
Questa che guarda sta con luna ghamma
Ne laltra tien la pietra che se dorme
Cadendogli del sonno gliocchi sbrama
Cosi doueria ciaschun cittadino
Luno collaltro essere conforme
Che non ueuisse lor terra al dechino
Ma tante questa inuidia che regna

Che sempre si disfacie el ben cōmuno
El luno de seguir laltro si disdegna
Lo senno de li gioueni qui ui uegio
Nonne chi faccia ben nonne sin uno
Per lutil si conseglia pur lo peggio
Et uegio cader diuiso questo regnio
Veggio che tolto lordine ello bene
Veggio regnar qua giu ogni malegnio
Veggio qui li buon non hauer locho
Veggio che tacer ciaschun conuene
Veggio arder qui loculto fuocho
Et ueggio uenire qui le piaghe noue
Dico se pieta cio non rimoue

ꝏDe la natura de la tortora, Capi. xxiii.

La

34. Cecco d'Ascoli, *L'acerba* [The acerbity]
(1521) page with a fine woodcut

Piero Paulo Sala Pittore, et
chirurgo ⁊

Lo illustro poeta Ce
cho Dascholi: con comēto nouamente tro
uato: & nobilmente historiato: reui
sto: & emendato: da multa in
correctiōe extirpato &
ad antiquo suo ue
stigio cxēpla
to &c.

☩

34. Cecco d'Ascoli, *L'acerba* (1521) title page

E tiene de pieta la spessa norma.

Glialtri animali. Qui solue la questione che si potrebbe fare perche li anima li bruti femine non hanno tale diffecto del mestro e dice che laltri animali che sono di uirtu nudi hano lestremita di fuore de la pelle e qlla materia si consuma i quella stremita cioei pelli pelle e ungia e corna & poi iuoca I dio ella sancta ternita lautore dicendo che la uirtu grade cioe dela deta unita qstaltre cose solamente per gratia del huomo come ne la lettera si comprende.

Œ De lordine di cieli & de le substanze separate & de alquanti loro effecti.

Capi.secon.   Polus mondi seu arcticus

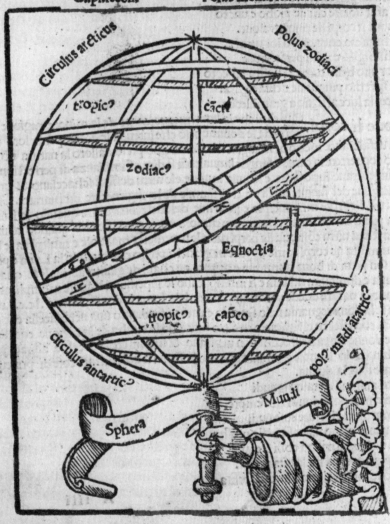

34. Cecco d'Ascoli, *L'acerba* (1521) a sphere

D. A. G.

DISSERTATIO ASTRONOMICA,

DE

CONSTELLATIONE ARIETIS,

QVAM

CONSENSU Ampliss. Fac. Ph. in REG. ACAD. Ups.

PRÆSIDE

VIRO CELEBERRIMO,

Mag. ANDREA CELSIO,

Astron. PROFESSORE Reg. et Ord.

AD PUBLICUM EXAMEN DEFERT

ANDREAS TULENIUS,

WESTMANNUS.

In Aud. Gust. Maj. ad D. XVI Jun. An. MDCCXL.

SOLITIS A. M. HORIS.

HOLMIÆ, Impressa Apud JOH. LAUR. HORRN,
REG. ANTIQV. ARCH. TYPOGR.

35. Celsius, *Dissertatio Astronomico* [Astronomical dissertation] (1740?) title page

37 CHERUBIN d'ORLEANS, le père, 1613–97

La Dioptrique oculaire, ou la théorique, la positive, et la méchanique de l'oculaire dioptrique en toutes ses espèces

Paris: Thomas Jolly & Simon Benard, 1671

38 cm. 250 leaves. First edition. Sixty fine engraved plates, some folding. Handsome engraved vignette, initial letters, head and tailpieces. Provenance, title page: "F. Willughby g:a:12." Francis Willughby (1635–72) was an English naturalist educated at Cambridge University where he began a lifelong association with John Ray (1627–1705). Willughby became one of the original fellows of the Royal Society (*DSB* v. 14, pp. 412–4).

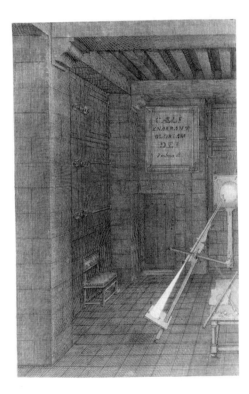

This is a seventeenth-century treatise describing the effect on the eye of various kinds of glasses. There are descriptions of microscopes and telescopes.

NUC: CU; DFo; DNLM; DSI; ICJ; KU-M; MBCo; MH; NCorniC; NIC; NN; NNC; NNNAM; PPF; PPULC; ViRA; WU

38 CHIARAMONTI, SCIPIONE, 1565–1652

De Tribus Novis Stellis

Cesena: J. Nerium, 1628

22 cm. 298 leaves. Illustrations. Diagrams. Contemporary vellum binding.

Zinner Collection

Lalande, p. 191-2

NUC: CSdS; MiU

39 *Cometa Scepticus. Oder Kurtzer Discurtz über Jüngst-Erschienenen Cometen*

Strasbourg?: n.p., 1681

19 cm. 24 pages. Two engraved folding plates by the Strasbourg artist, Johann Adam Seupel, 1662–1717.

NUC: NNC

40 COPERNICUS, NICOLAUS, 1473–1543

De Revolutionibus Orbium Coelestium

Basel: Henricpetrina, 1566

30 cm. 219 leaves. Diagrams, tables. Title vignette (printer's device). Ex libris Owen Gingerich.

Second edition of the famous sixteenth-century astronomical work, this copy has the signature of Guéneau De Montbéillard on the title page. Philibert Guéneau De Montbéliard (or Montbélliard, ca. 1720–85), French naturalist, was best known for his writings on birds and insects, as well as chemistry and experimental physics (*Nouvelle biographie générale.* Paris: Firmin Diderot, 1852–66, v. 22, p. 378).

   Included at the end of this edition is the *Narratio Prima* (First Report) of Georg Joachim Rhäticus, the German mathematician and astronomer who in 1539 arrived in Frauenburg to learn from Copernicus himself about the rumored new cosmology. Copernicus had long resisted entreaties to release his *De Revolutionibus* for publication, but he permitted Rhäticus to write the *Narratio Prima*, which was the earliest printed announcement of Copernicus's heliocentric system challenging the centuries-old Ptolemaic system. It was published at Gdánsk in early 1540. Rhäticus encouraged Copernicus to let *De Revolutionibus* be printed. Copernicus began putting finishing touches to the manuscript in 1541 (*DSB*, v. 11, pp. 395–8). Rhäticus took it to a Nürnberg printer in 1542 where that first edition appeared in 1543. It is said Copernicus held a copy of it in his hands a few hours before his death.

Houzeau, 652; Lalande, p. 90; Zinner, 2390

NUC: CLU-C; CtY; CU; DLC; DN-Ob; IaAS; InU; MB; MH; MWiW-C; MiU; NNNAM; NRU; PBL; RPB; ViU

le Pauvre delt.

La dioptrique oculaire
Par le Pere Cherubin d'Orleans
Capucin.

G. Edelinck sculp.

37. Chérubin, *La dioptrique oculaire*
[The optical lens] (1671) frontispiece

LA
DIOPTRIQVE
OCVLAIRE,
OV
LA THEORIQVE,
LA POSITIVE,
ET
LA MECHANIQVE,
DE L'OCVLAIRE DIOPTRIQVE
EN TOVTES SES ESPECES.

Par le Pere CHERVBIN D'ORLEANS, Capucin.

A PARIS,

Chez { THOMAS JOLLY, au Palais, } aux Armes de
{ & } Hollande.
{ SIMON BENARD, ruë S. Jacques. }

M. DC. LXXI.
AVEC PRIVILEGE DV ROY.

37. Chérubin, *La dioptrique oculaire* (1671) title page

COMETA
SCEPTICVS.

Oder

Kurtzer Discursz

Uber

Jüngst ⸱ Erschienenen

Cometen.

M. DC. LXXXI.

39. *Cometa Scepticus* [Amazing comet] (1681) title page

NICOLAI
COPERNICI TO-
RINENSIS DE REVOLVTIONI-
bus orbium cœlestium,

Libri VI.

IN QVIBVS STELLARVM ET FI-
XARVM ET ERRATICARVM MOTVS, EX VETE-
ribus atq recentibus obseruationibus, restituit hic autor.
Præterea tabulas expeditas luculentasq addidit, ex quibus eosdem motus ad quoduis tempus Mathe-
matum studiosus facillime calcu-
lare poterit.

ITEM, DE LIBRIS REVOLVTIONVM NICOLAI
Copernici Narratio prima, per M. Georgium Ioachi-
mum Rheticum ad D. Ioan. Schone-
rum scripta.

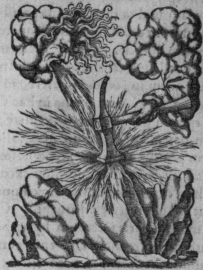

Cum Gratia & Priuilegio Cæf.Maiest.

BASILEAE, EX OFFICINA
HENRICPETRINA.

40. Copernicus, *De Revolutionibus Orbium Coelestium* [Concerning the revolutions
of the heavenly spheres] (1566) title page (reduced)

net, in quo terram cum orbe lunari tanquam epicyclo contineri
diximus. Quinto loco Venus nono mense reducitur. Sextum
deniq; locum Mercurius tenet, octuaginta dierum spacio circū
currens. In medio uero omnium residet Sol. Quis enim in hoc

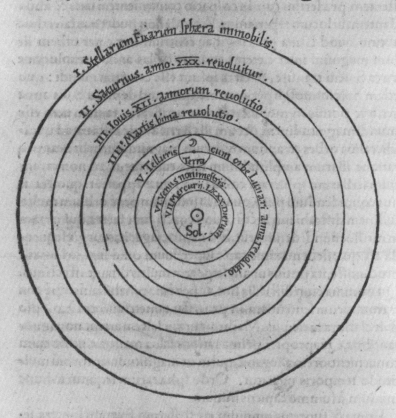

pulcherrimo templo lampadem hanc in alio uel meliori loco po
neret, quàm unde totum simul possit illuminare? Siquidem non
inepte quidam lucernam mundi, alij mentem, alij rectorem uo=
cant. Trimegistus uisibilem Deum, Sophoclis Electra intuentē
omnia. Ita profecto tanquam in solio regali Sol residens circum
agentem gubernat Astrorum familiam. Tellus quoque minime
fraudatur lunari ministerio, sed ut Aristoteles de animalibus ait,
maximam Luna cum terra cognationē habet. Cōcipit interea à
Sole terra, & impregnatur annno partu. Inuenimus igitur sub
hac

40. Copernicus, *De Revolutionibus Orbium Coelestium* (1566)
the heliocentric sphere (reduced)

41 CREUTZER, PETER

Planeten Büchlein

Frankfurt am Main: Nicolaus Basse, 1570

20 cm. 31 leaves. Woodcuts throughout. Title page printed in red and black.

Zinner Collection

Zinner, 1570

NUC: CSdS

42 CYSAT, JOHANN BAPTIST, ca. 1586–1657

Mathemata Astronomica de Loco, Motu, Magnitudine, et Causis Cometae

Ingolstadt: Ex Typographeo Ederiana, apud Elizabeth Angermar, 1619

21 cm. 47 leaves. Illustrations, diagrams, woodcut initials. Bound in modern half calf. Provenance, title page: "R.P. Joanni Sutori, auctor." First edition. Ex Libris Robert Honeyman IV.

Born in Lucerne, Cysat entered the Jesuit order in 1604. In 1611 he was at the Jesuit college in Ingolstadt as a pupil of Christoph Scheiner whom he assisted in observation of sunspots. In 1618 Cysat became professor of mathematics in Ingolstadt where he made observations on the comet of 1618–19 for which he is mainly known. He reports and analyzes these observations in his *Mathemata Astronomica* (*DSB*, v. 3, p. 528).

Contains a report of the first telescopic observation of a comet, showing at the same time that its orbit was parabolic, not circular. It also first mentions his discovery of the Orion nebula and two of Saturn's satellites. In 1631 he made the first recorded observation of a transit of Mercury.

Lalande, p. 174; Zinner, 4702

NUC: no copy

43 DEANE, WILLIAM, 1690–1738?

The Description of the Copernican System, with the Theory of the Planets

London: n.p., 1738

20 cm. 112 pages. Illustrations, eight folding copper plates. Calf binding.

First edition of a rare and beautifully illustrated work dealing with the construction and use of the author's grand orrery. Deane was a maker of all kinds of astronomical dials and was a mathematical instrument maker to His Majesty's Office of Ordnance and the Royal Mathematical School (King, H. C., *Geared to the Stars*, Toronto, 1978, p. 164).

NUC: CLU-C

44 DESAGULIERS, JOHN THEOPHILUS, 1683–1744

A Course of Experimental Philosophy

London: W. Innys, 1744–45

25 cm. Two volumes. Volume one is second edition corrected, Volume two, first edition. Bound in old calf rebacked, seventy-eight folded copper-engraved plates.

Desaguliers, a French Huguenot by birth, taught many years at Oxford. This work is the text of his course of lectures on astronomy, mechanics, and related subjects.

NUC: CLU-C; CSt; DLC; FU; ICJ; IU; KyU; MA; MB; MWiW-C; NN; NNC; PMA; PPAmP; PPF; PU

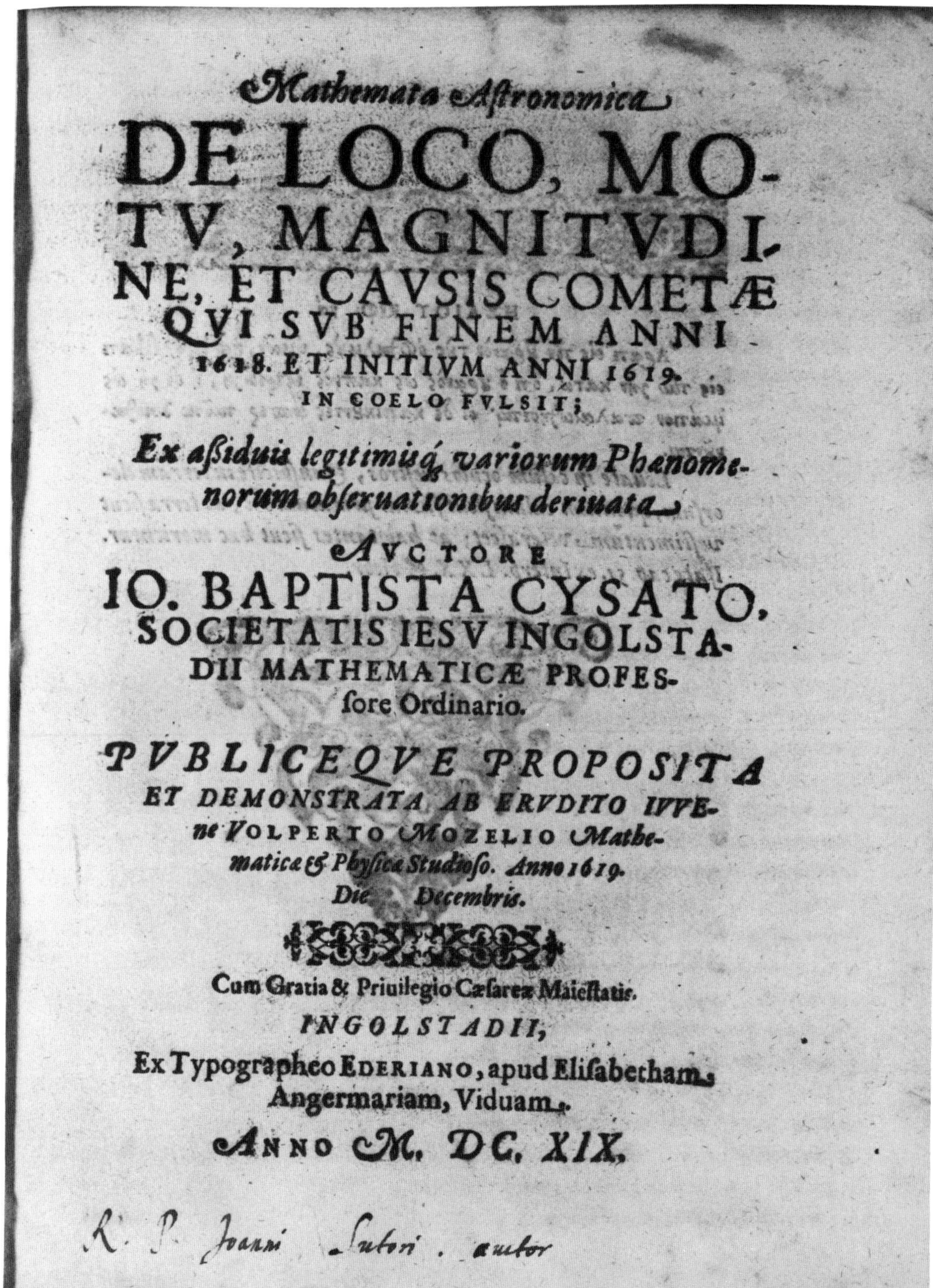

Mathemata Astronomica

DE LOCO, MOTV, MAGNITVDINE, ET CAVSIS COMETÆ QVI SVB FINEM ANNI 1618. ET INITIVM ANNI 1619. IN COELO FVLSIT;

Ex aßiduis legitimisq; variorum Phænomenorum obseruationibus deriuata.

AVCTORE

IO. BAPTISTA CYSATO, SOCIETATIS IESV INGOLSTADII MATHEMATICÆ PROFESSORE Ordinario.

PVBLICEQVE PROPOSITA ET DEMONSTRATA AB ERVDITO IVVENE VOLPERTO MOZELIO Mathematicæ & Physicæ Studioso. Anno 1619. Die Decembris.

Cum Gratia & Priuilegio Cæsareæ Maiestatis.

INGOLSTADII,

Ex Typographeo EDERIANO, apud Elisabetham Angermariam, Viduam.

ANNO M. DC. XIX.

R. P. Joanni Sutori. autor

42. Cysat, *Mathemata Astronomica* [Astronomical mathematics] (1619) title page

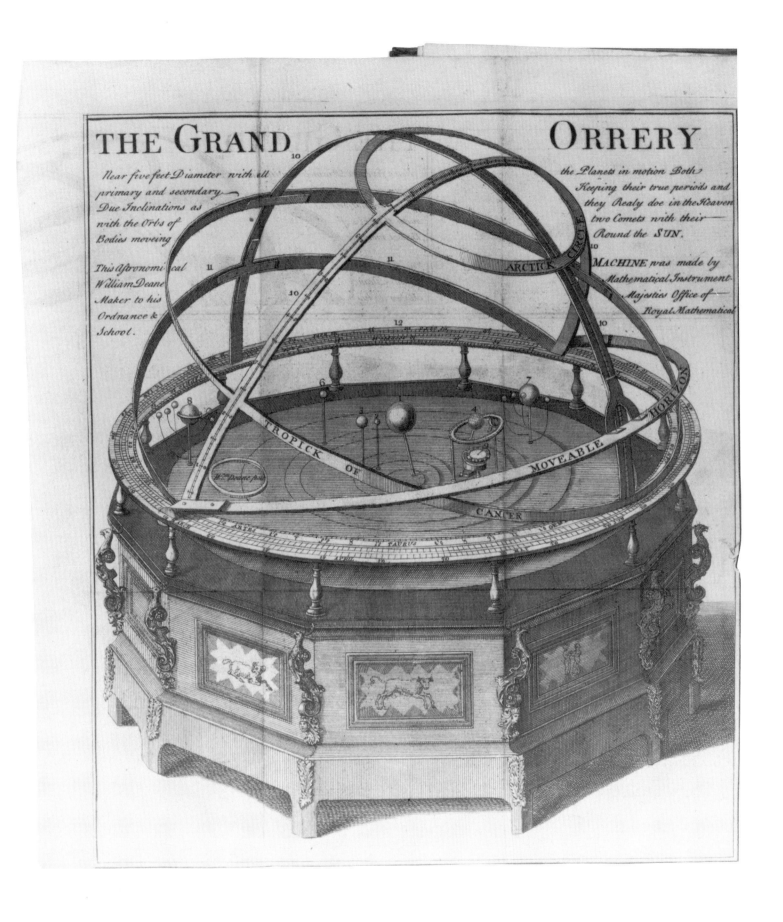

The labels visible within the engraving include: THE GRAND ORRERY, ARCTICK CIRCLE, HORIZON, MOVEABLE, CANCER, TROPICK OF, and the zodiac band labels.

The text within the engraving reads:

Near five feet Diameter with all primary and secondary Due Inclinations as with the Orbs of Bodies moveing

This Astronomical William Deane Maker to his Ordnance & Schoot.

the Planets in motion Both Keeping their true periods and they Realy doe in the Heaven two Comets with their Round the SUN.

MACHINE was made by Mathematical Instrument Majesties Office of Royal Mathematical

43. Deane, *The Description of the Copernican System* (1738) title page and folding frontispiece depicting an orrery

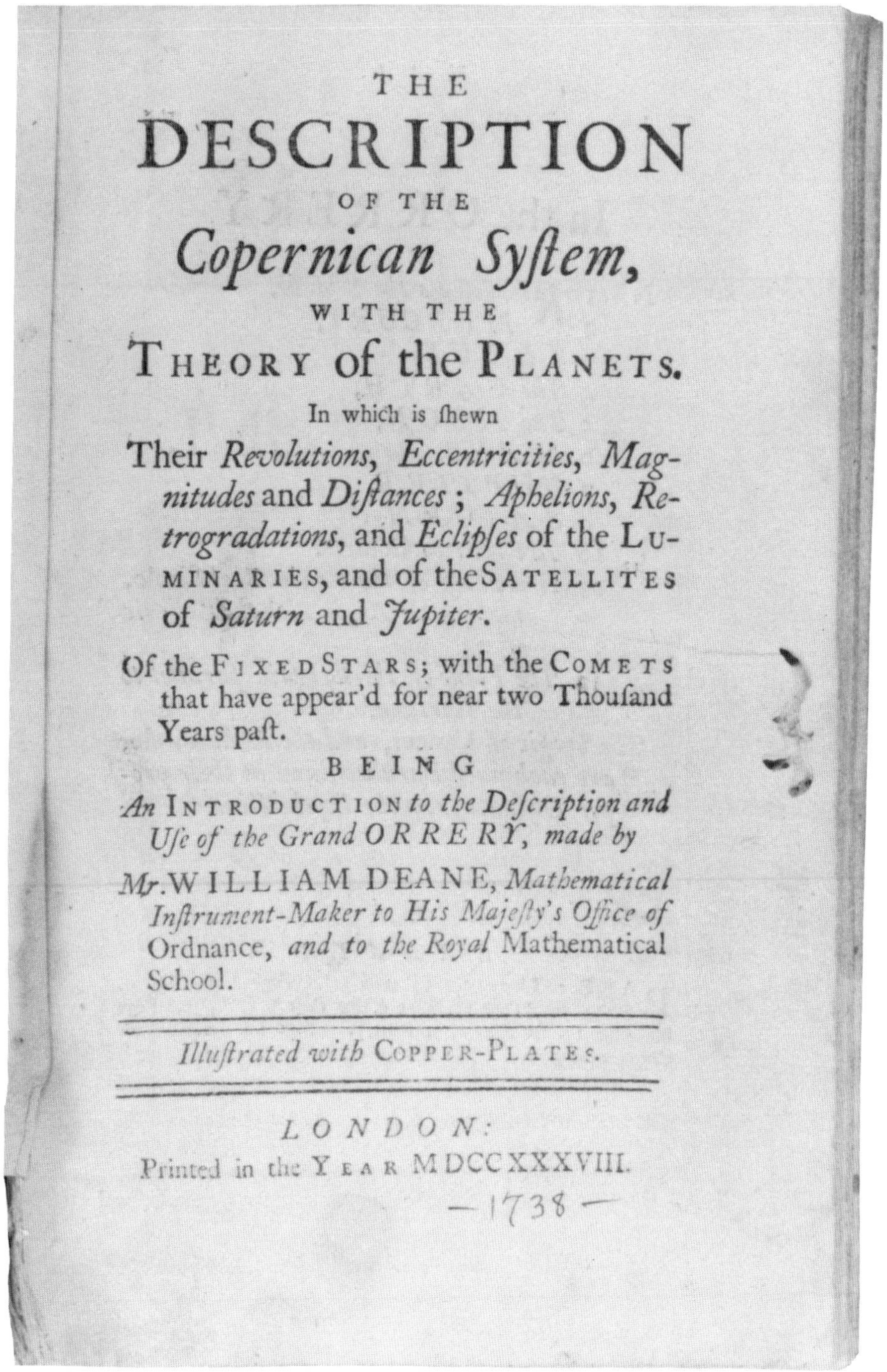

THE
DESCRIPTION

OF THE

Copernican System,

WITH THE

THEORY of the PLANETS.

In which is shewn

Their *Revolutions, Eccentricities, Magnitudes* and *Distances ; Aphelions, Retrogradations,* and *Eclipses* of the LUMINARIES, and of the SATELLITES of *Saturn* and *Jupiter.*

Of the FIXED STARS; with the COMETS that have appear'd for near two Thousand Years past.

BEING

An INTRODUCTION *to the Description and Use of the Grand* ORRERY, *made by*

Mr. WILLIAM DEANE, *Mathematical Instrument-Maker to His Majesty's Office of* Ordnance, *and to the Royal* Mathematical School.

Illustrated with COPPER-PLATES.

LONDON:

Printed in the YEAR MDCCXXXVIII.

— 1738 —

43. Deane, *The Description of the Copernican System* (1738) title page

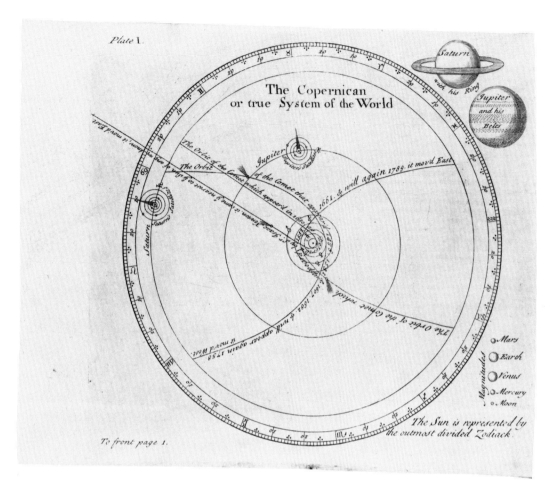

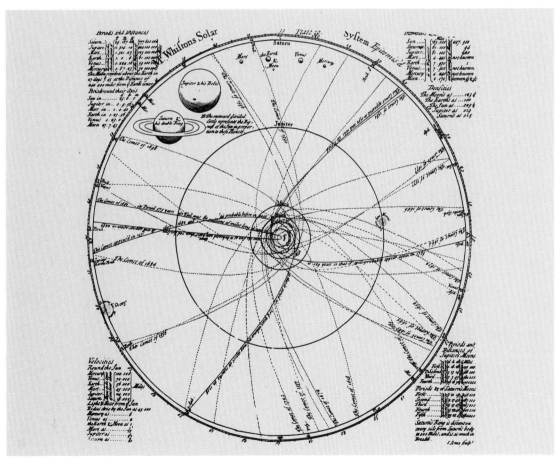

43. Deane, *The Description of the Copernican System* (1738)
diagram of the solar system showing comet paths (reduced)

44. Desaguliers, *A Course of Experimental Philosophy* (1744–45)
solar system showing paths of comets (reduced)

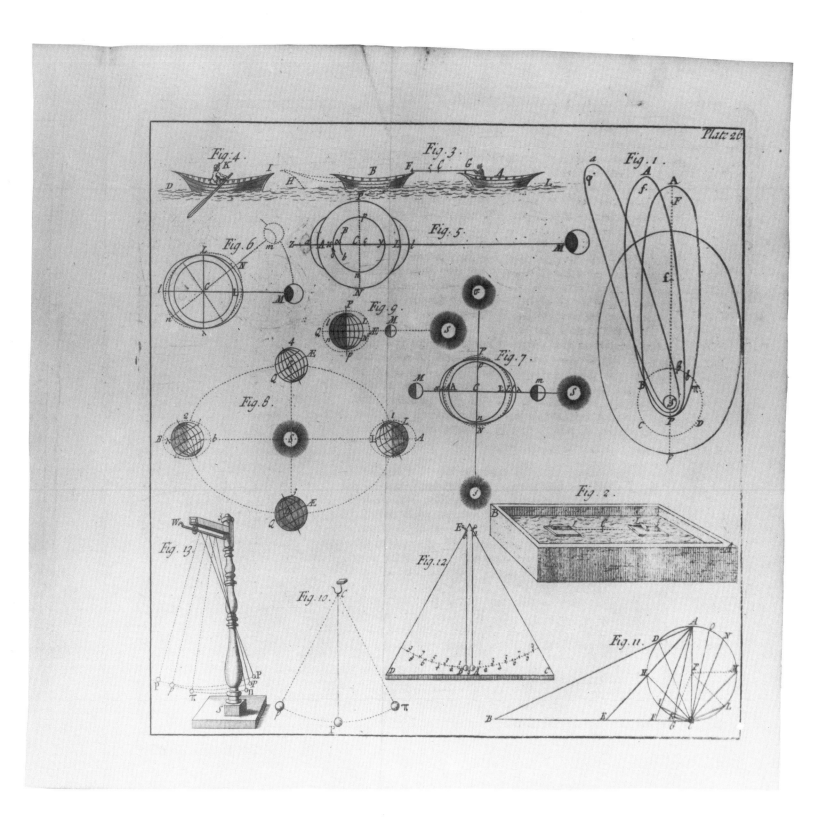

44. Desaguliers, *A Course of Experimental Philosophy* (1744–45) diagram

45 EIMMART, GEORG CHRISTOPH, 1638–1705

Ichnographia Nova Contemplationum de Sole

Nürnberg: J. E. Adelbulner, 1701

33 cm. 16 leaves. Title in red and black. Two historiated initials. Bound with Wurzelbau, J., *Uranies Noricae*, 1697 (item 211).

Georg Christoph Eimmart, called the younger, was an artist born at Regensburg, Germany. Skilled at drawing, painting, metal casting, and engraving, he achieved fame as an illustrator of astronomical works. At age sixteen he was studying metal working at Jena. It was there he came under the influence of the renowned mathematician Erhard Weigel (1625–99; items 197–204). After 1658 he went to Nürnberg where he worked both as an astronomer and as an engraver on copper. He designed and built astronomical instruments for the observatory there and was deeply engaged observing the comet of 1680–81. In 1683 King Charles XI of Sweden honored him in Stockholm with an award.

Zinner Collection

Lalande, p. 339.

NUC: CSdS; WU

46 ENGLEFIELD, SIR HENRY CHARLES, 1752–1822

On the Determination of the Orbits of Comets

London: Printed by Ritchie and Sammells for Peter Elmsly, 1793

30 cm. 204 pages. Folding plates, tables. Ex Libris William Howley. First and only edition.

Houzeau, 1249

NUC: CU; MeB; MBAt; MdBP; MH; NNC; NWM; PPL

47 EUCLIDES, fl. 300 B.C.

Preclarissimus Liber Elementorum… Geometrie

Venice: Erhard Ratdolt, 1482

31 cm. 138 leaves. Diagrams. Title printed in red on incipit page. Modern half morocco.

First printed edition of the oldest mathematical textbook still in use today. Campanus of Novara, ca. 1225–96, edited this *editio princeps* of Euclid's *Elements*. It is the work by which Campanus is best known and includes two non-Euclidian books, XIV and XV. It was reprinted at least thirteen times in the fifteenth and sixteenth centuries.

The printer of this work was Erhard Ratdolt (ca. 1443–1528) of Augsburg. It was the first and highly successful attempt to produce on the still new printing press a long mathematical book illustrated by numerous diagrams.

NUC: CSt; CU; CtNowa; CtY-M; DLC; ICJ; ICN; IU; MB; MWelC; MWiW-C; MiU; NjP; NIC; NN; PBL; PPF; PU; TxU; ViU

Goff: 58 copies

48 EUCLIDES, fl. 300 B.C.

Elementorum Sex Priores Libri

Leiden: Daniel, Abraham & Adrian a Gaesbeeck, 1673

14 cm. 306 pages. Frontispiece, vignette on title page, diagrams. This edition was edited by Christiaan Melder, fl. 1663, professor of mathematics.

Zinner Collection

NUC: CSdS; IU; MiU; NNC

49 FATIO DE DUILLIER, NICOLAS, 1664–1753

Navigation Improv'd

London: n.p., 1728

35 cm. 6 leaves. Bound with: Salusbury, T., *Mathematical Collections*, 1661 (item 166). One folding engraved plate.

Author's signed manuscript note on verso of title page: "London June the 5th 1728. I shall be further willing, upon proper Encouragement, to go to Sea a short Voyage, to demonstrate and teach the Method which I do here propose; As, for instance, a Voyage to Gottenburg, Copenhagen, or Portugal. /s/ N. Facio."

He was a friend of Newton and rebuked Leibnitz in the heated controversy over who developed integral calculus.

NUC: NN

ICHNOGRAPHIA
NOVA
Contemplationum

de

SOLE,

in

Desolatis

Antiquorum
PHILOSOPHORUM

Ruderibus

Concepta

à

Georgio Christophoro Eimmarto.

❧❧❧❧❧❧❧❧❧❧❧❧❧❧❧❧❧❧❧❧❧❧❧❧❧

NORIMBERGÆ,

Sumptibus Wolfgangi Mauritii Endteri.

Typis Johannis Ernesti Adelbulneri.

MDCCI.

4.

45. Eimmart, *Ichnographia Nova Contemplationum de Sole*
[Study of a new dimension concerning the sun] (1701) title page (reduced)

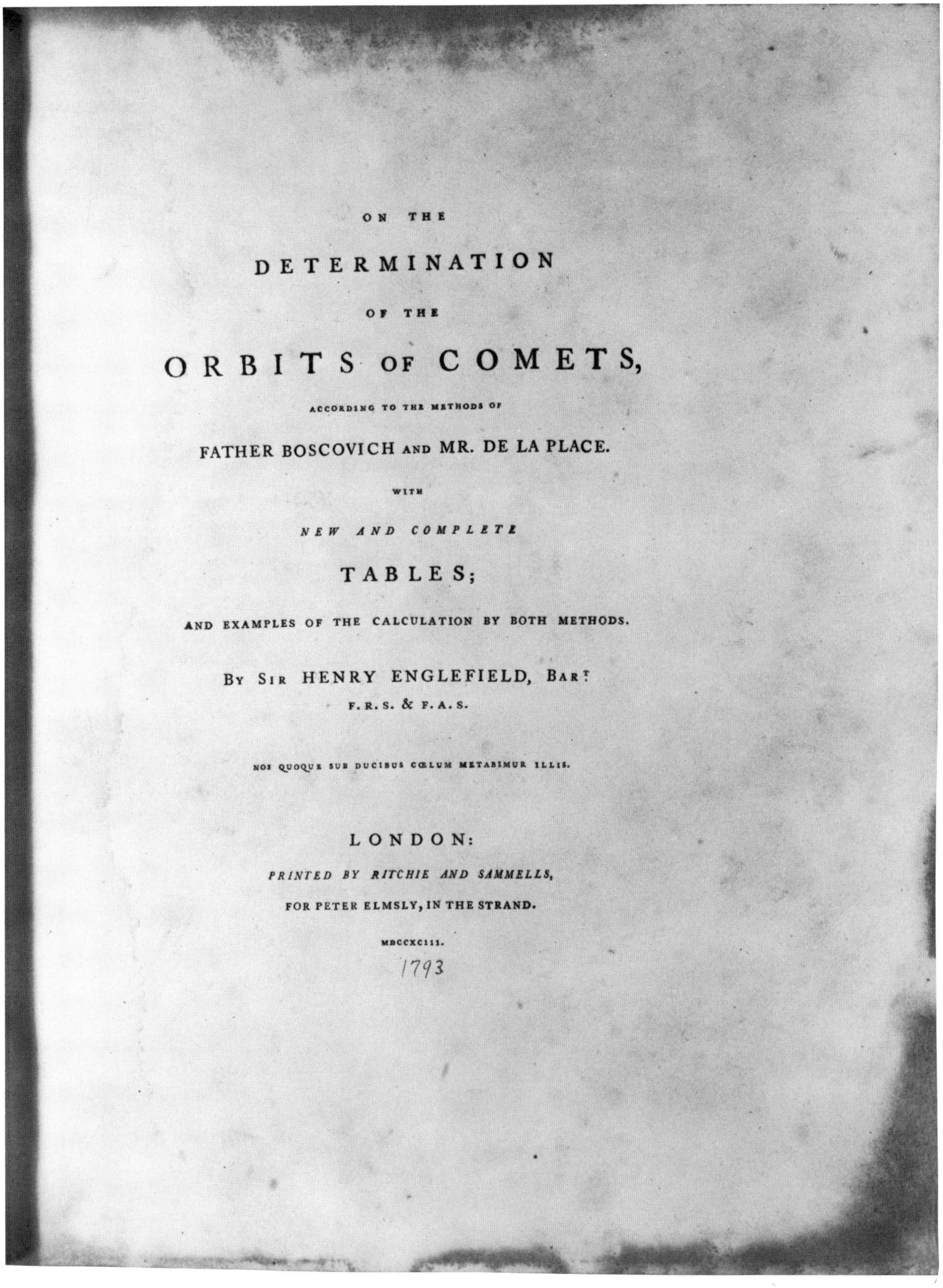

ON THE

DETERMINATION

OF THE

ORBITS OF COMETS,

ACCORDING TO THE METHODS OF

FATHER BOSCOVICH AND MR. DE LA PLACE.

WITH

NEW AND COMPLETE

TABLES;

AND EXAMPLES OF THE CALCULATION BY BOTH METHODS.

By Sir HENRY ENGLEFIELD, Barᵗ

F. R. S. & F. A. S.

NOS QUOQUE SUB DUCIBUS CŒLUM METABIMUR ILLIS.

LONDON:

PRINTED BY RITCHIE AND SAMMELLS,

FOR PETER ELMSLY, IN THE STRAND.

MDCCXCIII.

1793

46. Englefield, *On the Determination of the Orbits of Comets* (1793) title page (reduced)

C Erhardus ratdolt Augustensis impressor. Serenissimo
alme vrbis venete Principi Joanni Mocenico. S.

Solebam antea serenissime princeps mecum ipse cogitans admirari
quid cause esset q in hac tua prepotenti ↄ fausta vrbe cum varia au/
ctorum veterum nouorumq3 volumina quottidie imprimerent. In
hac mathematica facultate vel reliquarum disciplinarum nobilissima
aut nibil aut parua quedam et friuola in tanta impressorū copia qui
in tua vrbe agunt: viderentur impressa. Hec cum mecum sepius discu
terem inueniebam id difficultate operis accidisse. Non enim adhuc
quo pacto schemata geometrica: quibus mathematica volumina sca/
tent: ac sine quibus nibil i bis disciplinis sere intelligi optime potest
excogitauerant. Itaq3 cum boc ipsum tantūmodo cōmuni omniim
vtilitati que ex bis percipitur. obstaret mea industria nō sine maximo
labore effeci. vt qua facilitate litterarum elementa imprimuntur .ea
etiam geometrice figure conficerentur. Quamobrem vt spero boc
nostro inuento he disciplme quas mathemata greci appellant volu/
minum copia sicut relique scientie breui illustrabuntur. De quarum
laudibus ↄ vtilitate possem multa im presens adducere ab illustribus
collecta auctoribus: nisi studiosis iam omnibus bec nota esset. Illud
etiam plane cognitum est ceteras scientias sine mathematibus imper
se ras ac veluti mancas ee. Neq3 boc profecto negabunt Dialectici
neq3 Pbilosopbi abnuent: in quoↄ libris multa reperiuntur: que si
ne mathematica ratione minime intelligi possunt. Quam diuin9 ille
Plato mere veritatis arcanū. vt adipisceretur cyrenas ad .Tbeo/
dorum summum eo tempore mathematicuz ↄ ad egiptios sacerdotes
enauigauit. Quid q sine bac vna facultate viuendi ratio nō perfecte
constat. Nam vt de musice taceam: que nobis muneri ab ipsa natura
ad perferendos facilius labores concessa videtur: vt astrologiā pre/
teream qua exculti celum ipsum veluti scalis machinisq3 quibusdam
conscendentes verum ipsius nature argumentum cognoscimus: sine
aritbmetica ↄ geometria: quarum altera numeros altera mesuras do
cet ciuiliter: comodeq3 viuere q possum9: Sed quid ego i bis mo/
ror que iam omnibus vt dixi: notiora sunt q3 vt a me dicantur. Eu/
clides igitur megarensis serenissime princeps qui .xv. libris omnem
geometrie rationem consummatissime complexus est: quem ego sum
ma ↄ cura ↄ diligentia nullo pretermisso schemate imprimendum cu/
raui: sub tuo numine tutus felixq3 prodeat.

47. Euclid, *Preclarissimus Liber Elementorum…Geometriae* [Very clear book
of the elements of geometry] (1482) Erhard Ratdolt's introductory
statement and the incipit with diagrams in the margins (reduced)

De principijs p se notis:e pmo de diffini/
tionibus earundem.

Punctus est cuius ps nó est. C Linea est
lógitudo sine latitudine cui⁹ quidé ex/
tremitates sí duo púcta. C Linea recta
é ab vno púcto ad aliú breuissima exté/
sio i extremitates suas vtrúq3 eoz reci
piens. C Supficies é q lógitudiné z lati
tudiné tm b3:cui⁹termi quidé sút linee.
C Supficies plana é ab vna linea ad a/
liã extésio i extremitates suas recipiés
C Angulus planus é duarú lincarú al/
ternus ptactus:quaz expásio é sup sup/
ficié applicatioq3 nó directa. C Quádo aut angulum ptinét due
linee recte rectiline⁹ angulus noiaf. C Qñ recta linea sup rectá
steterit duoq3 anguli ytrobiq3 fuerit.eqles:eoz yterq3 rect⁹erit
C Lineaq3 linee supstás ei cui⁹supstat ppendicularis vocaf. C An
gulus vo qui recto maioz é obtusus dicif. C Angul⁹vo minoz re
cto acut⁹appellaf. C Termin⁹é qd vniuscuinsq3 finis é. C Figura
é q tmino vl termis ptinef. C Circul⁹é figura plana vna qdem li/
nea pteta: q circúferentia noiaf:in cui⁹medio púct⁹é: a quo⁹oés
linee recte ad circúferétiá exeútes sibiinuicez sút equales. Et hic
quidé púct⁹cétrú circuli dz. C Diameter circuli é linea recta que
sup ei⁹centz trásiens extremitatesq3 suas circúferétie applicans
circulú i duo media diuidit. C Semicirculus é figura plana dia/
metro circuli z medietate circúferentie ptenta. C Portio circu/
li é figura plana recta linea z parte circúferétie pteta: semicircu/
lo quidé aut maioz aut minoz. C Rectilinee figure sút q rectis li/
neis cótinenf quarú quedá trilatere q trib⁹rectis lineis: quedá
quadrilatere q qtuoz rectis lineis. qdá mltilatere que pluribus
q3 quatuoz rectis luneis continenf. C Figurarú trilaterarú:alia
est triangulus bñs tria latera equalia.Alia triangulus duo bñs
eqlia latera.Alia triangulus triú inequalium laterú. Max iterú
alia est ozthogoniú:vnú.s.rectum angulum habens.Alia é am/
bligonium aliquem obtusum angulum habens.Alia est oxigoni
um:in qua tres anguli sunt acuti. C Figurarú auté quadrilateraz
Alia est qdratum quod est equilaterú atq3 rectangulú. Alia est
tetragon⁹long⁹:q est figura rectangula : sed equilatera non est.
Alia est helmuaym: que est equilatera : sed rectangula non est.

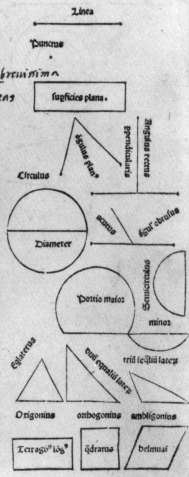

Linea

Punctus

breuissim

supficies plana.

Circulus

Angulus rectus

ppendicularis

angulus plan⁹

acutus

 figur obtusus

Diameter

Portio maior

Semicirculus

minoz

Egilaterus

duo equaliú laterz

triú ieqliú laterz

Origonius

orthogonius

ambligonius

Tetrago⁹ lóg⁹

qdratus

helmuai

48. Euclid, *Elementorum Libri Sex* [Six books of Euclid's elements]
(1673) preliminary title page

50 FERGUSON, JAMES, 1710–76

Astronomy Explained upon Sir Isaac Newton's Principles

Philadelphia: Mathew Carey, 1806

23 cm. 654 pages. Eighteen folding plates. Contemporary calf binding. First American edition. The first London edition was 1756.

NUC: ICJ; IU; KyLx; MB; MH; MiU; NcD; Nh; NjP; NNC; PPAmP; PSC; PU

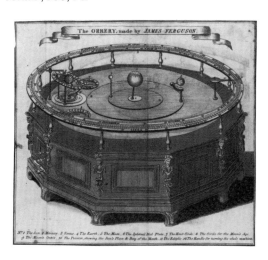

51 FIGATELLI, GIUSEPPE MARIA

Retta linea gnomonica

Forli: Gio. Cimatti, 1667

21 cm. 83 pages. Illustrations. Bound in gold-tooled contemporary vellum. First edition.

Zinner Collection

Lalande, p. 169

NUC: CSdS; CtY-M; MB

52 FINE, ORONCE, 1494–1555

De gli horologi solari

Italy?: ca. 1650?

32 cm. 80 leaves. Tables. Manuscript written on both sides of the paper in a neat hand. Bound in contemporary late seventeenth-century boards.

The text is an Italian translation of Volume one of the author's four-volume *...De Solaribus Horologiis et Quadrantibus, Libri Quatuor*, Paris: G. Cavellat, 1560. There is no Italian-language edition listed in *The National Union Catalog*, the British Museum, or Bibliothèque Nationale catalogues. The work treats sundials.

53 FINELLA, FILIPPO, ca.1584–ca.1649

Speculum Astronomicum

Naples: I. Cassari, 1649

21 cm. 64 leaves. Illustrations.

Lalande, p. 227

NUC: CSdS; MH; MiU

54 FIRMICUS MATERNUS, JULIUS, fl. A.D. 334–55

Astronomicon

Basel: J. Hervagen, 1533

30 cm. 246 leaves. Marginalia, diagrams, tables, historiated initials. Bound in old calf. Provenance, title page: "Robert Griffithie; Hugh Grove; W. C. Grove, Joannis Leith Rop de Arnage, 1814, Sir John Stowellis."

Firmicus Maternus lived in the time of Constantine the Great (280?–337) and his sons. Best known for his treatise on the errors of the pagan religions, some authorities also identify him as the author of a *Mathesios*, a work in eight books, and an introduction to astrology according to Egyptian and Babylonian lore (*Iselin*, v. 3, p. 481).

Zinner Collection

Lalande, p. 51; Zinner, 1533

NUC: CSdS; CtY; DNLM; GEU; RPB; RPJCB; WU

55 FIRMIN DE BELLEVAL, 14th century

Repertorium de Mutatione Aeris, tam Via Astrologica

Paris: J. Kerver, 1539

27 cm. 83 leaves. Printer's device and illegible ex libris on title page. Historiated initials and astrological tables.

Firmin was a fourteenth-century French astrologer and calendar reformer from Amiens. Known under various forms of his name, he is best known because Pope Clement VI (1291–1352; pope 1342–52) summoned him to Avignon in 1344 to advise him on calendar reform.

The original manuscript was written in 1338. Erhard Ratdolt issued the first printed edition anonymously at Venice in 1485. This 1539 edition is the last ever printed (Thorndike, L., *A History of Magic and Experimental Science*. New York: Macmillan, 1958, v. 3, pp. 268–80).

Lalande, p. 58

NUC: MH

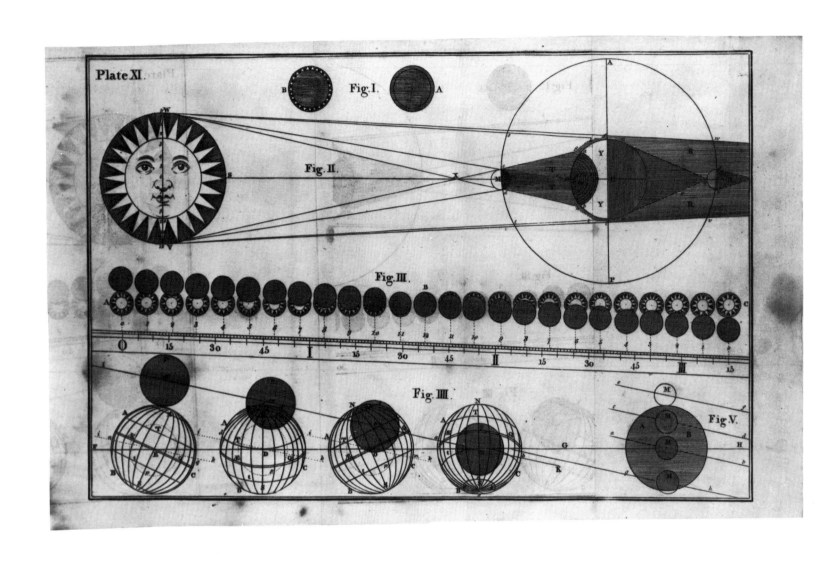

50. Ferguson, *Astronomy Explained upon Sir Isaac Newton's Principles* (1806)
folding plate (reduced)

ASTRONOMY

EXPLAINED UPON

SIR ISAAC NEWTON's PRINCIPLES,

AND

MADE EASY TO THOSE WHO HAVE NOT STUDIED MATHEMATICS.

TO WHICH ARE ADDED,

A PLAIN METHOD OF FINDING THE DISTANCES

OF ALL THE PLANETS FROM THE SUN,

BY THE

TRANSIT OF VENUS OVER THE SUN'S DISC,

In the year 1761:

AN ACCOUNT OF MR. HORROX's OBSERVATION

OF THE TRANSIT OF VENUS,

In the year 1639:

AND OF THE

DISTANCES OF ALL THE PLANETS FROM THE SUN,

AS DEDUCED FROM OBSERVATIONS OF THE TRANSIT

In the year 1761.

BY JAMES FERGUSON, F. R. S.

Heb. i. 3. The worlds were framed by the Word of God.
Job xxvi. 7. He hangeth the earth upon nothing.
——— 13. By his Spirit he hath garnished the heavens.

THE FIRST AMERICAN EDITION, FROM THE LAST LONDON EDITION;

REVISED, CORRECTED, AND IMPROVED,

BY ROBERT PATTERSON,

Professor of Mathematics, and Teacher of Natural Philosophy, in the
University of Pennsylvania.

PRINTED FOR AND PUBLISHED BY MATHEW CAREY.

FOR SALE BY JOHN CONRAD & CO. SAMUEL F. BRADFORD, W. W. WOODWARD,
JAMES CRUIKSHANK, W. P. FARRAND & CO. KIMBER, CONRAD & CO.
RONALDS & LOUDON. BERNARD DORNIN, P. A. MESIER.
ISAAC RILEY & CO. & EVERT DUYCKINCK.
1806.

50. Ferguson, *Astronomy Explained upon Sir Isaac Newton's Principles* (1806) title page

RETTA LINEA
GNOMONICA
DI
GIVSEPPE MARIA FIGATELLI
CENTESE,

Ouero breuiſſima eſtenſione inſtruttiua frà due punti di chiarezza, e facilità
per delineare Horologj Horizontali, Verticali, e Rifleſſi,
con alcuni pochi de' più vſati frà portatili.

Operetta aſſai diletteuole per il nuouo, & vniuerſal modo d'operare, in qual ſi ſia
Horologio Rifleſſo.

FEROX FERAXQ. LIVIA.

IN FORLI

Per Gio: Cimatti, Al Segno della LIVIA 1667. Con licenza de' Superiori.

51. Figatelli, *Retta linea gnomonica* [Resistance line gnomonics] (1667)
title page of work on gnomonics, the art of making or using sundials

52. Fine, *De gli horologi solari* [Concerning sundials] (1650) (reduced)

53. Finella, *Speculum Astronomicum* [Mirror of astronomy] (1649) portrait of the author

ꝛIVLII FIRMICI MA

TERNI IVNIORIS SICVLI V.C. AD MAVORTIVM
Lollianum Astronomicōn Lib. VIII. per NICOLAVM
PRVCKNERVM Astrologum nuper ab
innumeris mendis uindicati.

HIS ACCESSERVNT.

CLAVDII PTOLEMAEI Pheludiensis Alexandrini ἀποτιλεσμάτωμ, quod
Quadripartitum uocant, Lib. IIII

De inerrantium stellarum significationibus Lib. I

Centiloquium eiusdem.

EX ARABIBVS ET CHALDEIS.

HERMETIS uetustissimi Astrologi centum Aphoris. Lib. I

BETHEM Centiloquium.

EIVSDEM de Horis Planetarum Liber alius.

ALMANSORIS Astrologi propositiones ad Saracenorum regem.

ZAHELIS Arabis de Electionibus Lib. I

MESSAHALAH de ratione Circuli & Stellarum, & qualiter in hoc seculo ope=
rentur, Lib. I

OMAR de Natiuitatibus Lib. III

MARCI MANILII Poëtae disertissimi Astronomicōn Lib. V

Postremo, OTHONIS BRVNFELSII de diffinitionibus & terminis Astrolo=
giae libellus isagogicus.

BASILEAE EX OFFICINA IOANNIS HERVAGII,
MENSE MARTIO, ANNO M. D. XXXIII

54. Firmicus, *Astronomicon* [Compendium on astronomy] (1533)
title page with signatures of former owners (reduced)

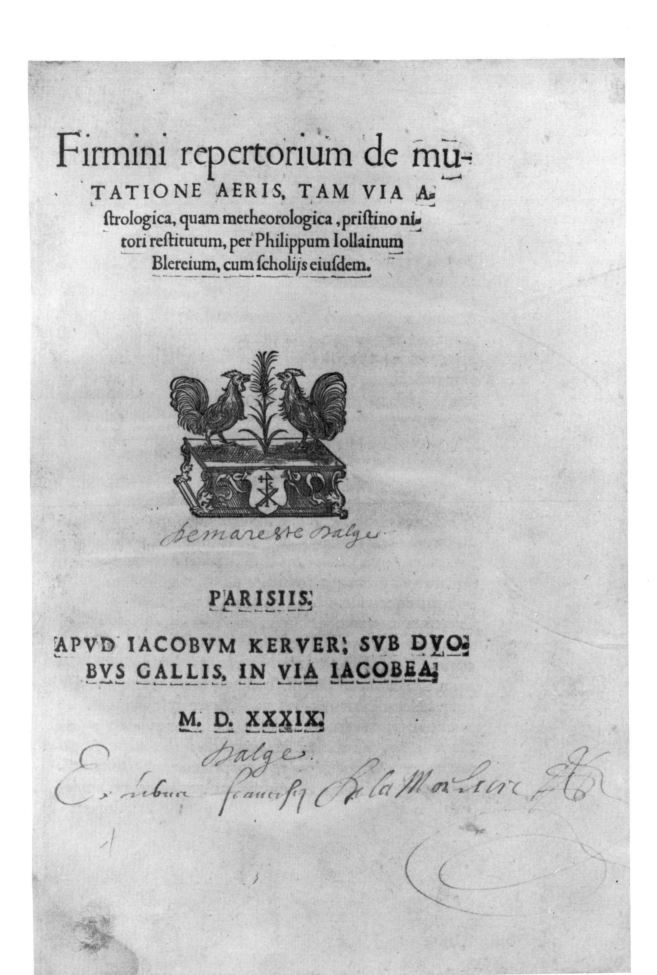

Firmini repertorium de mu-
TATIONE AERIS, TAM VIA A-
strologica, quam metheorologica, pristino ni-
tori restitutum, per Philippum Iollainum
Blereium, cum scholijs eiusdem.

PARISIIS.

APVD IACOBVM KERVER, SVB DVO-
BVS GALLIS, IN VIA IACOBEA.

M. D. XXXIX.

55. Firmin de Belleval, *Repertorium de Mutatione Aeris, tam Via Astrologica*
[Source materials on the changing heavens, according to the astrological way] (1539) title page

56 FIXMILLNER, PLACIDUS F., 1721–91

*Decennium Astronomicum Continens Observationes
Praecipuas ab Anno MDCCLXV ad Annum MDCCLXXV*

Steyr: A. Wimmer, 1776

24 cm. 150 leaves. Four folding engraved plates. Printer's
vignette on title page and decorative initials and devices
throughout. First and only edition. Bound with his
Meridianus Speculae, 1765 (item 57).

Fixmillner was a Benedictine monk and astronomer
at the Krems monastery in Austria.

Zinner Collection

Houzeau, 3385; Lalande, p. 550

NUC: CSdS

57 FIXMILLNER, PLACIDUS F., 1721–91

Meridianus Speculae Astronomicae Cremifanensis

Steyr: G. Menhardt, 1765

24 cm. 75 leaves. Three folding copper-engraved plates.
Printer's decorative devices. Three-quarter leather binding. Ex Libris Heinz Kreutz. First and only edition.

Zinner Collection

NUC: CSdS

58 FLAMSTEED, JOHN, 1646–1719

Atlas Coelestis

London: n.p., 1753

57 × 39.5 cm. 7 leaves of text, 28 double-page engraved
star maps delicately hand-colored and mounted on linen
stubs. The large volume is handsomely bound in vellum
over boards.

Lalande describes this second folio issue as "the great
and magnificent celestial atlas, the best ever made."
Flamsteed was the first Astronomer Royal at
Greenwich. He had a passion for precision and accuracy in astronomical data. The first issue of the *Atlas*
was in 1729. The plates show the stars as positioned
by Abraham Sharp. The glorious constellation figures
were drawn by Sir James Thornhill.

Lalande, p. 338

NUC: MdBP; NjP

59 FLAMSTEED, JOHN, 1646–1719

Historiae Coelestis Britannicae

London: H. Meere, 1725

40 cm. 3 large folio volumes. Frontispiece (portrait of
Flamsteed), folding plates, rare and important astronomical tables. There is another copy of the Flamsteed portrait
in the Zinner Collection of Portraits of Scientists. First
edition.

Contains the results of Flamsteed's many important
observations. Volume three contains the British Catalogue of 2,935 stars observed at Greenwich, exceed-
ing all former catalogues in number and accuracy.

Houzeau, 3360; Lalande, p. 379

NUC: CtY; DLC; DN-Ob; IU; InU; MBAt; MH; MNS;
MWiW; MiU; NN; NWM; OClCS; PPAmP; PPL; ViU;
WU

60 FONTENELLE, BERNARD LE BOVIER DE, 1657–
1757

Entretiens sur la pluralité des mondes

Amsterdam: E. Roger, 1719

17 cm. 85 leaves. New edition augmented from the seventh
edition by the author. Engraved plates.

Fontenelle was not an astronomer, but a well-educated rational thinker, author of numerous works,
and investigator in the natural sciences. He was
accorded every possible academic honor in France
including acceptance into the renowned French
Academy (1691) and was elected to the Royal Society,
London, in 1733.

His most famous and most frequently pub-
lished and translated work was *Entretiens sur la pluralité
des mondes*. First published at Paris in 1686, no less
than forty editions and reprints appeared up to 1911.
English translations appeared in 1715 and 1728, Greek
in 1794 and Italian in 1748 (*DSB*, v. 5, pp. 57ff.;
Bibliothèque Nationale, *Catalogue générale des livres
imprimés* v. 53).

Lalande, p. 372

NUC: NjP; NN; TxDaM-P

MERIDIANVS
SPECVLAE ASTRONOMICAE
CREMIFANENSIS
SEV
LONGITVDO EIVS GEOGRAPHICA
PER MAGNVM ILLVD SOLIS DELIQVIVM,
IPSIS CALENDIS APRILIS ANNI M. DCC. LXIV.
SPECTATVM, EXAMINATIS VARIORVM CELEBRIVM
LOCORVM OBSERVATIONIBVS ACCVRATE INVESTIGATA
ATQVE INVENTA,

ET

ADIECTIS PLVRIBVS ALIIS SPECTACVLIS
CAELESTIBVS, AD REM PRAESENTEM ILLVSTRAN-
DAM FACIENTIBVS, PVBLICI IVRIS FACTA

A

P. PLACIDO FIXLMILLNER,
ORDINEM S.P. BENEDICTI IN EODEM MONA-
STERIO PROFESSO, NOTARIO APOSTOLICO IN CVRIA
ROMANA INSCRIPTO, ACADEMIAE ILLVSTRIVM REGENTE,
ALTIORVM SCHOLARVM DECANO, ET SS. CANONVM
PROFESSORE ORDINARIO.

FELICIBUS AVSPICIIS

CVM FACVLTATE SVPERIORVM.

STYRAE,
TYPIS GREGORII MENHARDT ANNO M.DCC. LXV.

57. Fixmillner, *Meridianus Speculae Astronomicae Cremifanensis* [Astronomical
studies of the meridian at Krems] (1765) title page

118

HISTORIÆ COELESTIS
BRITANNICÆ
VOLUMEN Primum.

Complectens

STELLARUM FIXARUM

Nec non

PLANETARUM OMNIUM

OBSERVATIONES

Sextante, Micrometro, &c. peractas.

Quibus subjuncta sunt

PLANETARUM LOCA

ab iisdem OBSERVATIONIBUS deducta.

Observante JOANNE FLAMSTEEDIO, A.R.

In OBSERVATORIO Regio

GRENOVICENSI

CONTINUA SERIE

Ab Anno 1675, ad Annum 1689.

LONDINI: Typis H. MEERE, M.DCC.XXV.

59. Flamsteed, *Historiae Coelestis Britannicae Volumen Primum* [Volume one of the Britannic history of the heavens] (1725) title page (reduced)

JOHANNES FLAMSTEEDIUS Derbiensis
Astronomiæ Professor Regius. Anno Ætatis 74 Obijt
Decem 31 1719

59. Flamsteed, *Historiae Coelestis Britannicae Volumen Primum* (1725) frontispiece (reduced)

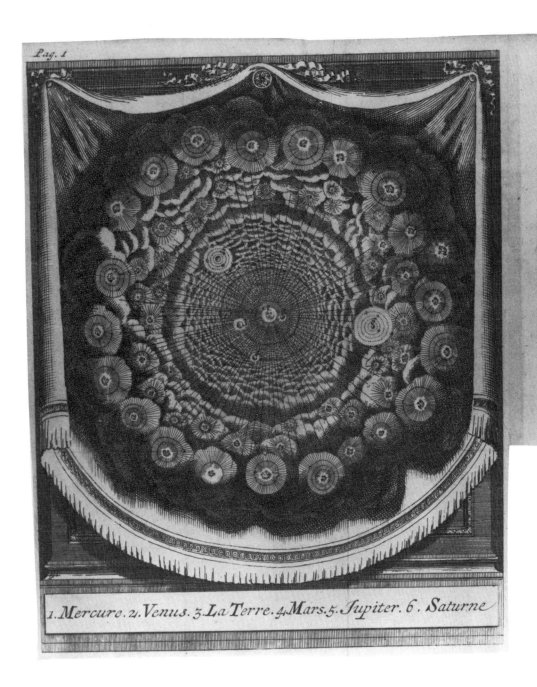

1. Mercure. 2. Venus. 3. La Terre. 4. Mars. 5. Jupiter. 6. Saturne

ENTRETIENS
SUR
LA PLURALITÉ
DES MONDES.
A MONSIEUR L***

VOUS voulez, Monsieur, que je vous rende un compte exact de la maniére dont j'ai passé mon tems à la campagne, chez Madame la Marquise de G ***. Sçavez-vous bien que ce compte exact sera un Livre, & ce qu'il y a de pis, un Livre de Philosophie ? Vous vous attendez à des Fêtes, à des Parties de Jeu ou de Chasse, & vous aurez des Planètes, des Mondes, des Tourbillons; il n'a presque été question que de ces choses-là. Heureusement vous êtes Philosophe, & vous ne vous en moquerez pas tant qu'un autre. Peut-être même serez-vous bien-aise que j'aye attiré Madame la Marquise dans le party de la Philosophie. Nous ne pouvions faire une acquisition plus considerable; car je compte que la beauté & la jeunesse sont toûjours des choses d'un grand prix. Ne croyez-vous pas que si la Sagesse elle-même

A 7   vou-

60. Fontenelle, *Entretiens sur la pluralité des mondes* [Communications concerning the plurality of the worlds] (1719) first page of the text and facing folding plate (reduced)

61 FRACASTORO, GIROLAMO, 1483–1553

Homocentrica

Venice: n.p., 1538

22 cm. 146 pages. Illustrations. Portrait of Fracastoro. Bound with Amico, *De Motibus Corporum Coelestiū...* (item 4).

Fracastoro was a famous physician, poet, and astrologer born at Verona. It is said that as a child while being held in his mother's arms a bolt of lightning struck and killed her, but miraculously he was untouched.

He was the physician in attendance at the historic Council of Trent (1545–63) and persuaded the prelates present to move the council to Bologna because from his star observations he foresaw a great pestilence coming. Thereafter he lived at Verona where he made astronomical observations and wrote descriptions of the world (*Iselin*, v. 3, pp. 526–7).

Zinner Collection

Houzeau, 636.

NUC: DFo; DLC; DNLM; ICJ; MB; MH; NNC; NNNAM; PBL; PPC

62 FRISI, PAOLO, 1728–84

Elogio del Galileo

Milano: F. Agnelli, 1775

22 cm. 135 pages. First edition. Vignette on title page. Provenance, front free endpaper "D Arch Whitehouse." Bound in contemporary vellum.

Frisi was an Italian astronomer who studied the daily movement of the earth. He was the author of books on mathematics, physics, and astronomy.

NUC: no copy

63 FULKE, WILLIAM, 1538–89

A Most Pleasant Prospect. Into the Garden of Naturall Contemplation, to Behold the Naturall Causes of All Kinde of Meteors

London: W. Leake, 1640

15 cm. 74 leaves. Bound in nineteenth-century calf. Ex Libris Robert B. & Marian S. Honeyman.

Late edition of a work first published in 1563. Fulke, a Puritan divine, wrote on natural phenomena. He matriculated at Saint John's College, Cambridge, in 1555, graduated B.A. in 1558, and received his M.A. in 1563. He studied mathematics, languages, and theology and was appointed principal lecturer at Saint John's in 1565.

NUC: CtY; DFo; MH; MiD; NcD; NcU; OkU; TxU

64 FURTENBACH, JOSEPH, 1591–1667

Dess Aeltern Mannhaffter Kunst-Spiegel

Augsburg: Johann Schultes, 1663

31 cm. 292 pages, 33 leaves of plates. Title printed in red and black. Diagrams, plans. Superb copper-engraved folding plates.

The chapter headings include among others: arithmetic, geometry, planimetria, geography, astronomy, and navigation.

Amelang Collection, San Diego State University Library.

NUC: CSmH; DFo; ICJ; IU; MiU; N; NIC; NN; OO

65 GABRIELE, GIACOMO, 1510–50

Dialogo di M. Iacomo Cabriele, nel quale de la sphera, et de gli orti et occasi de le stelle

Venice: G. de Farri, 1545.

22 cm. 64 leaves. Printer's vignette on title page, historiated initials.

Lalande, p. 65

NUC: DFo; DLC; MB; NN

HIERONYMI FRACASTORII.

61. Fracastoro, *Homocentrica* [Spheres having the same center] (1538) portrait of the author

ELOGIO

DEL

GALILEO.

IN MILANO)(MDCCLXXV.

Per Federico Agnelli.
CON LICENZA DE' SUPERIORI.

62. Frisi, *Elogio del Galileo* [Eulogy on Galileo] (1775) title page

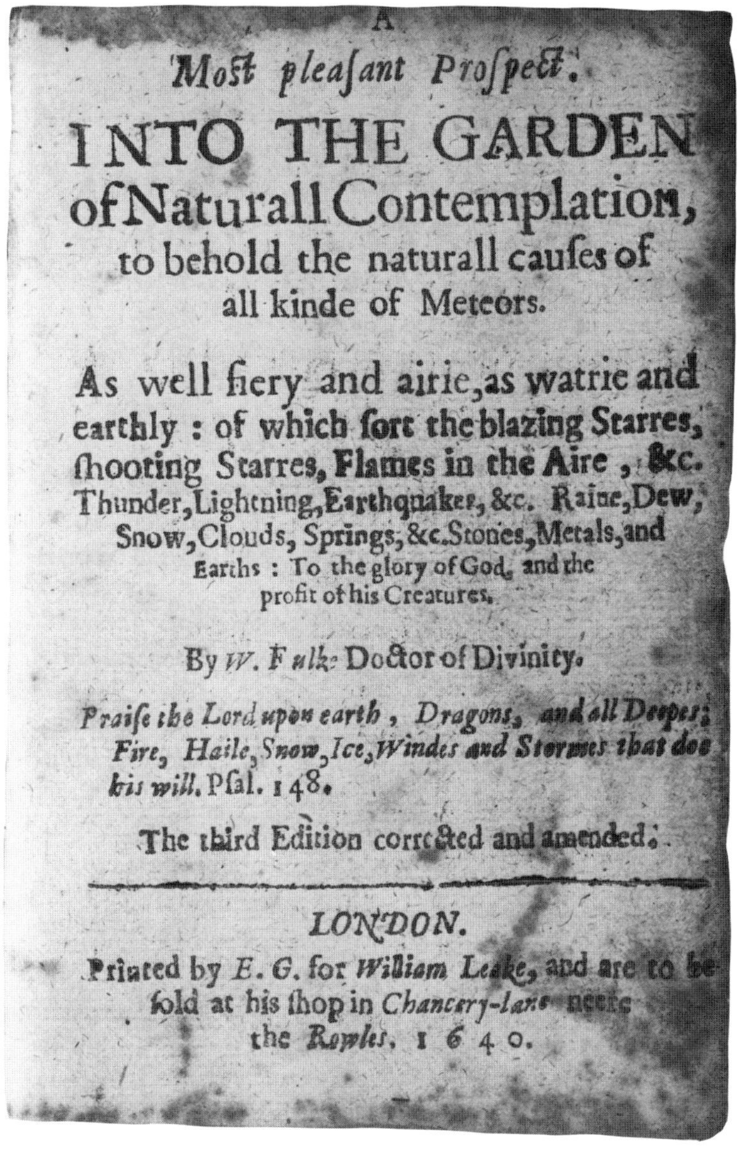

A

Most pleasant Prospect.

INTO THE GARDEN of Naturall Contemplation, to behold the naturall causes of all kinde of Meteors.

As well fiery and airie, as watrie and earthly : of which sort the blazing Starres, shooting Starres, Flames in the Aire, &c. Thunder, Lightning, Earthquakes, &c. Raine, Dew, Snow, Clouds, Springs, &c. Stones, Metals, and Earths : To the glory of God, and the profit of his Creatures.

By *W. Fulke* Doctor of Divinity.

Praise the Lord upon earth, Dragons, and all Deepes; Fire, Haile, Snow, Ice, Windes and Stormes that doe his will. Psal. 148.

The third Edition corrected and amended.

LONDON.

Printed by *E. G.* for *William Leake*, and are to be sold at his shop in *Chancery-lane* neere the *Rowles*. 1640.

63. Fulke, *A Most Pleasant Prospect* (1640) title page

64. Furtenbach, *Dess Aeltern Mannhaffter Kunst-Spiegel* [Concerning the ancient
strong optical mirror] (1663) map of the Italian coast near Rapallo (reduced)

DIALOGO DI

M. IACOMO GABRIELE,

NELQVALE DE LA SPHERA,

ET DE GLI ORTI ET OCCASI DE
LE STELLE, MINVTAMEN=
TE SI RAGIONA.

VIRTVTE DVCE

COMITE FORTVNA.

CO'L PRIVILEGIO DEL SOMMO PONTEFI=
ce Paulo III, & dell'Illuſtriſſ. Senato Vinitiano per anni X.

65. Gabriele, *Dialogo…de la sphera* [Dialogue concerning the sphere] (1545) title page

66 GALGEMAIR, GEORG, 15??–1619

Practica. Das ist: Beschreibung dess Gewitters, auss der Planeten Lauff und Finsternuss genommen, auff das Jar M.DCI

Augsburg: J. Schultes, 1601

20 cm. 11 leaves. Armorial device on title page.

Zinner Collection

Zinner, 3886a

NUC: CSdS

67 GALGEMAIR, GEORG, 15??–1619

Practica. Das ist: Beschreibung dess Gewitters, auss der Planeten Lauff...auff das Jar MDC.X

Haunssheim: n.p., 1610

18 cm. 14 leaves. Armorial device on title page.

Zinner Collection

Zinner, 4270

NUC: CSdS

68 GALILEI, GALILEO, 1564–1642

Opere di Galileo Galilei Linceo Nobile Fiorentino

Bologna: HH. del Dozza, 1655–56.

22.5 cm. Nineteen parts in two volumes. Frontispieces, illustrations (including tables and diagrams), folding plates. Title vignettes, initials, head and tailpieces. Volume two contains a MS leaf between pages 128–9 of *Il saggiatore*. Full leather binding. First edition of his collected works.

The dedication, signed by Carlo Manolessi, is dated Bologna 17 February 1650. The nineteen parts each have a special title page and for the most part separate pagination. Volume one has a portrait of Galileo on the verso facing the first special title page.

Houzeau, 794; Lalande, p. 243

NUC: CU; CoU; CtY; DFo; DLC; FU; IaU; MA; MCM; MH; NcGU; NjP; OCU; OU; PBm; PPF; PPL-R; TxU

69 GALILEI, GALILEO, 1564–1642

Systema Cosmicum [Dialogo]

Strasbourg: Elzevir, 1635

20 cm. 495 pages, 20 leaves. Illustrations, diagrams, copper-engraved plates. Contemporary vellum over boards.

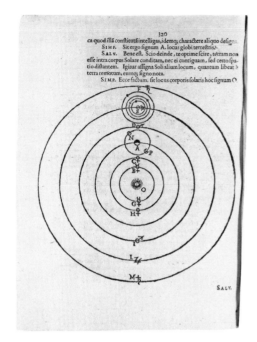

Galileo's heliocentric celestial sphere (reduced)

This is the first Latin edition of the famous *Dialogo* translated by Matthaeus Bernegger from the original Italian edition of 1632, the book that brought Galileo the condemnation of the Inquisition on 22 June 1633.

Lalande, p. 204

NUC: CtY; DLC; ICJ; IEN; MB; MH; MiU; NjP; NN; NNE; NcU

70 GASSENDI, PIERRE, 1592–1655

Institutio Astronomica, juxta Hypotheseis tam Veterum, quam Copernici & Tychonis

London: Eliz. Flesher, 1675

19 cm. 108 leaves. Fifth edition. Thirty-five woodcut illustrations, bound in full calf. Title printed in red and black.

Presents the classical planetary system with the earth at its center along with the hypotheses of Copernicus and Tycho Brahe.

Gassendi was a renowned seventeenth-century philosopher/astronomer who received his doctorate at Avignon in 1614. He was a professor at Digne while still young. His observation of the transit of Mercury 7 November 1631 confirmed Kepler and, indirectly, Copernicus, which caused widespread discussion. He was an influential thinker, experimenter, skeptic, astronomical observer, correspondent, and the author of many books (*DSB*, v. 5, pp. 284ff).

Houzeau, 684; Lalande, p. 233

NUC: CLU-C; CtY; MH; NNC; NcD

PRACTICA.
Das ist:
Beschreibung deß Ge-
witters/auß der Planeten lauff/vnd
Finsternuß genommen/auff das Jar
IESV CHRISTI

M. DCI.

Mit allem fleiß beschrieben / vnnd zu glückseliger
Regierung dediciert:

Dem Durchleuchtigen/Hochgebornen Fürsten vnd Herrn/ Herrn
Philipps Ludwig/Pfaltzgrafen bey Rhein/Hertzogen in Bayrn/Grafen
zu Veldentz vnd Sponhaim/Meinem gnedigen Fürsten vnd Herrn.

Durch M. Georgium Galgemair Danuuerdanum Pfaltzgräffischen Pfar-
rern zu Leibstatt/In der Herrschafft Haydeck.

66. Galgemair, *Practica. Das ist: Beschreibung dess Gewitters, auss der Planeten Lauff*
[Practica. That is: A description of the danger from the planetary movement and eclipse]
(1601) title page

OPERE
DI GALILEO GALILEI
LINCEO
NOBILE FIORENTINO

Già Lettore delle Matematiche nelle Vniuersità
di Pisa, e di Padoua, di poi Sopraordi-
nario nello Studio di Pisa.

*Primario Filosofo, e Matematico del Serenissimo
Gran Duca di Toscana.*

In questa nuoua editione insieme raccolte, e di varij
Trattati dell'istesso Autore non più Stam-
pati accresciute.

AL SERENISSIMO
FERDINANDO II.
GRAN DVCA DI TOSCANA.

In BOLOGNA, Per gli HH. del Dozza.   MDCLVI.

68. Galilei, *Opere* [Works] (1655–56) title page

68. Galilei, *Opere* (1655–56) frontispiece depicting Galileo receiving honors

69. Galilei, *Systema Cosmicum…Dialogo* [The cosmic system…dialogue] (1635) portrait of Galileo (reduced)

69. Galilei, *Systema Cosmicum…Dialogo* (1635) depiction of Aristotle, Ptolemy, and Copernicus in earnest consultation (reduced)

SYSTEMA COSMICVM,
Authore
GALILÆO GALILÆI
LYNCEO, ACADEMIÆ PISANÆ
Mathematico extraordinario,

SERENISSIMI
MAGNI- DVCIS HETRVRIÆ
PHILOSOPHO ET MATHEMATICO
PRIMARIO:

In quo

QVATVOR DIALOGIS,

DE

Duobus Maximis Mundi Systematibus,

PTOLEMAICO & COPERNICANO,

Vtriusq; rationibus Philosophicis ac Na-
turalibus indefinite propositis,
disseritur.

Ex Italica Lingua Latine conuersum.

Accessit

Appendix gemina, qua SS. Scripturæ dicta
cum Terræ mobilitate conciliantur.

Alcinous.
Δεῖ δ᾽ ἐλεύθεριον εἶναι τῇ γνώμῃ τὸν μέλλοντα Φιλοσοφεῖν.
Seneca
Inter nullos magis quàm inter Philosophos esse
debet æqua LIBERTAS.

AVGVSTAE TREBOC.
Impensis ELZEVIRIORVM,
Typis DAVIDIS HAVTTI.
Anno 1 6 3 5.

69. Galilei, *Systema Cosmicum…Dialogo* (1635) title page

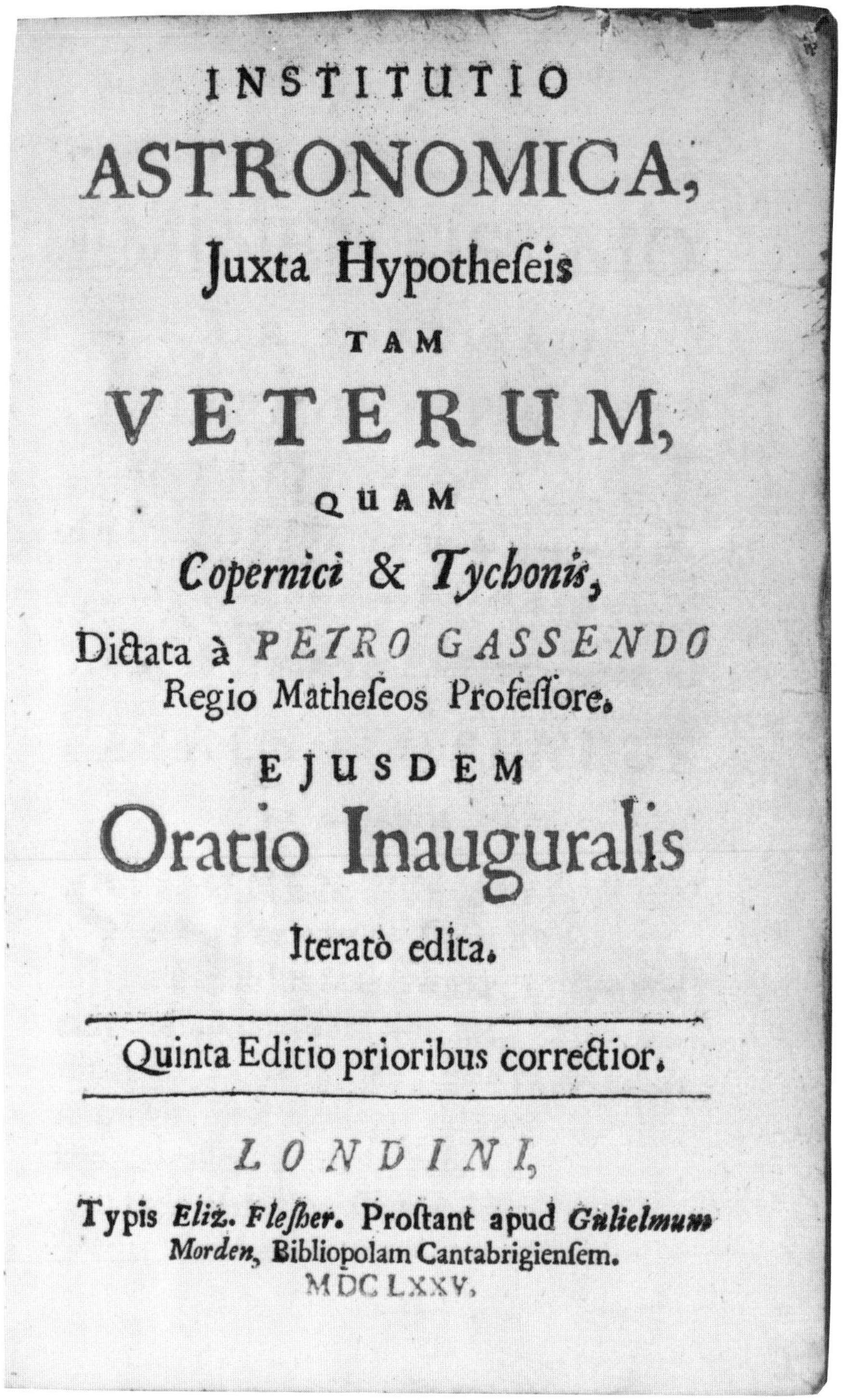

INSTITUTIO
ASTRONOMICA,

Juxta Hypotheseis

TAM

VETERUM,

QUAM

Copernici & Tychonis,

Dictata à *PETRO GASSENDO*
Regio Matheseos Professore.

EJUSDEM
Oratio Inauguralis

Iteratò edita.

Quinta Editio prioribus correctior.

LONDINI,

Typis *Eliz. Flesher.* Prostant apud *Gulielmum
Morden,* Bibliopolam Cantabrigiensem.
MDCLXXV.

70. Gassendi, *Institutio Astronomica* [Fundamentals of astronomy] (1675) title page

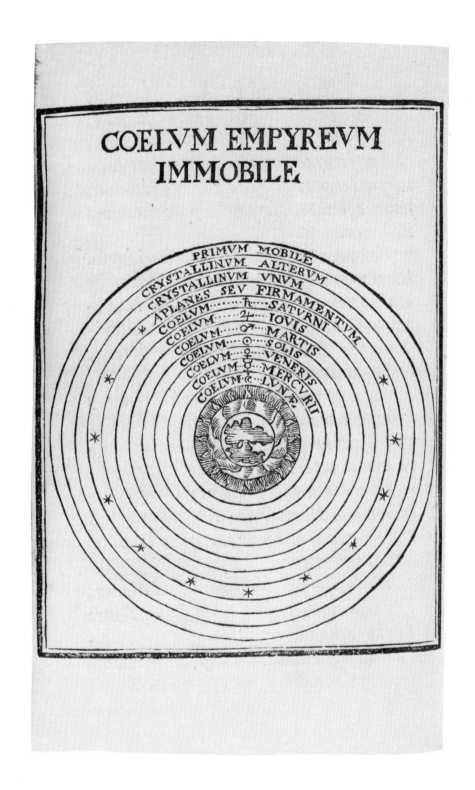

70. Gassendi, *Institutio Astronomica* (1675) earth-centered celestial sphere

71 *Geistlicher Betrachtungs-Lust. Oder Geistliche Ausslegung dess Comet Prophetens und Himmlischen Ambassadeurs... Beschrieben und erkläret durch M. Z. G.*

n.p.: n.p., 1681

19 cm. 8 leaves.

NUC: no copy

72 GEMMA FRISIUS, REINERUS, 1508–55

De Principiis Astronomiae et Cosmographiae

Antwerp: Ioan. Steels, 1548

17 cm. 72 leaves. Woodcut on title page and verso of leaf 5. Bound with this work are his *Usus Annuli Astronomici*, 1548 (item 73); J. Schöner, *De Usu Globi Astriferi Opusculum*, 1548 (item 170); *Typus Globi Astriferi*, 1548 (item 188); and *Sphaerici ac Solidi Corporis sive Globi Astronomici*, 1548.

Gemma Frisius, native of Friesland in the Netherlands, first published this work in 1530. It was reprinted numerous times. He designed globes and astronomical instruments well known throughout Europe. Some of them were completed by Gerard Mercator, who had attended mathematical lectures Gemma Frisius gave at his home.

Zinner Collection

Lalande, p. 67

NUC: DLC; InU; NN

73 GEMMA FRISIUS, REINERUS, 1508–55

Usus Annuli Astronomici

Antwerp: Ioan. Steels, 1548

17 cm. 16 leaves. Title-page vignette; woodcut decorative initials and illustrations on leaves 83–6. Bound with his *De Principiis Astronomiae et Cosmographiae* (item 72).

Zinner Collection

Lalande, p. 67

NUC: DLC; InU; NN

74 GLAREANUS, HENRICUS, 1488–1563

De Geographia Liber Unus ab Ipso Authore Iam Tertio Recognitus

Venice: D. Melchior Sessa, 1538

16 cm. 40 leaves. Twenty-one woodcuts, printer's device on title page and verso of last leaf, woodcut initials. Extensive marginalia. Bound with Sacro Bosco, J. *Liber de Sphaera*, 1541 (item 161).

Glareanus was an erudite Swiss of the Renaissance, who was born at Glarus from which he took his Latinized name. A member of the Loritus family, he early turned to the pursuit of knowledge. He was educated at the University of Basel and later taught there and at the universities of Cologne and, lastly, Freiburg, where he died in 1563.

Maximilian I (1459–1519), Holy Roman Emperor in Vienna, honored him with a laurel wreath and a ring in recognition of his superb poetry.

Extraordinarily knowledgeable and resourceful, he also displayed a crudity and arrogance that offended many. A colorful anecdote has it that on one occasion at the University of Basel to show his contempt for the learned professors after they had voted to deny him professorial rank, "he rode a donkey into the auditorium and remained seated on it," presumably during an academic assembly (*Iselin*, v. 4, pp. 814–5).

Desiderius Erasmus (1466?–1536) became attracted to him because of his remarkable erudition, but was never favorably disposed toward him personally. A jealous rivalry ensued largely because Glareanus publicly attacked Erasmus with withering ridicule and scornful criticism.

Glareanus was the author of more than twenty books mostly on literary and philosophical subjects. A few were on mathematics.

NUC: no copy

ANTVERPIÆ,
In ædibus Ioannis Steelsii.
M. D. XLVIII.

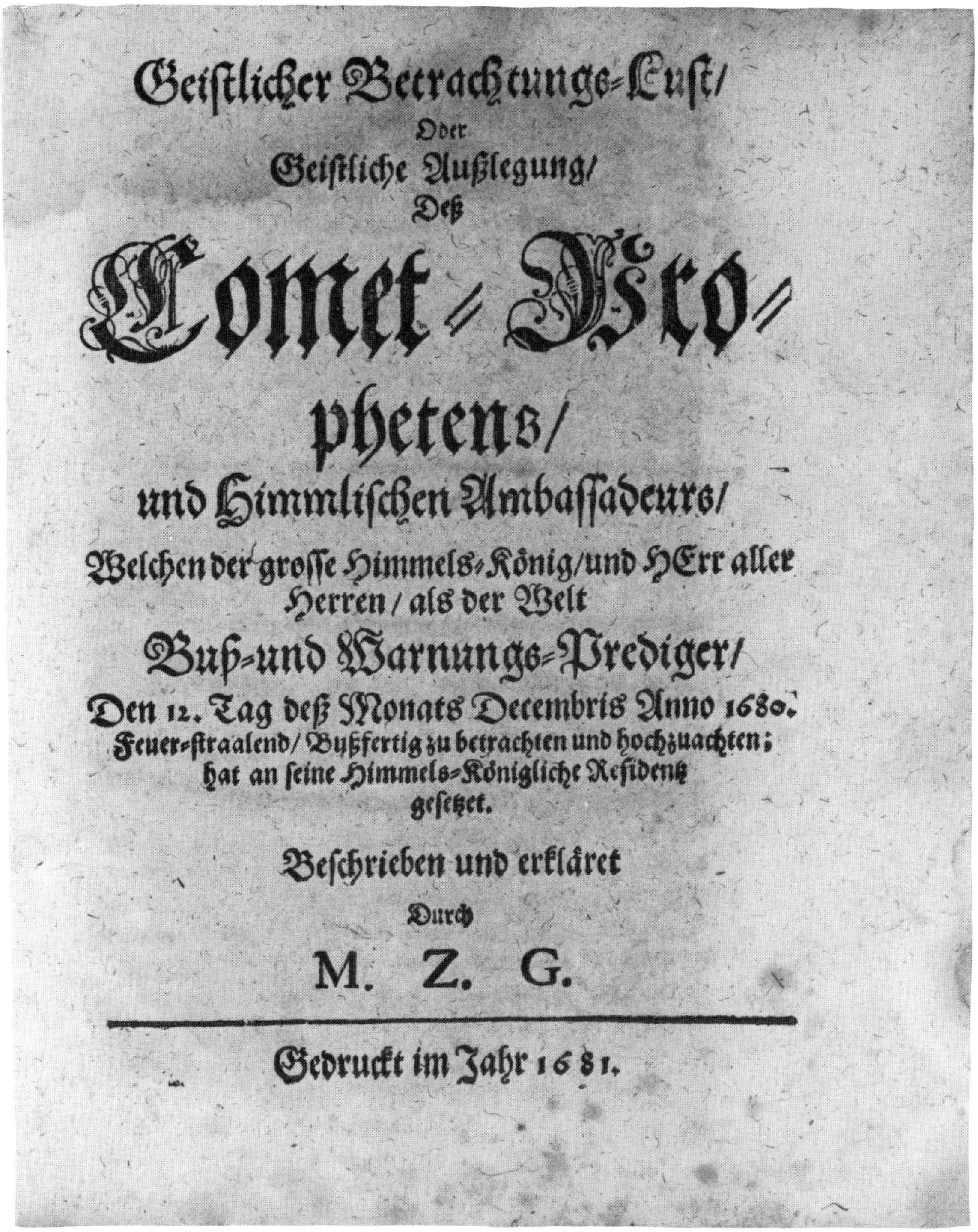

Geistlicher Betrachtungs-Lust/
Oder
Geistliche Außlegung/
Deß

Comet-Pro-
phetens/
und Himmlischen Ambassadeurs/

Welchen der grosse Himmels-König/und HErr aller
Herren / als der Welt

Buß-und Warnungs-Prediger/

Den 12. Tag deß Monats Decembris Anno 1680.
Feuer-straalend/Bußfertig zu betrachten und hochzuachten;
hat an seine Himmels-Königliche Residentz
gesetzet.

Beschrieben und erkläret

Durch

M. Z. G.

Gedruckt im Jahr 1681.

71. *Geistlicher Betrachtungs-Lust…Comet Prophetens* [Spiritual meditation
on the prophetic comet] (1681) title page

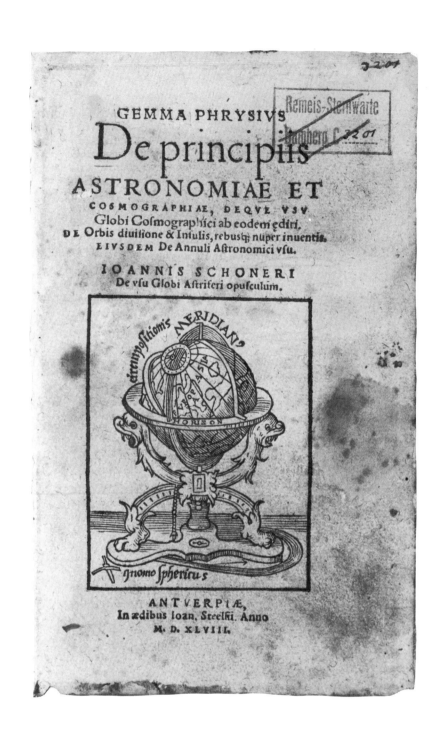

GEMMA PHRYSIVS
De principiis
ASTRONOMIAE ET
COSMOGRAPHIAE, DEQVE VSV
Globi Cosmographici ab eodem editi.
DE Orbis diuisione & Insulis, rebusq; nuper inuentis.
EIVSDEM De Annuli Astronomici vsu.

IOANNIS SCHONERI
De vsu Globi Astriferi opusculum.

ANTVERPIÆ,
In ædibus Ioan. Steelsii. Anno
M. D. XLVIII.

72. Gemma Frisius, *De Principiis Astronomiae et Cosmographiae* [Concerning the principles of astronomy and cosmography] (1548) title page

VSVS
Annuli Aſtro=
NOMICI GEMMA
FRISIO MATHEMATICO
Autore.

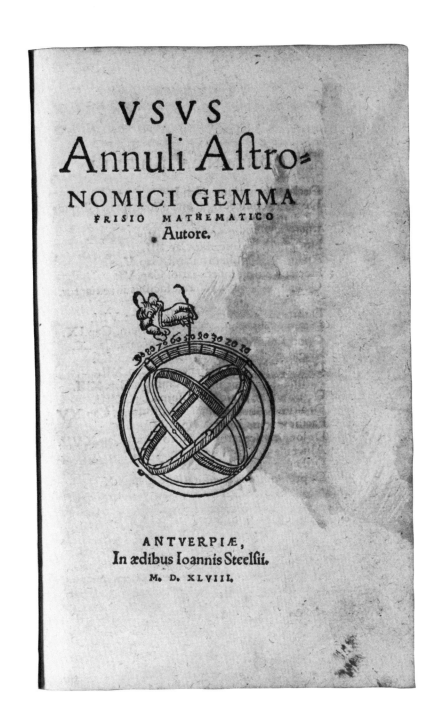

ANTVERPIÆ,
In ædibus Ioannis Steelſii.
M. D. XLVIII.

73. Gemma Frisius, *Usus Annuli Astronomici* [Application
of the astronomical circle] (1548) title page

HENRICI

GLAREANI HELVETII

POETÆ LAVREATI DE

Geographia Liber unus ab
ipso authore iam tertio
recognitus.

Diſſimiliuz inſi da ſocietaſ.

VENETIIS.

74. Glareanus, *De Geographia Liber* [Book of geography] (1538) title page

75 GRAAF, ABRAHAM DE, 1635–1717

De geheele Mathesis of Wiskonst

Amsterdam: Jacobus de Veer voor Jan ten Hoorn, 1694

25 cm. 318 pages. Illustrations. Many folding engraved plates. Contemporary vellum. First published in 1676; this is the first reprinting.

Graaf was a Dutch mathematician, astronomer, teacher, and author of many books and pamphlets on mathematics, astronomy, and navigation. Several of his books were widely used in schools. He corresponded with Christian Huygens (1629–95) and other mathematicians.

Zinner Collection

NUC: CSdS; MiU; NN

76 GREGORII, JOHANN GOTTFRIED, 1685–1770

Cosmographia Novissima, oder allerneueste und accurate Beschreibung... aus der Astronomia, Geographia, Physica...

Erfurt: Johann C. Stoessels Erben, 1715

21 cm. 534 leaves. Frontispiece, diagrams, tables. Title page printed in red and black.

Gregorii (or Gregorius) was a pastor at Dornheim, Germany. He studied widely in theology, geography, astronomy, and other subjects and wrote several popular books using the pseudonym Melissantes. "His works had errors and his writings tended to superficiality" (*Allgemeine deutsche Biographie*, v. 9, pp. 630–31).

Amelang Collection, San Diego State University Library

NUC: no copy

77 GREGORY, DAVID, 1661–1708

Astronomiae Physicae & Geometricae Elementa

Oxford: E Theatro Sheldoniano, 1702

37 cm. 6 leaves, 496 pages. Copper-engraved vignette on title page, numerous diagrams. Manuscript corrigendum to page 476 on the verso of the last leaf. First edition.

DSB gives 1659 as the year of Gregory's birth. The first English language edition of this work appeared in 1715.

Gregory is known for his work in mathematics, astronomy, and optics. He graduated from Marischal College, Aberdeen, and took his M.A. in 1683 at Edinburgh University where he was also elected chair of mathematics. In 1691 he was appointed professor of astronomy at Oxford with the support of John Flamsteed, but opposed by Edmund Halley. In 1692 he was elected a fellow of the Royal Society (*DSB* v. 5, pp. 520ff).

Lalande, p. 345

NUC: DLC; FU; InU; MB; MBAt; MH; MiU; NIC; NN; WU

78 *Das Grosse Planeten Buch sampt der Geomanci, Physiognomi....*

Erfurt: Tobias Fritzschen, 1644

16 cm. 217 leaves. Bound in an old vellum manuscript page. Title page printed in red and black. Vignette on title page, many curious small woodcuts.

Popular treatment naming the sun, moon, planets, and many stars useful in casting horoscopes.

Amelang Collection, San Diego State University Library

NUC: no copy

DE GEHEELE
MATHESIS
OF
WISKONST,
Herſtelt in zijn natuurlijke gedaante:
Door ABRAHAM de GRAAF.

t'AMSTERDAM,
Gedrukt, by JACOBUS de VEER,

Voor JAN ten HOORN, Boekverkooper over 't Oude Heeren Logement,
in de Hiſtory Schryver, 1714. 1694.

Ptolomäisch=Alphon=
Welt=
Welche der H. Schrift ge=
mäß ist/ nach wel=
chem die Erde un=
beweglich und fest

sinische Ordnung der
Kugeln:
in Mittelpunct der Welt
ist/ die Planeten
sich aber bewe=
gen,

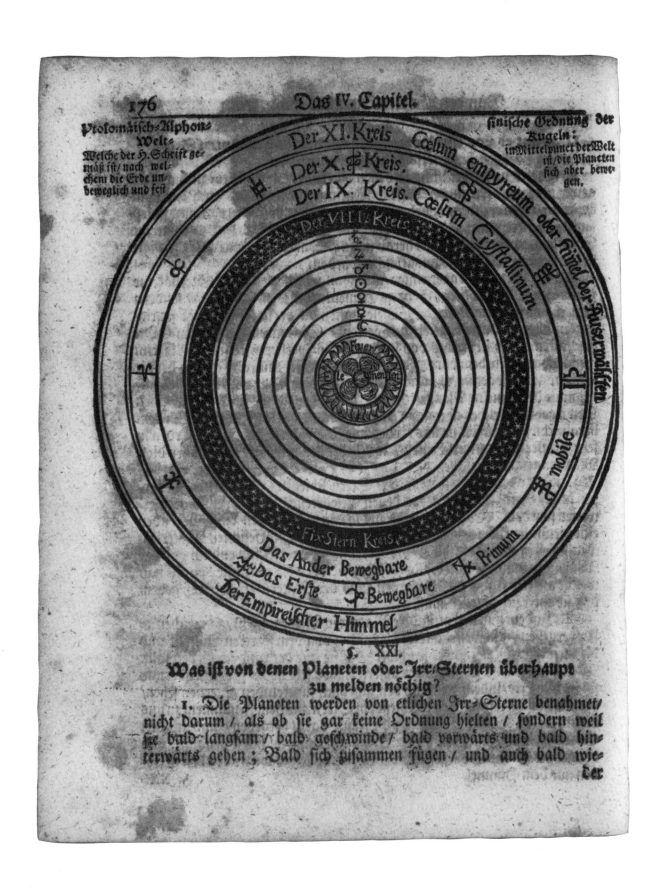

§. XXI.

Was ist von denen Planeten oder Irr=Sternen überhaupt zu melden nöthig?

1. Die Planeten werden von etlichen Irr=Sterne benahmet/ nicht darum / als ob sie gar keine Ordnung hielten / sondern weil sie bald langsam / bald geschwinde / bald vorwärts und bald hin= terwärts gehen ; Bald sich zusammen fügen / und auch bald wie= der

76. Gregorii, *Cosmographia Novissima* [The latest cosmography]
(1715) a Ptolemaic celestial sphere

COSMOGRAPHIA
NOVISSIMA,
Oder
Allerneueste und accurate
Beschreibung
Der gantzen wunderbaren Welt,

Samt denen merckwürdigsten/ curieusen und auserle=
sensten Sachen aus der ASTRONOMIA, GEOGRAPHIA,
PHYSICA, POLITICA, und HISTORIA.

Darinnen

Erstlich von der höchst wunderbahren und unbegreifflichen Erschaf-
fung dieses gantzen Welt=Gebäudes, von denen Globis oder natür= und künst-
lichen Himmels= und Erd=Kugeln/sowohl mit einer richtigen und leichten Anweisung und Un=
terricht, zu dererselben nützlichen Gebrauch, als auch ausführlichen Erklärung aller daran befindlichen Circkel,
insonderheit auch von allen Planeten, Stern=Bildern, Cometen und deren Bedeutung, von der Zeit,
Lufft, Feuer, Wasser, Bergen und der Erd=Beschreibung insgemein;

Zum Andern

Von denen vier Theilen der Welt/ als EUROPA, ASIA, AFRICA, AMERICA, samt deren
Eintheilung in ihre vornehmste Reiche und Länder/ als Käyserthümer/ Königreiche/ Staaten/ Republiquen/
Herrschafften/und dergleichen/ wie auch von allen und jeden Fatis/ Aufnahme und Zerrüttungen/von denen Müntzen
und Flüssen ausführlich gehandelt und in schönster Ordnung vorgestellet wird.

Auch mit einer Vorrede und dreyfachen Registern versehen, und ausgefertiget

Von
MELISSANTES.

Mit Königlichen und Chur=Sächsischen Allergnädigsten PRIVILEGIO.

FRANCKFURT und LEIPZIG,
In Verlegung Johann Christoph Stössels seel. Erben in Erffurt/ 1725.

76. Gregorii, *Cosmographia Novissima* (1715) title page

ASTRONOMIÆ

PHYSICÆ & GEOMETRICÆ

ELEMENTA.

Auctore DAVIDE GREGORIO M. D.
Astronomiæ Profeſſore Saviliano OXONIÆ,
& Regalis Societatis Sodali.

OXONIÆ,

E THEATRO SHELDONIANO, An. Dom. MDCCII.

77. Gregory, *Astronomiae Physicae & Geometricae Elementa* [The elements of astronomy,
physics, and geometry] (1702) title page (reduced)

79 GROTHAUSEN, JOANNE

Summa Mathesios sive Cursus Disciplinarum Mathematicarum

Cologne: 1645–46

17 cm. 95 leaves. Illustrations. Numerous diagrams and tables. Contemporary vellum over boards. Marginalia.

Manuscript written in Germany in Latin script. A considerable portion concerns astronomy. Related subjects include mathematics, optics, physics, and geography. The author was a Jesuit and professor.

Zinner Collection

NUC: no copy

80 HARRIS, JOHN, 1667?–1719

Astronomical Dialogues Between a Gentleman and a Lady

London: J. Horsfeild, 1725

20 cm. 190 pages. Second edition. Illustrations. Full contemporary calf binding. Library also has 1729 and 1745 editions.

Harris took his B.A. at Trinity College, Oxford, in 1686 and his M.A. in 1689. He became a fellow of the Royal Society in 1696. Harris early began his studies of natural science. He lectured at Oxford and in his home there on mathematics and astronomy.

Lalande, p. 390

NUC: CSdS; NjP

81 HARTMANN, JOHANN JACOB, 1671–1728?, preses; Respondens, FRIDER. CHRISTOPHOR KROHN

De Usu Refractionum Astronomico

Wittenberg: Christian Schrödter, 1694

21 cm. 8 leaves.

Zinner Collection

NUC: CSdS

82 HEIDEN, CHRISTIAN

Practica... auf das M.D.LXVII. Jar....

Nürnberg: Nicolaus Knorr, 1567?

22 cm. 12 leaves. Illustrations.

Zinner Collection

Zinner, 2421

NUC: CSdS

detail from the title page

83 HEVELIUS, JOHANNES, 1611–87

Firmamentum Sobiescianum, sive Uranographia

Gdánsk: [J.Z. Stollius] 1687

32 x 39 cm. Folio. 54 double-page star maps and two folding plates of the hemispheres. Title on spine is *Atlas des gestirnten Himmels* (Atlas of the Starry Heavens). This 1687 first edition was reissued as part two of Hevelius's *Prodromus Astronomiae*, 1690, with a special title page and text added. Charles de La Haye (1614–ca. 1712) engraved the plates after designs by Andreas Stech (1635–97).

Educated at Gdánsk and later taught by Peter Crüger (1580–1639), teacher of mathematics and astronomy, Hevelius early learned the art of instrument making. He began systematic astronomical observations in 1639. He is perhaps best known for his work *Selenographia*, 1647 (*DSB*, v. 6, pp. 360ff).

Zinner Collection

Lalande, p. 322

NUC: CSdS; MH

79. Grothausen, *Summa Mathesios* [Summary of mathematics] (1645-46) title page of a generously illustrated manuscript book of mathematics and astronomy

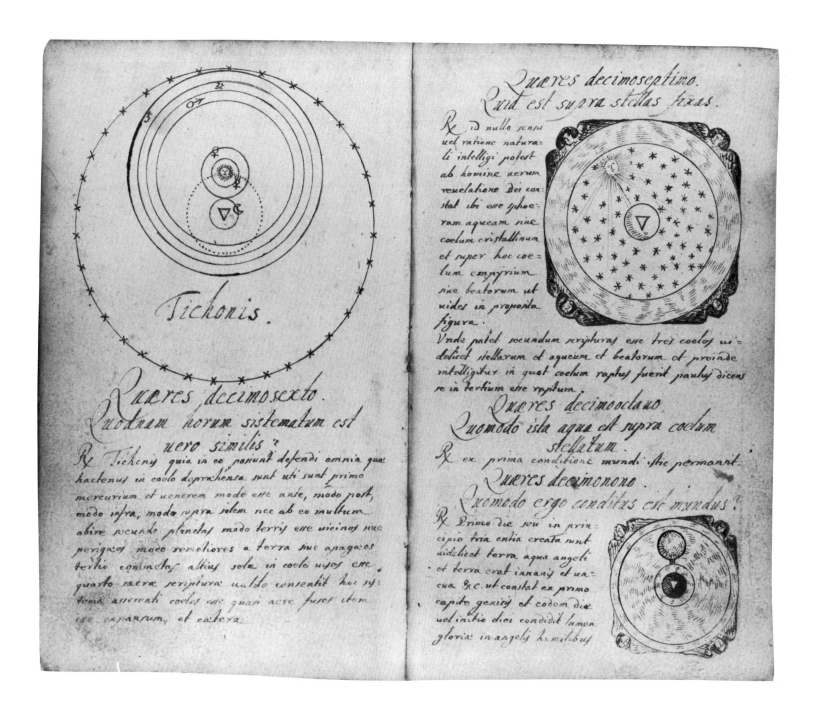

Tichonis.

Quaeres decimosexto.
Quotnam horum sistematum est vero similis?

Rx Tichonis quia in eo possunt defendi omnia quae hactenus in coelo deprehensa sunt uti sunt primo mercurium et venerem modo esse ante, modo post, modo infra, modo supra solem nec ab eo multum abire secundo planetas modo terris esse vicinos sive perigaeos, modo remotiores a terra sive apogaeos tertio cometas altius sole in coelo visos esse quarto sacra scriptura valde consentit huic systemati asserenti coelos esse quasi aere puros item esse expansum, et caetera

Quaeres decimoseptimo.
Quid est supra stellas fixas.

Rx id nullo sensu vel ratione naturali intelligi potest ab homine verum revelatione Dei constat ibi esse sphaeram aqueam sive coelum cristallinum et super hoc coelum empyrium sive beatorum ut vides in proposita figura.

Unde patet secundum scripturas esse tres coelos videlicet stellarum et aqueum et beatorum et proinde intelligitur in quot coelum raptus fuerit paulus dicens se in tertium esse raptum.

Quaeres decimooctavo.
Quomodo ista aqua est supra coelum stellatum.

Rx ex prima conditione mundi stie permanent.

Quaeres decimonono.
Quomodo ergo conditus est mundus?

Rx Primo die seu in principio tria entia creata sunt videlicet terra aqua angeli et terra erat inanis et vacua &c. ut constat ex primo capite genesis et eodem die vel initio diei condidit lumen gloriae in angelis humilibus

79. Grothausen, *Summa Mathesios* (1645–46)

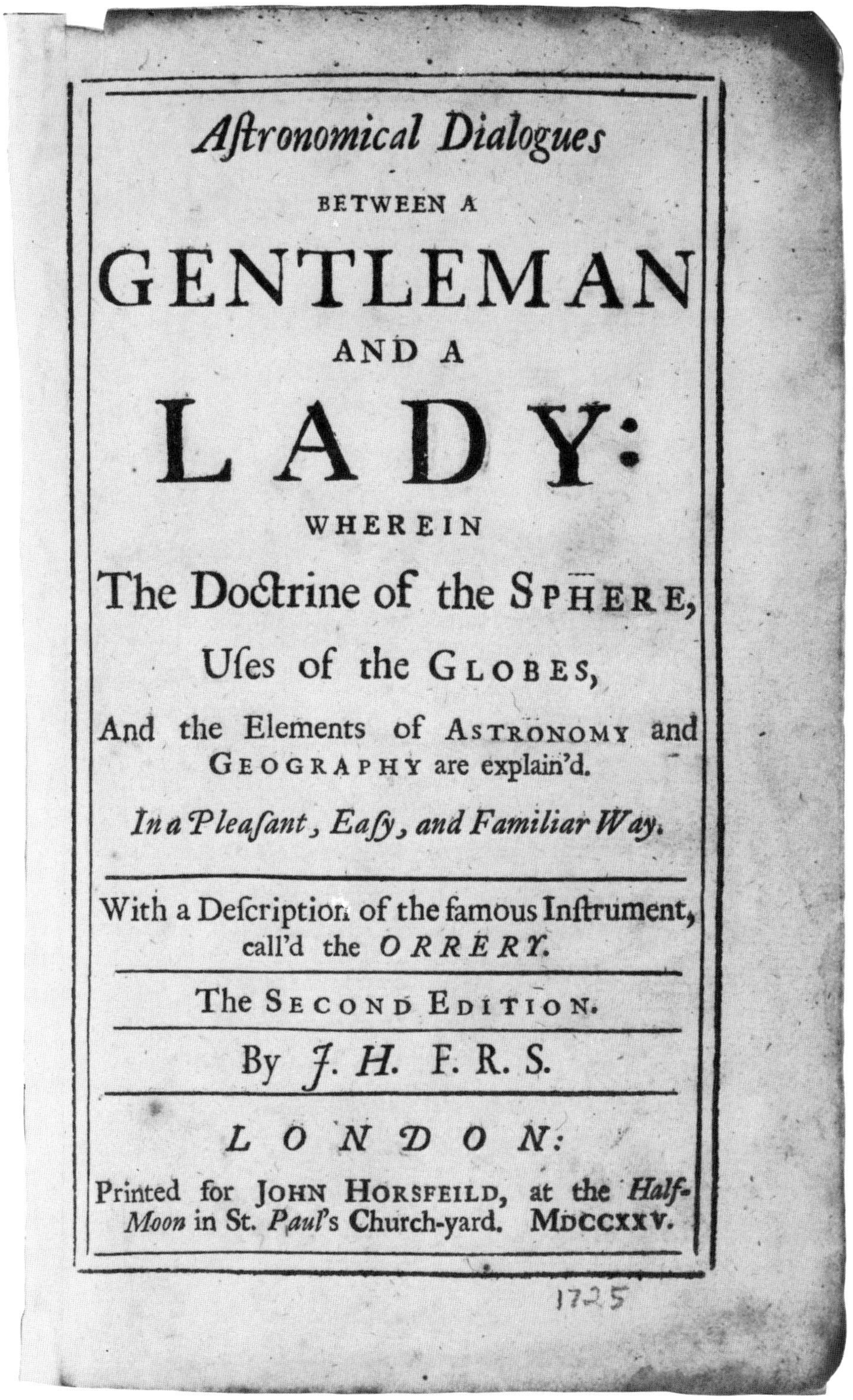

Astronomical Dialogues

BETWEEN A

GENTLEMAN

AND A

LADY:

WHEREIN

The Doctrine of the Sphere,

Uses of the Globes,

And the Elements of Astronomy and
Geography are explain'd.

In a Pleasant, Easy, and Familiar Way.

With a Description of the famous Instrument,
call'd the *ORRERY.*

The Second Edition.

By *J. H.* F. R. S.

LONDON:

Printed for John Horsfeild, at the *Half-Moon* in St. *Paul's* Church-yard. MDCCXXV.

1725

80. Harris, *Astronomical Dialogues* (1725) title page

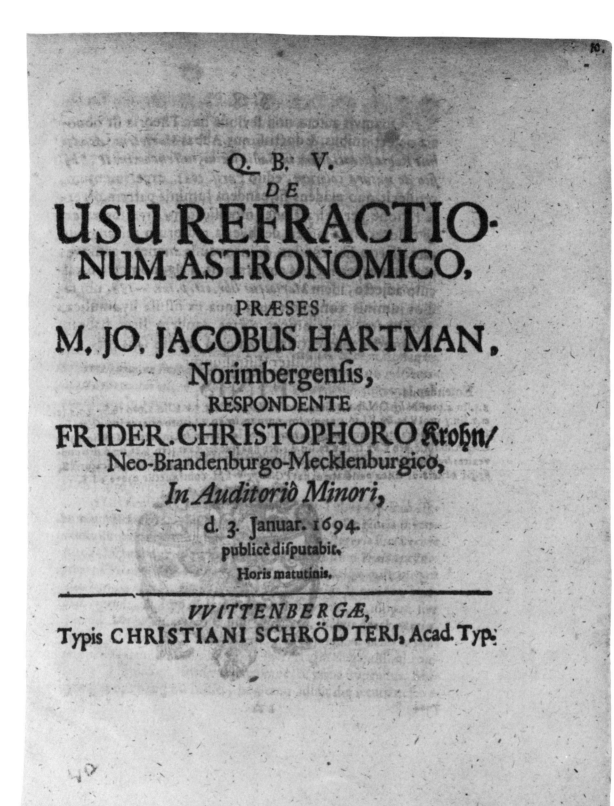

Q. B. V.

DE

USU REFRACTIO-
NUM ASTRONOMICO,

PRÆSES

M, JO, JACOBUS HARTMAN,

Norimbergensis,

RESPONDENTE

FRIDER. CHRISTOPHORO Krohn/

Neo-Brandenburgo-Mecklenburgico,

In Auditoriô Minori,

d. 3. Januar. 1694.

publicè disputabit.

Horis matutinis.

VVITTENBERGÆ,
Typis CHRISTIANI SCHRÖDTERI, Acad. Typ.

81. Hartmann, *De Usu Refractionum Astronomico* [Concerning the use of refraction in astronomy] (1694)
title page of an academic disputation

82. Heiden, *Practica…auf das M.D.LXVII. Jar*
[Practica for the year 1567] (1567?) title page

83. Hevelius, *Firmamentum Sobiescianum, sive Uranographia* [Sobiescian firmament and uranography] (1687) constellation with a charging taurus (reduced)

83. Hevelius, *Firmamentum Sobiescianum, sive Uranographia* (1687) constellation (reduced)

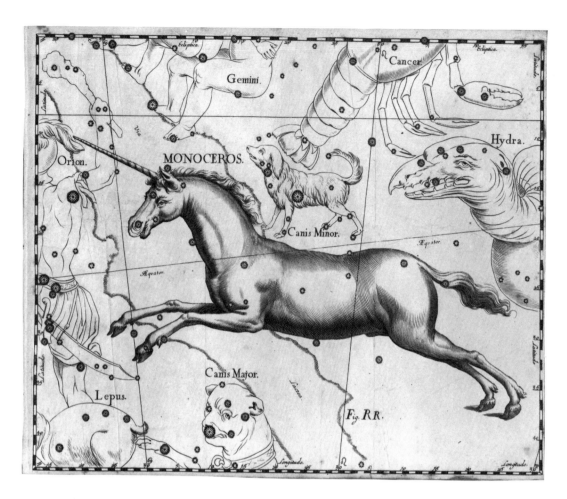

83. Hevelius, *Firmamentum Sobiescianum, sive Uranographia* (1687)
above: constellation showing a dashing unicorn (reduced)
below: constellation (reduced)

83. Hevelius, *Firmamentum Sobiescianum, sive Uranographia* (1687)
two plates showing constellations (reduced)

84 HILL, JOHN, 1716?–75

Urania or, a Compleat View of the Heavens; Containing the Antient and Modern Astronomy

London: T. Gardner, 1754

24 cm. 618 pages. Frontispiece, twelve engraved plates. Title page in red and black. First and only edition.

DSB gives 1707? as the year of Hill's birth. John Hill, a controversial figure in eighteenth-century English science, possessed a wide range of interests. Known best as a botanist, he was the author of a great number of publications in science. Besides botany and gardening, he published books and pamphlets in medicine, zoology, entomology, mineralogy, and astronomy. The king of Sweden knighted him in 1774, but the English refused to recognize the title "Sir" that he assumed thereafter (*DSB*, v. 6, p. 400).

Houzeau, 234; Lalande, p. 453

NUC: DAU; DN-Ob; FU; ICU; MH; MdBP; MiU; MnU; OkU; PKsL; PPAmP; WU

85 HOLDER, WILLIAM, 1616–98

A Discourse Concerning Time

London: Printed by F. Heptinstall, for L. Meredith, 1694

17 cm. 120 pages. First edition.

Holder matriculated at Pembroke Hall, Cambridge, in 1633 where he received the M.A. in 1640. He was later awarded the D.D. at Oxford. He was known for teaching the deaf to speak and as a composer of music. In *A Discourse Concerning Time*, he explained natural day, the lunar month, the solar year, and the Julian Calendar as natural phenomena. (*DSB*, v. 9, pp. 1015–6).

NUC: CLU-C; CU; CtY; DFo; DLC; ICJ; InU; MH; NNC; PPL

86 HORTENSIUS, MARTINUS, 1605–39

Dissertatio de Mercurio in Sole Viso et Venere Invisa

Leiden: Isaac Commelin, 1633

20 cm. 95 pages. First edition. Woodcut text figures, decorative initials. Bound in contemporary vellum. Ex Libris: Albert Edgar Lownes.

Hortensius was a Dutch astronomer. He began lecturing on mathematics at the Amsterdam Atheneum in 1635 where he also became professor in the Copernican theory. He corresponded with Descartes, Mersenne, Gassendi, Huygens, and Galileo. He made observations on eclipses and on transits and endeavored to improve existing telescopes. Kepler criticized his findings concerning the angular diameter of the sun, which resulted in a vigorous exchange of conflicting opinions (*DSB*, v. 6, p. 520).

NUC: NNC; RPB

87 HULSIUS, LEVINUS, ca. 1565–1606

Theoria et Praxis Quadrantis Geometrici

Nürnberg: Gerlachianis, Sumptibus Cornelii de Judaeis, 1594

22 cm. 35 leaves and one folding plate. Numerous engraved plates, historiated initials.

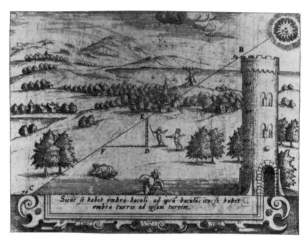

Hulsius, born at Gent, came in 1590 to Nürnberg where he taught languages and operated a book printing press. He printed Brahe, *Astronomiae Instauratae Mechanica* (item 28). In 1602 he left Nürnberg and became a book dealer. He wrote on various subjects including mechanics, especially the quadrant. He is best known for this book, which describes all the mathematical and mechanical instruments known at that time.

Zinner Collection

Zinner, 3573

NUC: CSdS; DLC; MiU; NN; NNC

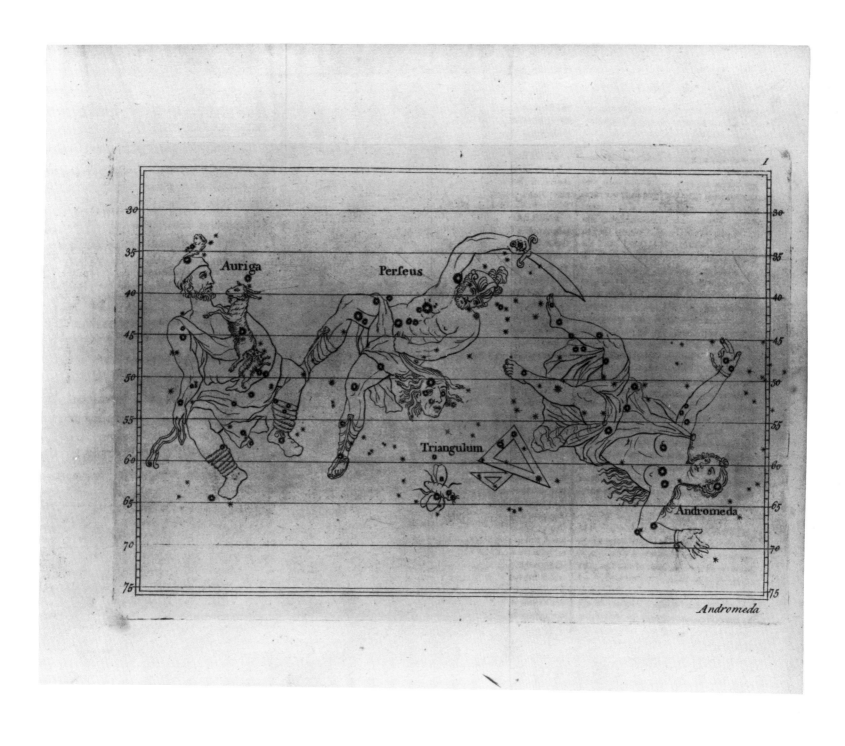

84. Hill, *Urania* (1754) folding plate (reduced)

MARTINI HORTENSI
Delfensis

DISSERTATIO
DE

MERCVRIO IN SOLE VISO
ET

VENERE INVISA:

Instituta cum

Clarissimo, ac Doctissimo Viro , D. PETRO
GASSENDO, Cathed. Ecclesiæ *Diniensis*
Canonico, Theologo, Philosopho, ac
Mathematico celeberrimo.

LVGDVNI BATAVORVM,
Apud ISAACVM COMMELINVM.
ANNO cIↃIↃcXXXIII.

86. Hortensius, *Dissertatio de Mercurio in Sole Viso*
[Dissertation on the single appearance of Mercury] (1633) title page

Cap. XXIII.
Beschreibung der andern seiten di=
ses Instruments.

Vff der andern seiten hat diß Instrument ein Bussolle oder Magnet Compaß (darzu gehört der Deckel/mit dem Buchstaben D, verzeichnet) auff welchen die 3 2. wind/deren jeder in 4. Minuten abgetheilt/abgerissen sein. Die= net alle distantias oder weiten von Flüssen/ Weyern oder Gräben abzumessen. Vnd solches zu brauchen / leget man das flach mit dem löchlein G, auff den stecken von 4. schuch/ in das nägelein H, also das der Magnet frey vmbschwebe.

Mehr ist hie an der seiten ein Lineal abgetheilt in zwey schuch/jeder schuch in 8. finger/je=
G der fin=

87. Hulsius, *Theoria et Praxis Quadrantis Geometrici*
[Theory and use of the geometric quadrant] (1594)

THEORIA

Et Praxis Quadrantis Geometrici &c.

Das ist/

Beſchreibung/ Vnterricht vnd

Gebrauch/des gevierdten Geometriſchen vnd an-

derer Inſtrument / damit ein jede ebne/höhe/breite/länge/weite/tieffe/vnd ge-
wiſſe diſtantz/eines jeglichen dings/ nach des Euclidis,vnd anderer geleh-
ter Mathematiken Regel / abzuſehen vnd zumeſſen.

Item/ein Statt/Garten/Weyer/oder Land von 5.6.oder mehr
meile groß/nach dem kleinen Schuch zuverjüngen/vnd in
Grund zu legen.

Mit xxxvii. Kunſtreichen Kupfferſtücken gezieret.

Beſchriben durch

Levinum Hulſium, Gallicæ linguæ Noribergæ ludimagiſtrum, Not. Imp.
der Mathematiſchen Kunſt Liebhaber.

NORIBERGAE, TYPIS GERLACHIANIS,
Sumptibus Cornelii de Iudæis. 1594.

Cum Priuilegio Cæsareæ Maieſtatis.

87. Hulsius, *Theoria et Praxis Quadrantis Geometrici* (1594) title page

vnd hencke das Inſtrument mit dem löchlein G, in das nägelein H, Richte auch nach dem perpendiculo, ſo von A, nach B, frey hinunterwarts hencket/das Inſtrument/vnd ſchraube es veſt an den ſtecken / mit der ſchrauben K , alſo daß die ſeiten des Inſtruments A, B, vnd D, C, ſchnurrecht ſtehen.

Sicut ſe habent partes V. rectæ abſciſſæ ad totā ſcalā, ita ſe habet altitudo baculi ad diſtantiā queſitū.   In mediū aūt Scalæ incidente Dioptra, diſtantia erit æqualis altitudini baculi.   Itē ſicut ſe habet integra Scala ad partes V. Verſæ abſciſſas, ita ſe habet diſtātia M.N. ad baculi altitudinem M.A.

Als denn ſetze dein auge in A, vnd rucke den Zeiger oder Regel ſo lange/biß du durch beide abſehen den punct oder gemerck/ davon du die weite wiſſen wilt/ſeheſt : Als hie in dem abſehen nach O, fällt die Regel in I, umbræ rectæ, nun iſt die höhe des ſteckens M, A, gröſſer/ als die weite M, O. Eben wie die ſtehende höhe A, B, des Inſtruments/höher iſt/als das theil B, I, des ligenden umbræ rectæ, vnd wie auff dem Inſtrument die ligende ſeite/I, B, 6. ſich proportionirt helt/gegen der ſtehenden ſeiten / A, B, 12. alſo helt ſich die weite des Feldes/ M, O, 4. proportionirt gegen der höhe/ M, A. Nun iſt aber B, I, das halbe theil von B, A, alſo iſt auch O, M, das halbe theil von M, A.

Vnd ſeind diſe zween Triangel A, I, B, auff dem Inſtrument/vnd A, O, M, im Feld/ gleich : Wie auß der 28. vnd 29. Propoſit. des erſten Buchs Element. Euclidis, vnd auß des Chriſtoph. Clavii Corollario, Propoſit. 4. lib. 6. Euclidis, zu ſehen/Darinn er diſen bey-

87. Hulsius, *Theoria et Praxis Quadrantis Geometrici* (1594)

88 HYGINUS, GAIUS JULIUS, mythographer, fl. first century B.C.

Fabularum Liber

Basel: Johannes Hervag, 1549

34 cm. 147 leaves. Title-page vignette, historiated initials, and forty-eight woodcut illustrations. Modern vellum over boards.

Modern scholars question the authorship of this work. Roman Emperor Augustus (63 B.C.–A.D. 14) appointed Hyginus librarian of the Palatine Library in Rome. Hyginus was a very learned man, author of several books and a friend of Ovid. Internal criticism of the *Fabulae* convinces Latin scholars that he could not have been the author of the "vast number of absurdities" found in this work. It is assumed that some earlier authority mistakenly attributed the MS (now lost) to Hyginus. The *editio princeps* (1482) was printed from it and all subsequent editions repeated the questionable attribution. (Rose, H.J. *A Handbook of Latin Literature*. London: Methuen, 1966, pp. 445f.).

Lalande lists 11 printings from 1482 to 1674. Houzeau, 861; Lalande, p. 68; Zinner, 1958

NUC: CtY; DFo; InU; MH; NN; NNC; NcU; OCU

89 HYGINUS, GAIUS JULIUS, mythographer, fl. first century B.C.

Fabularum Liber

Basel: Johannes Hervag, 1570

34 cm. 143 leaves. Contemporary half-vellum binding. Marginalia. Title-page vignette, historiated woodcut initials, forty-eight woodcut illustrations.

Houzeau, 861; Lalande, p. 94; Zinner, 2523

NUC: DLC; IEN; MiEM; NNC; PPL; TU

90 INDAGINE, JOANNES AB, 1467–1537

Astrologia Naturalis

Strasbourg: Lazar Zetzners Erben, 1630

16 cm. 156 leaves. Woodcuts. Title-page vignette. Bound in full contemporary vellum.

Text covers palmistry, astrology, numerology, sun, moon, and stars.

Also called Johannes Sagen, Indagine was a parish priest at Steinheim am Main near Mainz. Because of his unusual talents he peformed many functions for the Archbishop of Mainz and for other German princes. He was adept at astrology and wrote books on it and other subjects (*Iselin*, v. 4, p. 394).

Zinner, 5182

NUC: CtY

91 JEANNIN, PIERRE, 1540–1622

Les négotiations de monsieur le président Ieannin

Amsterdam: J. de Jonge, 1659

15 cm. 838 leaves. Two volumes bound in eighteenth-century-style full leather. Fine engraved portrait of the author.

Jeannin, a celebrated French statesman, was sent to The Hague in 1607 to negotiate an important treaty with the Dutch. First published in one volume in 1656, it contains the important collection of correspondence including his letter from The Hague in October 1608 on Hans Lipperhey's telescope. He recruited a French soldier to uncover the secret of the new telescope and sent him back to France with letters describing the new instrument in detail.

NUC: CLU; MeB; MH

92 JEBINGER, STEPHAN

Prognosticon Astrologicon

Regensburg: n.p., 1590

21 cm. 7 pages. Illustrations.

Jebinger was a doctor of medicine, an astronomer, and a mathematician at Regensburg.

Zinner Collection

Zinner, 1592 edition only

NUC: CSdS

93 KEILL, JOHN, 1671–1721

Inleidinge tot de Waare Natuur-en Sterrekunde

Leiden: J. and H. Verbeek, 1741

27 cm. 332 leaves. Forty-eight folding plates. Bound in contemporary vellum over boards. Fine historiated initials.

Dutch translation of his *Introductio ad Veram Astronomiam*, Oxford, 1718. The English translation, *An Introduction to the True Astronomy*, was published at London in 1721. Keill was born and educated at Edinburgh where he studied under David Gregory (1661–1708). He received his M.A. before going to Oxford where he was professor of astronomy until his death. He was one of Newton's very important disciples (*DSB*, v. 7, pp. 275–7).

Zinner Collection

Houzeau, 137

NUC: CSdS

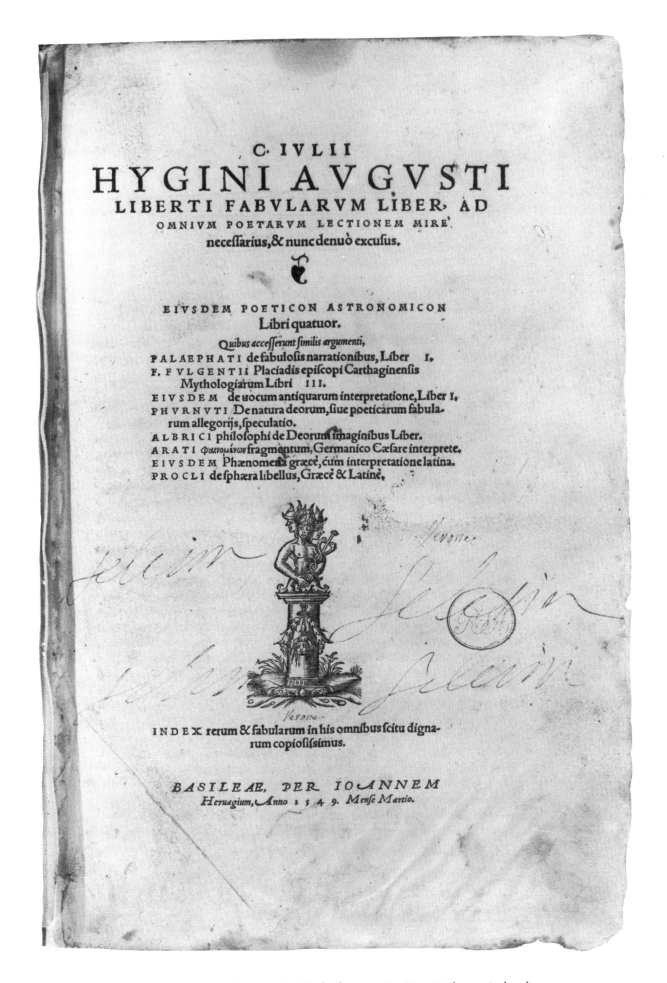

C · IVLII
HYGINI AVGVSTI
LIBERTI FABVLARVM LIBER, AD
OMNIVM POETARVM LECTIONEM MIRE'
necessarius, & nunc denuò excusus.

℘

EIVSDEM POETICON ASTRONOMICON
Libri quatuor.
Quibus accesserunt similis argumenti,
PALAEPHATI de fabulosis narrationibus, Liber I.
F. FVLGENTII Placiadis episcopi Carthaginensis
  Mythologiarum Libri III.
EIVSDEM de uocum antiquarum interpretatione, Liber I.
PHVRNVTI De natura deorum, siue poeticarum fabula-
  rum allegorijs, speculatio.
ALBRICI philosophi de Deorum imaginibus Liber.
ARATI Φαινομένων fragmentum, Germanico Cæsare interprete.
EIVSDEM Phænomena græcè, cùm interpretatióne latina.
PROCLI de sphæra libellus, Græcè & Latinè,

INDEX rerum & fabularum in his omnibus scitu digna-
rum copiosissimus.

BASILEAE, PER IOANNEM
Heruagium, Anno 1 5 4 9. Mense Martio.

88. Hyginus, *Fabularum Liber* [Book of conversations] (1549) title page (reduced)

Nauis.

Nauis unam habet primæ magnitudinis, qui Cano-
pus uocatur, ponitur̃q; in præcipuo remo, sed quæ lon-
gè deflectit ad austrum. Habet sex¹ secundæ magnitu-
dinis, unam in transitro, aliam in sectione transtri, er̃c.
habet quoq; multas tertiæ, er̃ item multas quartæ ma-
gnitudinis: quæ in malo ponuntur, sunt quartæ ma-
gnitudinis.

ARgo. Huius puppis hyemalem
circulum, & maioris canis caudam contingens inferiore parte, no-
uissimè nauis inclinata Antarcticum
circulum tangit. Occidens sagittario
& capricorno exorto, ut in mari col-
locata, exoriens cum uirgine & chelis. Hæc habet in puppi ad singula guberna-
cula, ad primum stellas quinque, ad alterum quatuor, circum carinam quinque,
& sub reiectum quinq;, ad malum quatuor : in tota est stellarum uigintitrium.
Quæ, quare non sit tota in mundo collocata, prius diximus.

Phillyris.

Centaurus in pede dextro duas habet stellas pri-
mæ magnitudinis, in pede verò sinistro habet unam se-
cundæ magnitudinis, similiter super coxam dextram,
er̃ sub uentre, atq; super calcaneum pedis dextri, er̃
super genu sinistrum, habet er̃ multas tertiæ, quartæ,
er̃ quintæ magnitudinis.

CEntaurus. Hic ita figuratur, ut
in antarctico circulo niti pedibus, humeris hyemalem sustinere ui-
deatur, capite prope caudam hydræ
coniungens, hostiam dextra manu
tenens supinam, quæ pedibus & ex-
tremo ore circulum hyemalem tangit, inter eum & antarcticum orbem collocata. Centauri autem crura à reliquo corpore diuidit circulus qui Lacteus appella-
tur. Hic spectans ad ortus signorum, totus occidit aquario & piscibus exortis:
exoritur autem cũ scorpione & sagittario, habet aũt stellas supra caput tres ob-
scuras, in utrisq; humeris singulas claras, in cubito sinistro unam, in manu unam,
in medio pectore equino unam, in prioribus poplitibus utrisq; singulas, in interscapilio quatuor, in uentre duas claras, in cauda tres, in lumbo equino unam, in
genubus posterioribus singulas, in poplitibus singulas. omnino sunt 24. Hostia
autem habet in cauda duas, in pede de posterioribus primo unam, in utrisq; pedibus unam, in interscapilio unam claram, & in priore parte pedum unam, infrà alteram, in capite tres dispositas. Omnino sunt num. 10.

Ara.

Ara habet septem stellas, ex quibus quinq; sunt
quartæ magnitudinis, er̃ duæ quintæ.

ARa antarcticum circulum prope tangens, inter hostiæ caput
& scorpionis caudam extremã col-
locatur; occidẽs arietis exortu, exoriens cum capricorno. Hęc habet in
summo cacumine circuli ubi forma-
tur, stellas duas, & in imo alteras. Et
ita est omnino stellarum quatuor.

Hydra.

LES
NEGOTIATIONS
DE MONSIEVR
LE
PRESIDENT
IEANNIN.

Iouxte la Copie de Paris.
Chez PIERRE LE PETIT.
1659.

91. Jeannin, *Les négotiations* [The negotiations] (1659) title page

91. Jeannin, *Les négotiations* (1659) portrait of Jeannin and page of text

INLEIDINGE

TOT DE WAARE

NATUUR-EN STERREKUNDE,

OF DE

NATUUR- EN STERREKUNDIGE LESSEN

VAN DEN HEER

JOHAN KEILL, M.D.

Saviliaanfch Hoogleeraar in de Sterrekunde te Oxfort, en Medelid
van de Koninglyke Maatfchappy der Wetenfchappen te Londen.

Waar by gevoegt zyn deszelfs Verhandelingen

OVER DE

PLATTE EN KLOOTSCHE DRIEHOEKS-REKENINGE,

OVER DE

MIDDELPUNTS-KRAGTEN

EN OVER DE

WETTEN DER AANTREKKINGE.

Uit het Latyn vertaald, en met eenige Aantekeningen en
Byvoegzels verrykt

DOOR

JOHAN LULOFS, M.D.V.K.

Doctor in de Regten en in de Philofophie, Medelid van de Koninglyke
Maatfchappy der Wetenfchappen te Berlyn.

TE LEIDEN,

By JAN en HERMANUS VERBEEK,

MDCCXLI.

94 KEPLER, JOHANN, 1571–1630

De Cometis Libelli Tres

Augsburg: Typis Andrea Aspergeri, Sumptibus Sebastiani Mylii Bibliopolae, 1619

20 cm. 78 leaves. First edition. Illustrations, two folding plates, three folding tables. Contemporary vellum over soft boards. Imprint date of book three is 1620.

Lalande, p. 172; Zinner, 4739

NUC: MB; MH; NN; NNC; PPL

95 KEPLER, JOHANN, supposed author, 1571–1630

De Novis ab Autore Inventis Instrumentis

n.p.: n.p., n.d.

16 cm. 6 leaves. Illustrations. First edition.

Zinner (item 5221, p. 409) attributed authorship of this small anonymous pamphlet on newly invented astronomical instruments to Kepler. No author, place, publisher, or date of publication appears on the publication. The title is not listed among Kepler's original printed works in the *DSB* (v. 7, pp. 308–9).

Zinner Collection

Zinner, 5221

NUC: no copy

Not by Kepler – per letter 1/30/93 – Dr. Jurgen Hamel of Bibliographia Kepleriana is Adrian Metius

96 KEPLER, JOHANN, 1571–1630

Eclogae Chronicae

Frankfurt: Johannes Bringer, 1615

21 cm. 4 leaves, 215 pages. First edition.

Kepler treats on the calendar, attempting to date Christ's birth accurately by computing lunar positions, eclipses, and star positions.

Lalande, p. 163; Zinner, 4514

NUC: NN

97 KIRCH, GOTTFRIED (?), 1639–1710

Kurtze Beschreibung und auf das fleissigst deducirte Calculation der in diesem 1699sten Jahr... grossen und sichtbaren Sonnenfinsternis von einem der gelehrtesten Astronomorum dieser Zeit G. K. an das Tagslicht gebracht

Nürnberg: Johann Andrea Endters Seel. Söhne, 1699

22 cm. 9 leaves. Engraved vignette on title page, one plate and a table in the text.

Zinner Collection

NUC: CSdS

98 KIRCH, GOTTFRIED, 1639–1710

Kurtze Betrachtung derer Wunder am gestirnten Himmel

Leipzig: C. Kirchner, 1677

19 cm. 12 leaves. Illustrations. Woodcut on title page, one full-page woodcut, and one large engraving in text.

First edition of an astronomical treatise on the comet of 1676 and the reasons for its appearance. Kirch later became known as the discoverer of the famous comet of 1680.

Kirch was the staff astronomer of the Royal Prussian Society of the Sciences, Berlin, from 1700 to 1710. The son of a tailor, he first educated himself in mathematics and astronomy. He later studied at Jena under Erhard Weigel (1625–99) who recommended him to Hevelius in Gdánsk. He studied astrology and published calendars, ephemerides, and a treatise, *Neue Himmels-Zeitung* (Nürnberg, 1681). He lived at Gdánsk, Leipzig, and other places and eventually settled at Berlin in 1700. In 1692 he married Maria Margaretha Winckelmann, daughter of Matthias Winckelmann, pastor at Pomitzsch. She had learned astronomy during her youth from a townsman named Christoph Arnold, and besides bearing fourteen children, she assisted her husband with his observations, calendar making, and mathematical calculations on planetary movements. She achieved recognition as an astronomer before her death in 1720. Among her patrons was Gottfried Wilhelm von Leibnitz (1646–1716). (*Iselin*, v. 4, p. 513).

NUC: NNC

DE COMETIS
LIBELLI TRES.

I. *ASTRONOMICVS*, *Theoremata continens de motu Cometarum, vbi Demonstratio Apparentiarum & altitudinis Cometarum qui Annis 1607. & 1618. conspecti sunt, noua & παράδοξος.*

II. *PHYSICVS*, *continens Physiologiam Cometarum nouam & παράδοξον.*

III. *ASTROLOGICVS*, *de significationibus Cometarum Annorum 1607. & 1618.*

AVTORE
IOHANNE KEPLERO,
SAC. CÆS. MAIEST. MA-
thematico,

Seneca Nat. Quæst. lib. 6. cap. 26.

Erit qui demonstret aliquando, in quibus Cometa partibus errent, cur tam seducti à cæteris eant, quanti qualesq̃, sint. Contenti simus inuentis: aliquid veritati & posteri conferant.

Cum Priuilegio Sac. Cæsareæ Maiest.
ad Annos XV.

AVGVSTÆ VINDELICORVM,
Typis Andreæ Apergeri, Sumptibus Sebastiani Mylii Bibliopolæ Augustani, M. DC. XIX.

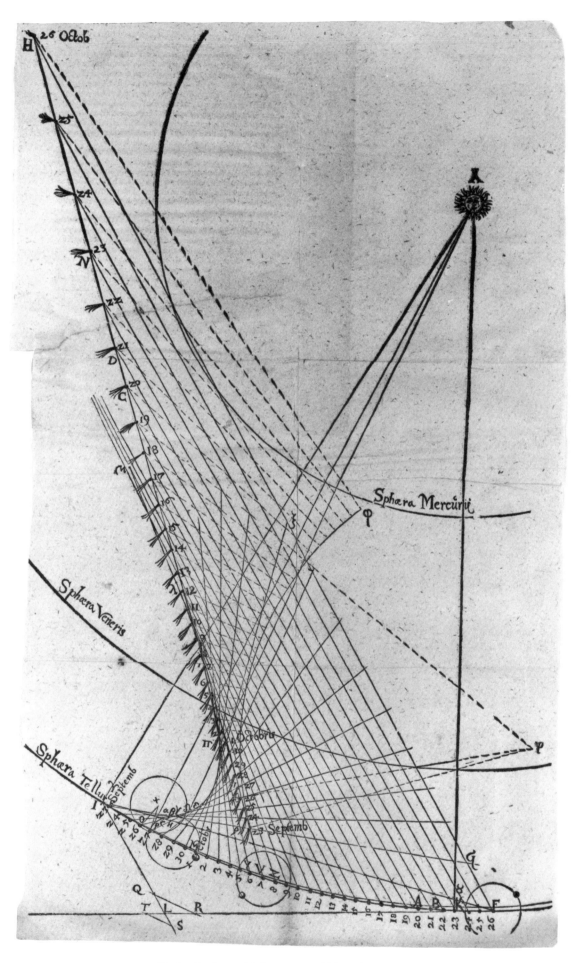

94. Kepler, *De Cometis Libelli Tres* (1619) folding plate (reduced)

95. Kepler, *De Novis ab Autore Inventis Instrumentis* [Concerning the author's newly invented instruments] (n.d.) title page

transversariū Majus, DE, in longitudine

firmiter continetur. Circuli superficies

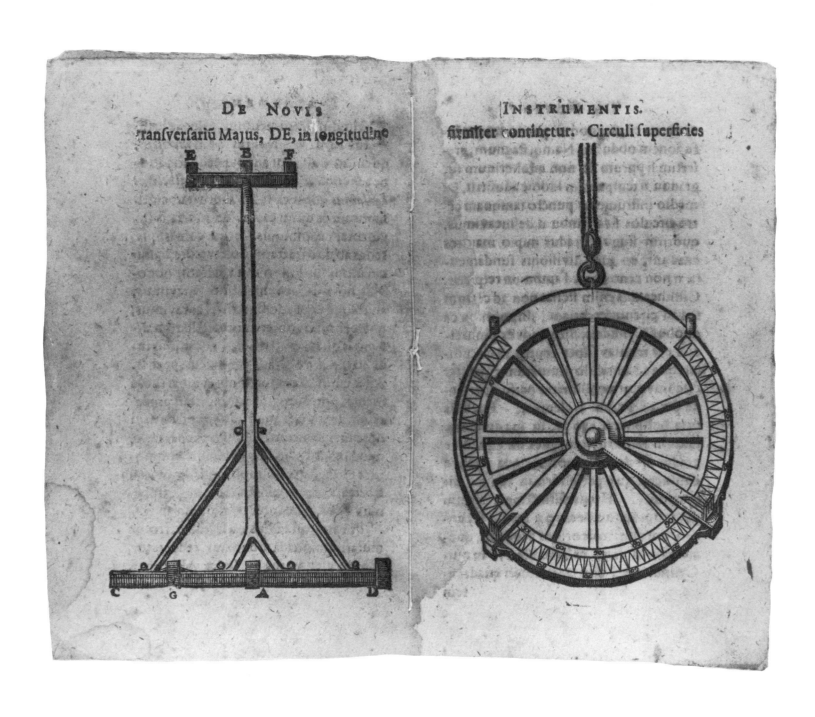

95. Kepler, *De Novis ab Autore Inventis Instrumentis* (n.d.)

JOANNIS KEPPLERI

Mathematici

ECLOGÆ CHRONICÆ

EX EPISTOLIS DOCTISSIMORVM

aliquot Virorum, & Suis mutuis,

Quibus examinantur tempora nobilissima

I. Herodis Herodiadumque.
II. Baptismi & Ministerii Christi annorum non plus $2\frac{1}{4}$.
III. PASSIONIS, MORTIS ET RESVRRECTIONIS DN N. Iesu Christi, anno æræ nostræ vulgaris, 31. non, vt vulgo, 33.
IV. Belli Iudaici, quo funerata fuit cum Ierosolymis & Templo Synagoga Iudaica, sublatumque Vetus Testamentum.

Inter alia & Commentarius luculentus in locum Epiphanij obscurissimum de cyclo veteri Iudæorum.

Cum Priuilegio   ad annos XV.

FRANCOFVRTI,

Typis Ioannis Bringeri, Impensis vero GODE-
FRIDI TAMPACHII.

M. DC. XV.

96. Kepler, *Eclogae Chronicae* [Time] (1615) title page

Kurtze Beschreibung

und
auf das fleissigst deducirte
CALCULATION
Der
in diesem 1699sten Jahr am $\frac{13}{23}$ September
sich ereignenden
Grossen und sichtbaren

Sonnenfinsternis/

Von einem
der gelehrtesten Astronomorum dieser Zeit
G. K.
an das Tagslicht gebracht.

Nürnberg/
In Verlegung Johann Andreä Endters Seel. Söhne.
M DC XCIX.

97. Kirch, *Kurtze Beschreibung…Calculation…der Sonnenfinsternis*
[Short description and calculation of the eclipse of the sun] (1699) title page

Kurtze Betrachtung
derer
Wunder am gestirnten Himmel/
welche veranlaßet der itzige recht
Merckwürdige neue Comet/
Die feurige Kugel/welche im vergangenen Jahre durch
Italien geflogen/ und anderes mehr.
Mit flüchtiger Feder auffgesetzet von
Gottfried Kirchen.

Die nächst verfloßene sichtbare Martis Finsterniß/den
22. Aug. 1676.

Die nächst künftige sichtbare
Saturns-Finsterniß / den
4. Octob. 7761.

LEIPZIG/
In Christian Kirchners Buchladen zufinden.
Gedruckt/ bey Michael Vogten.
Anno 1677.

98. Kirch, Kurtze Betrachtung derer Wunder am gestirnten Himmel...merckwürdige neue Comet
[Brief consideration of the miracle in the starry heavens, the remarkable new comet] (1677) title page

99 KIRCHER, ATHANASIUS, 1602?–1680

Iter Exstaticum Coeleste

Würzburg: J. A. Endter, 1671

22 cm. 364 leaves. Illustrations. Bound in calf. Illegible signature on title page.

A major Jesuit astronomer, Kircher was educated at the Jesuit Gymnasium at Fulda. He entered the Jesuit order in 1616. At Paderborn he studied humanities, natural science, and mathematics. Later at Mainz he first used the telescope for observations of sunspots. In the same year he was appointed professor of philosophy and mathematics at Würzburg. In 1631 he fled to Lyons where he worked in astronomy, hieroglyphics, and surveying and published a book on astronomical observations obtained at the planetarium he designed.

Zinner Collection

Houzeau, 691; Lalande, p. 275

NUC: CU; CtY; DLC; MB; MH; MiU; NIC; OU

100 LEADBETTER, CHARLES, fl. 1728

A Treatise of Eclipses

London: John Wilcox, 1731

17 cm. 93 leaves. Second edition. Numerous woodcuts. Bound in contemporary full calf.

Leadbetter was an eighteenth-century English astronomer who taught mathematics, navigation, and astronomy at a school in London. The first edition of this work was published in 1727. He was an early commentator on Newton (*DSB*, v. 11, pp. 755–6).

Lalande, p. 392

NUC: CLU-C; CtY; ICU; MiU; PBa

101 LE CLERC, JEAN, 1657–1736

Opera Philosophica

Leipzig: T. Georg, 1710

18 cm. 133 leaves. Four volumes bound in one, vellum over boards. Volume three is on astronomy. Four folding engraved plates. Frontispiece is an engraved portrait of the author. Provenance: "E.F.C. Doehner, 1794" on recto of first flyleaf.

title-page vignette

LeClerc was a philosopher, theologian, and prolific writer. He was born and educated at Geneva. He spent most of his adult life in Amsterdam and became known above all as a celebrated critic. He was extraordinarily erudite, a champion of liberty, and an enemy of intolerance. His volume on astronomy begins with Ptolemy, describes the Copernican system, and includes the discoveries of Edmund Halley.

NUC: ICU; NcU; NjP; PPAmP; PU;·OrU; ViU

102 LE FEVRE, JACQUES D'ETAPLES, ca. 1455–1537

Introductorium Astronomicum Theorias Coporum Coelestium

Paris: Henry Stephan, 1517

32 cm. 65 leaves. Woodcut illustrations and historiated initials. Variant spelling of Corporum in the title noted. Provenance: "Joachim ese Braur Suosz(?) Amicon, S." appears on the recto after the colophon.

Le Fèvre was a renowned French polygraph born at Étaples in ca. 1455. He received his M.A. at Paris and soon thereafter traveled to Italy where he studied the mathematics and philosophy of the ancients. Although he wrote more on biblical and theological subjects, he nevertheless published many works on mathematics and astronomy including editions of Euclid's *Elements* and Sacro Bosco's *Sphaera Mundi* along with his own commentaries. *The National Union Catalog* shows he was author or editor of fifty-one different works.

Lalande, p. 39

NUC: DLC; ICN; MB; MH; NNC

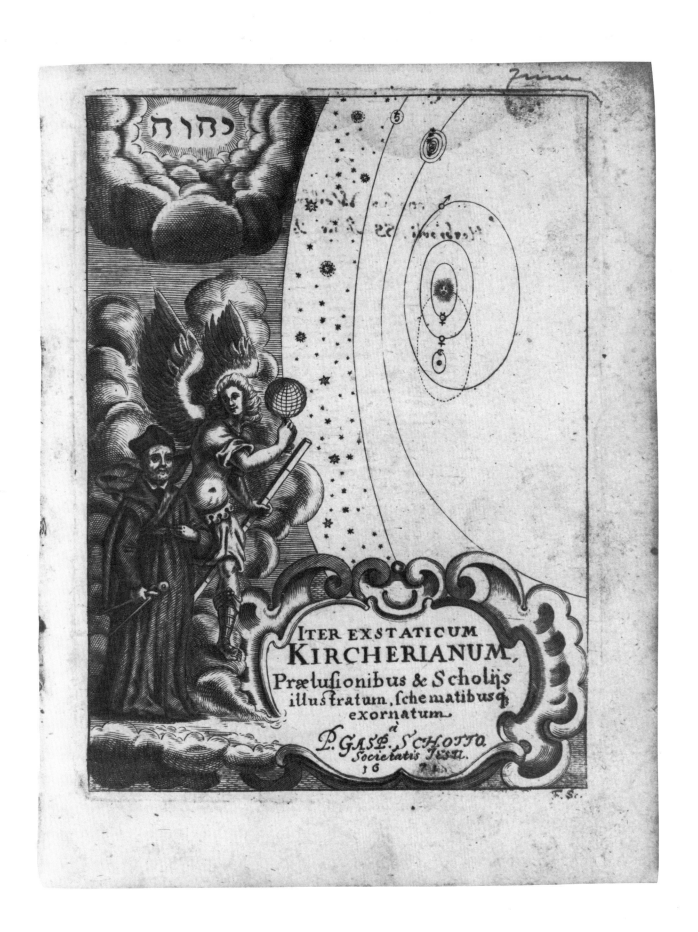

99. Kircher, *Iter Exstaticum* [Amazing journey] (1671) title page

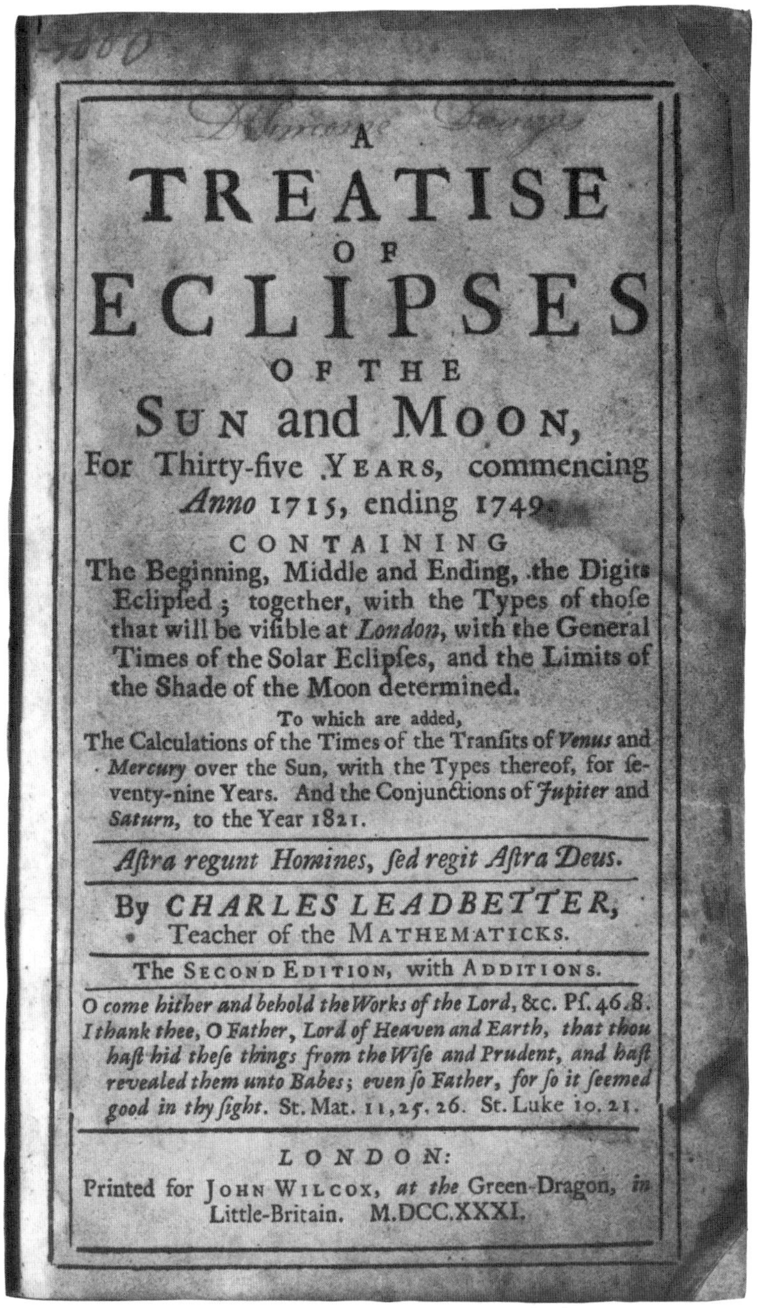

A
TREATISE
OF
ECLIPSES
OF THE
Sun and Moon,

For Thirty-five Years, commencing
Anno 1715, ending 1749.

CONTAINING

The Beginning, Middle and Ending, the Digits
Eclipſed; together, with the Types of thoſe
that will be viſible at *London*, with the General
Times of the Solar Eclipſes, and the Limits of
the Shade of the Moon determined.

To which are added,

The Calculations of the Times of the Tranſits of *Venus* and
Mercury over the Sun, with the Types thereof, for ſe-
venty-nine Years. And the Conjunctions of *Jupiter* and
Saturn, to the Year 1821.

Aſtra regunt Homines, ſed regit Aſtra Deus.

By *CHARLES LEADBETTER*,
Teacher of the MATHEMATICKS.

The SECOND EDITION, with ADDITIONS.

O come hither and behold the Works of the Lord, &c. Pſ. 46.8.
*I thank thee, O Father, Lord of Heaven and Earth, that thou
haſt hid theſe things from the Wiſe and Prudent, and haſt
revealed them unto Babes; even ſo Father, for ſo it ſeemed
good in thy ſight.* St. Mat. 11,25.26. St. Luke 10,21.

LONDON:
Printed for JOHN WILCOX, *at the* Green-Dragon, *in*
Little-Britain. M.DCC.XXXI.

100. Leadbetter, *A Treatise of Eclipses* (1731) title page

JOANNES CLERICUS
Natus
an. 1657.
Vita labore dedit
Nil sine magno mortalibus

JOANNIS CLERICI
OPERA
PHILOSO-
PHICA
IN IV. TOMOS
DIGESTA.
EDITIO IN GERMANIA PRIMA ET
NOVISSIMA.
PRÆFATIONEM
NOVAM
ADDIDIT
GOTTL. FRID. JENICHEN.

LIPSIÆ
Apud THEOPH. GEORGI, MDCCX.
Cum Privilegio S. R. M. Pol. & Elect. Sax.

101. Le Clerc, *Opera Philosophica* [Philosophical Works] (1710)
title page and frontispiece portrait of Le Clerc

102. Le Fèvre, *Introductorium Astronomicum Theorias Coporum Coelestium*
[Astronomical introduction to theories of the heavenly bodies] (1517) title page (reduced)

❧De mercurio/eiuſqʒ latitudine. Cap. XI.

153 **M**Ercurius triplicem/vt venus: ſortitur latitudinem. Primã deuiationis circu li eccentri ab ecliptica. Secundã inclinationis diametri verarum abſidum epicyclij: a ſuperficie eccẽtri deferentis. Tertiam vero: reflexionis diametri mediarũ longitudinum a deferentis planicie. Diffinitiones autem earũ la titudinum/ſunt eædem: quæ in venere circa præcedentis cap. principium

154 ſunt aſſignatæ. ❧Nonnihil tamẽ inter venerem & mercurium eſt diſcriminis. Nam qᷓ in deuiatione inclinatione aut reflexione eccentri aut illarum diametrorum : in venere flectitur ad boream atqʒ ſeptẽtrionem in mercurio conſimilibus ex locis idem conuertit̃

155 ad auſtrum/partemqʒ meridionalem. ad quã ſolam: mercurij tẽdit deuiatio. ❧Quo fit : vt mercurialis epicyclij centrum nunᷓ deuiet ad boream. Nam ex præcedente propoſi tione/quod in deuiatione tendit ad arcton in venere: in mercurio deuergit ad auſtrum. Atqui ſemper centrum epicyclij venerjs in toto deuiationis motu flectitur ad ſeptentri onem/& nunᷓ ad meridiem: vt numero 143 dictum eſt. Igitur e diuerſo ſemper cẽtrum mercurialis epicyclij deuiat ad meridiem & nunᷓ ad boream: in quacũqʒ eccentri defe

156 rentis parte feratur. ❧Maxima mercurij deuiatio ab ecliptica/& vltra quam non poteſt ab ea magis aberrare: continet quinqʒ & quadraginta minuta. Et hanc maximam lati tudinis quantitatem tunc habet mercurius: cum eſt in vmbilico medietatis eccentri in qua apogium eſt deferentis/aut perigium. In vtroqʒ enim illorum punctorum: maxime ab ecliptica deuiat/cũ a nodis vtrinqʒ æquo diſtet interuallo: in quibus ipſi ecliptiçᷓ cõ iungitur. quẽadmodum de alijs planetis etiam eſt dictum. ❧Et hæc pro aſtronomicæ huius introductionis elucidatione dicta ſufficiant. quæ ſolam fere litteræ declarationem exemplorumqʒ aſſignationem cum figuratione ſenſibili/vbi locus efflagitat/ afferunt. Nam illa ad rudem introductorij compendij intelligentiam/vtqʒ peruia eius reddatur ſententia : & neceſſaria ſunt & ſufficiunt. Non equidem inficior / plurima quinimo fere omnia quæ hoc in opere diſſeruntur : ratiocinatione doctrinali oſtendi poſſe/ac demon ſtrari. Sed non ferunt demõſtrationũ pondus iſagogicæ ꝓparationes: neqʒ in eis paſſim adduci debent/quin potius ad ipſam diſciplinam cuius parãt introitum : adhiberi atqʒ reſeruari. Qᷓ ſi quis demõſtrationes harum rerum efflagitat : poſt huius operis lectionẽ ad Purbachianam ſe cõferat theoricã. cui adiectus a Frãciſco Capuano viro vtiqʒ ma thematum peritiſſimo cõmentarius/complura eorum quæ hic diſcutiuntur: rationaliter & exacte demõſtrat. aut ad epithomata Ioannis de monte regio in ipſum Ptolõmæũ. aut ad magnam Ptolomæi compoſitionem (quod almageſtum vulgo dicunt) ſe tranſ ferat: vbi modo doctrinali demonſtrantur omnia. Nam & ad Purbachium intelligendũ itidem & Ptolomeum/quinimo & ad epithomen in illum modo analytico & doctrinali elaboratam: magnam hoc opus introductorium affert opem atqʒ preſidium.

Purbachiꝰ,
Franciſcus
Capuanus
Ioannes de
mõte regio
Ptolomeus

❧Secundi libri aſtronomici theorici corporum cœleſtium & adiectæ eidem commentationis : finis.

❧Excudit hoc opus & impreſſit Henricus Stephanus/effor mãdorum librorumſedulus & induſtrius artifex: Pa riſijs in ſua officina libraria e regione ſcholæ Decretorum. Anno Chriſti cœloᷓ rum totiuſqʒ nature condi toris. 1517. die nona decembris.

103 LE MONNIER, PIERRE CHARLES, 1715–99

Description et usage des principaux instruments d'astronomie

Paris: Académie Royale des Sciences, 1744

48 × 32 cm. 31 leaves. First edition. Bound in contemporary paper covers. Fourteen large copper-engraved plates illustrating French astronomical instruments of the mid-eighteenth century.

Le Monnier was a noted French astronomer and favorite of King Louis XV, who procured the best astronomical instruments in France for him. He was admitted to the Académie des Sciences in 1736 at age twenty. In 1746 he became professor at the Collège Royale and was admitted to the Royal Society, London, and the Akademie der Wissenschaften, Berlin. His most prominent pupil was Jérôme Lalande (1732–1807).

NUC: CU; MH; NjP; OCl

104 LEOPOLD OF AUSTRIA, ASTRONOMER, fl. ca. 1200

Compilatio Leupoldi Ducatus Austrie Filii de Astrorum Scientia Decem Continentis Tractatus

Venice: Melchior Sessa, 1520

22 cm. 94 leaves. Woodcut illustrations and historiated initials throughout. Printer Erhard Ratdolt's name appears on the verso of the second leaf. The colophon shows Melchior Sessa as printer of this book. A manuscript index to the contents appears on the verso of the third leaf.

Leopold of Austria was a medieval astrologer about whose life very little can be ascertained. His birth and death dates are unknown. The Italian astronomer

the sphere

Giambattista Riccioli (1598–1671) referred to him as "the very famous astrologer who flourished ca. 1200." The National Library in Vienna has a manuscript of Leopold's *Compilatio* dated 1332, while the State Library in Munich has another dated between 1445 and 1450. Erhard Ratdolt (ca. 1443–1528) published the first printed edition at Venice in 1489. Since no Austrian duke named Leopold can be identified as the astrologer-author of the *Compilatio, Allgemeine deutsche Biographie* suggests "ducatus Austrie filius" might be interpreted to mean "son of the land of Austria."

Zinner Collection

Lalande, p. 41

NUC: CtY; DFo; ICN; ICU; MB; NN

105 LEOVITIUS, CYPRIANUS L., 1524–74

Eclipsium Omnium ab Anno Domini 1554 usque in Annum Domini 1606

Augsburg: Philipp Ulhard, 1556

30 cm. 114 leaves. Numerous woodcut illustrations. Bound in contemporary limp vellum. Hand-drawn and colored coat of arms on inside front cover.

Pictorial representations of the eclipses of the sun and moon at Augsburg with explanatory text appear throughout.

Leovitius was an astronomer and astrologer born at Hradec Kralové in Bohemia. He came to Augsburg in 1552 where he remained most of his life. He was an author of books on astronomy and ephemerides and was well known among contemporary astronomers.

Lalande, p. 79; Zinner, 2154

NUC: DLC; DN-Ob

106 LEOVITIUS, CYPRIANUS L., 1524–74

Ephemeridum Novum atque Insigne Opus ab Anno Domini 1556 usque in 1606

Augsburg: Philipp Ulhard, 1557

40 cm. 684 unnumbered leaves. Illustrations, diagrams, tables. Bound in hand-tooled parchment over boards and dated 1575. Extensive marginalia. Provenance, title page: "M. Jacobus Hallius, anno 1615." The date of publication is taken from the colophon.

Zinner Collection

Lalande, p. 81; Zinner, 2176

NUC: NN; WU

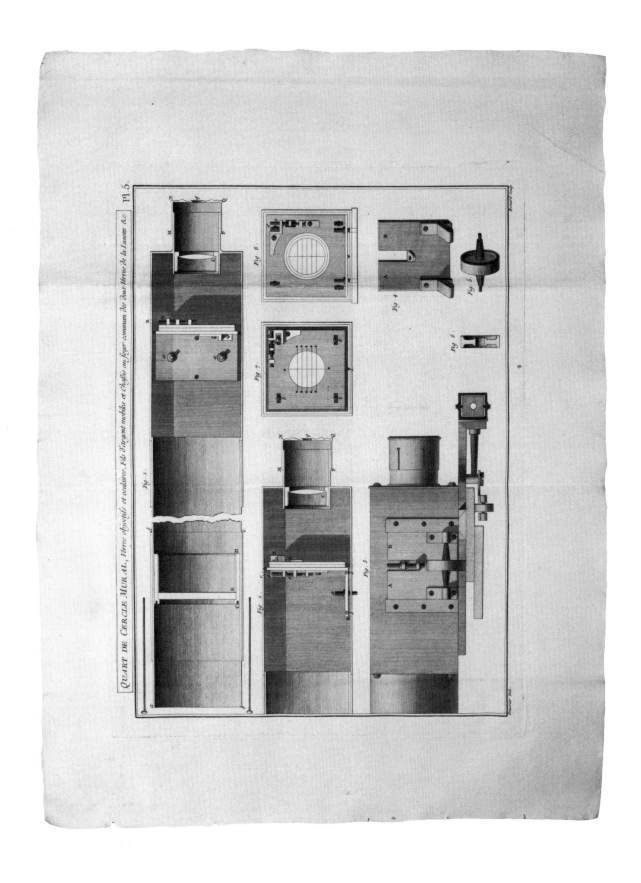

103. Le Monnier, *Description et usage des principaux instruments d'astronomie*
[Description and use of the principal astronomical instruments] (1744) plate 5 (reduced)

103. Le Monnier, *Description et usage des principaux instruments d'astronomie*
(1744) plate 10 (reduced)

♈ **Aries**   ♉ **Thaurus**   ♊ **Gemini**

♋ **Cancer**   ♌ **Leo**   ♍ **Uirgo**

♎ **Libza**   ♏ **Scorpius**   ♐ **Sagittarius**

♑ **Capricornus**   ♒ **Aquarius**   ♓ **Pilces**

℄ Manſiones lūne in predictis duodecim ſignis ſūnt.28. quartum cuilibet
de zodiaco cedunt gradus.12.minuta.ſ1.ſecunda.26.fere: τ ſunt iſte.
1 Cornua ♈ habet ſtellas duas
2 Uenter ♈ habet tres ſtellas
3 Caput ♉ habet ſex ſtellas
4 Cor ♉ habet nouem ſtellas
5 Caput canis validi quinꝗ habet ſtellas

104. Leopold of Austria, *Compilatio…de Astrorum Scientia*
[Compilation of knowledge of the stars] (1520) signs of the zodiac

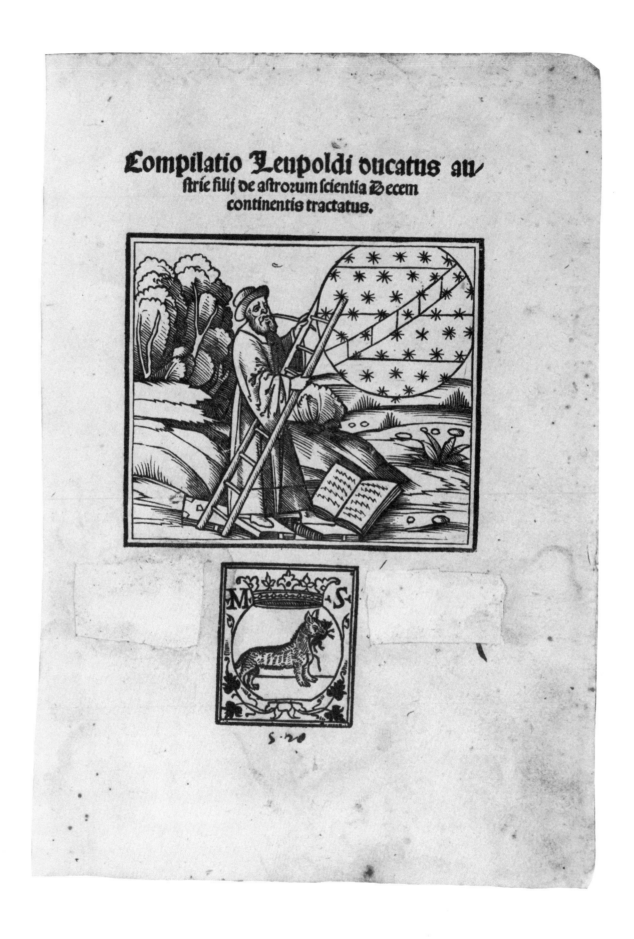

104. Leopold of Austria, *Compilatio…de Astrorum Scientia* (1520) title page

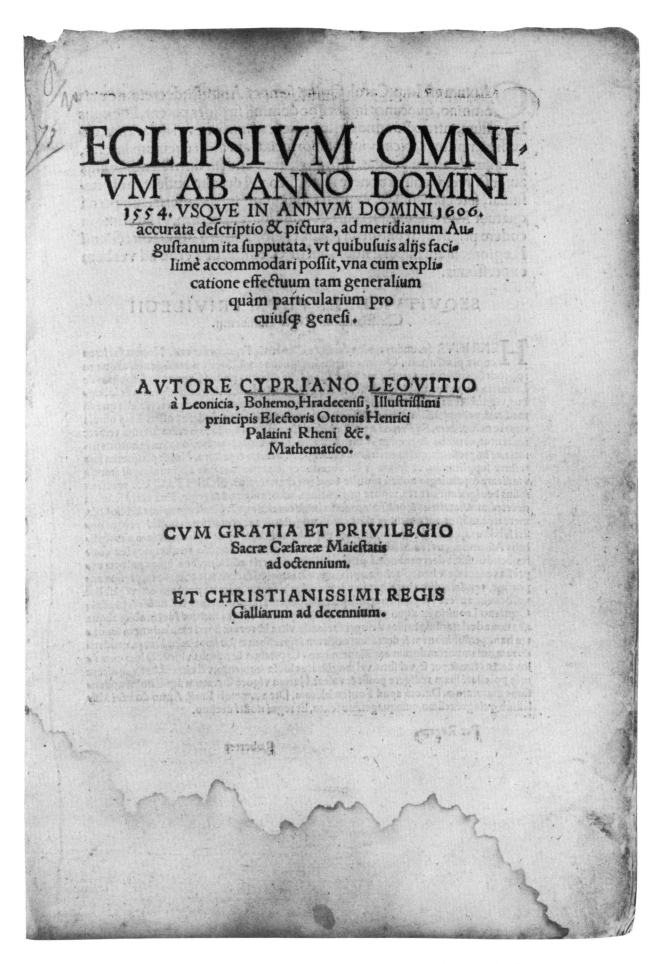

ECLIPSIVM OMNI-
VM AB ANNO DOMINI

1554. VSQVE IN ANNVM DOMINI 1606,
accurata deſcriptio & pictura, ad meridianum Au-
guſtanum ita ſupputata, vt quibuſuis alijs faci-
lime accommodari poſſit, vna cum expli-
catione effectuum tam generalium
quàm particularium pro
cuiuſꝗ geneſi.

AVTORE CYPRIANO LEOVITIO
à Leonicia, Bohemo, Hradecenſi, Illuſtriſſimi
principis Electoris Ottonis Henrici
Palatini Rheni &c̄.
Mathematico.

CVM GRATIA ET PRIVILEGIO
Sacræ Cæſareæ Maieſtatis
ad octennium.

ET CHRISTIANISSIMI REGIS
Galliarum ad decennium.

105. Leovitius, *Eclipsium Omnium* [All of the eclipses] (1556) title page (reduced)

EPHEMERIDVM NOVVM

ATQVE INSIGNE OPVS AB ANNO DOMINI

1556. vſφ in 1606. accuratiſſimè ſupputatum : cui præter
alia ommia in cæteris editionibus addi ſolita,
etiam hæc acceſſerunt .

I   **ECLIPSIVM TYPI ELEGANTISSIMI.**

II   **EXPEDITA RATIO CONSTITVENDI COELESTIS**
thematis, cum tabulis, è quibus motus planetarum tam in natiuitatibus quàm reuolutionibus citra laborem haberi poſſunt.

III   **LOCA STELLARVM FIXARVM AB ANNO**
domini 1349. vſφ in 2029. diligenter annotata.

IIII   **BREVIS RATIO GENESES IVDICANDI, CVM NO-**
uis quibuſdam obſeruationibus & electionum methodo tam
vniuerſali quàm ad cuiuſφ geneſin accommodata·

V   **THEMATA QVATVOR ANNI TEMPORVM, CVM**
breui declaratione reuolutionis mundi, aliaφ plura, quæ diligens
lector in ipſo opere facile perſpiciet.

AVTORE CYPRIANO LEOVITIO A LEONICIA

Bohemo Hradecenſi, Illuſtriſſimi principis Electoris Ottonis
Henrici Palatini Rheni &c̄. Mathematico.

EXCVDEBAT AVGVSTÆ VINDELICORVM

Philippus Vlhardus, Anno domini 1556.
Menſe Octobri.
5

106. Leovitius, *Ephemeridum Novum* [New ephemerides] (1557) title page (reduced)

107 LEOVITIUS, CYPRIANUS L., 1524–74

Letter, 11 October 1560, Lauingen, Bavaria, to Ludwig von Oettingen

28 cm. 1 leaf holograph signed.

Leovitius offers to draw up a horoscope for Ludwig XVI, Count of Oettingen, after having received a letter from him with the record of his birth. An English translation and commentary by Harvey I. Dunkle appeared in *Manuscripts* (v. 33, No. 3 (Summer 1975), pp. 216–9).

Zinner Collection

108 LEOVITIUS, CYPRIANUS L., 1524–74

Omissa Utilitati Eclypsium

1560?

32 cm. 82 leaves. Manuscript with numerous diagrams and illustrations in a fine hand.

Zinner Collection

NUC: CSdS

109. frontispiece (reduced)

109 LEVERA, FRANCESCO, 17th century

Prodromus Universae Astronomiae Restitutae de Anni Solaris

Rome: Angeli Bernabo, 1663

34 cm. 211 leaves. First edition. Frontispiece, tables, historiated initials, printer's vignettes. Bound in contemporary limp vellum.

Levera was an Italian astronomer at Rome. In this extensive astronomical-astrological compendium he gives a survey of the history of astronomy up to the time of Tycho Brahe. He also tells the story of how Copernicus withheld publication of *De Revolutionibus* for thirty years.

Lalande, p. 254

NUC: DLC; NN; OkU

110 LINE, FRANCIS, 1595–1675

An Appendix to Clavis Horologiae: Or an Explication of the Pyramidical Dyal

London: n.p., 1685

21 cm. 40 leaves (including the 18 plates). Inscribed on cover leaf, "An Herrn Professor Ernst Zinner mit herzlichem Gruss. P. Couinder."

Francis Line, who also wrote under the pseudonym Francis Hall, was an English Jesuit who was ordained in 1628. He was a professor of mathematics and Hebrew at the Jesuit college in Liège for many years. In 1669 he constructed the curious sundial installed at Whitehall, London.

Zinner Collection

Lalande, p. 280

NUC: CSdS; CtY; DP; ICN; MB; MH; NNC

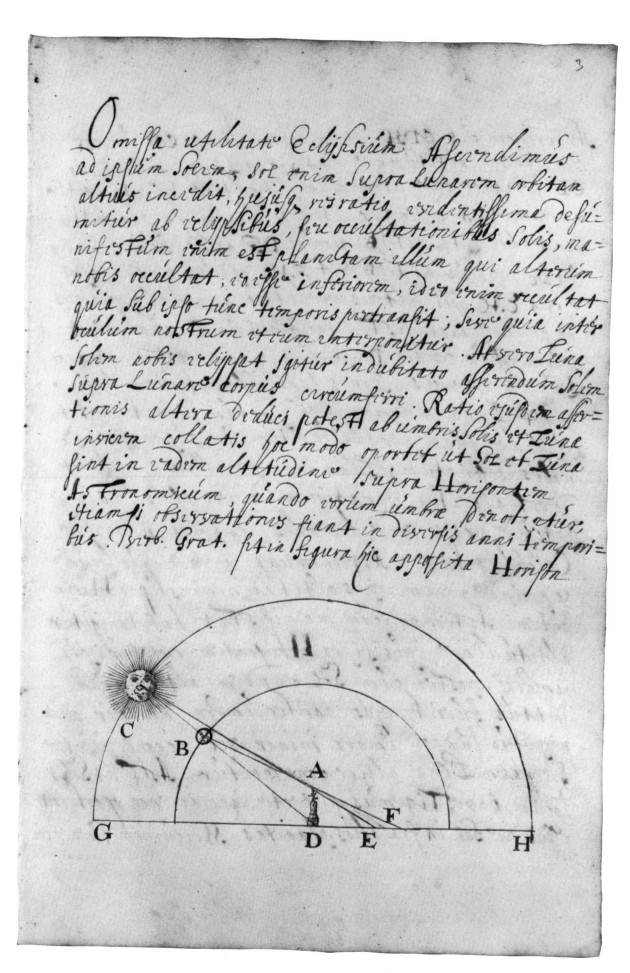

108. Leovitius, *Omissa Utilitati Eclypsium* [Reports on the usefulness of the eclipses]
(1560?) first page of a manuscript work (reduced)

FRANCISCI
LEVERAE
ROMANI
PRODROMVS

VNIVERSAE ASTRONOMIAE RESTITVTAE

De Anni Solaris, & Siderei, ac Dierum magnitudine in omni Æuo, &
de reliquis Periodis, Motibus, & Circulationibus Solaribus admi-
randis, adhuc incognitis, ac etiam Sidereis, ab Authore explora-
tis, & inuentis, ac plenè dilucidatis per demonstrationes
Arithmeticas, aliafque plures probationes.

Et propterea exhibentur Radices, & Tabulæ multiplices dictorum Motuum, Periodorum,
& Reuolutionum perpetuo veracissimæ ab eodem Authore exantlata ad longitudinem
Almæ Vrbis, & exindè Vniuersales per differentiam Meridianorum aliarum
Vrbium, & Locorum, quorum hic datur Catalogus; cum noua Metho-
do supputandi ad quælibet secula exactissimè dictos motus Sola-
res, & Sidereos omnes, ad vsus, & vtilitates præclariſ-
fimas infrà explicatas.

Motus omnes Solares primo editi sunt, quia ab his, tanquam fundamento, & basi,
præcognitis, maximè pendet integra adinuentio, & supputatio motuum
reliquorum Planetarum, nec non Terreni Globi immobilitas,
de quibus vberrimè in sequentibus editionibus.

ROMÆ M. DC. LXIII.

Ex Typographia Angeli Bernabò.   *Superiorum Permissu.*

AN APPENDIX

TO

CLAVIS HOROLOGIÆ:

OR AN

EXPLICATION

OF THE

PYRAMIDICAL DYAL

Set up

In His Majesties Garden at *White-Hall*, Anno 1669.

IN WHICH

Very many Sorts of DYALS are contained; by which besides the Hours of all Kinds diversly expressed, many things also belonging to *Geography*, *Astrology*, and *Astronomy*, are by the Suns Shadow made visible to the Eye.

AMONGST WHICH,

Very many Dyals, especially the most Curious, are new Inventions, hitherto divulged by none.

All these Particulars are shortly, yet clearly set forth for the common Good,

By the Reverend Father *Francis Hall*, otherwise *Line*, of the Society of *Jesus*, Professor of *Mathematicks*.

Printed at *Liege*, by *Guillaume Streel*, in the Year of ourLord 1673. And Reprinted at *London*, 1685.

110. Line, *An Appendix to Clavis Horologiae* (1685) title page

111 MAIGNAN, EMANUEL, 1601–76

Perspectiva Horaria sive de Horographia Gnomonica

Rome: Philipp Rube, 1648

32 cm. 705 pages, 43 leaves of plates (2 folding). Magnificently illustrated with superb copper-engraved plates. Marginalia including corrections. First edition.

Born at Toulouse, France, Maignan entered the religious order of Minims in 1619. Early in life he showed a strong interest in mathematics. He taught philosophy at the Minim convent of Monte Pincio, Rome, from 1636 to 1650. He was an original and individualistic thinker. *Perspectiva Horaria* is an exhaustive study of sundials (*DSB*, v. 9, p. 25).

Lalande, p. 226

NUC: IU; MH

---

112 MANILIUS, MARCUS, fl. Rome, ca. A.D. 9–14

Astronomicon

Nürnberg?: n.p., 1471?

23 cm. 78 leaves. Marginalia. Verso of the leaf following the colophon has a one-page inscription in two different hands beginning: "Anno 1478...." Bound in vellum over boards.

Lalande (p. 9) says this edition was the first printed book on astronomy and was printed at Nürnberg undated between 1471 and 1473. He also attributes its printing to Regiomontanus (1436–76) although his name does not appear in the book.

Manilius's life is a mystery. He is known only through this incomplete Latin poem on astrology, the *Astronomicon*, which its author began to compose while Augustus was still Roman emperor. The text concerns the sphere, the zodiac, constellations, comets, and related topics.

Lalande, p. 9

NUC: no copy

Goff: ChL; HarvCL; HEHL; NYHisSL

---

113 MANILIUS, MARCUS, fl. Rome, ca. A.D. 9–14

Astronomicon.

Strasbourg: J. J. Bockenhofer, 1655

22 cm. 136 pages. Frontispiece. Bound with this work is Scaliger, J., *Castigationes et Notae in M. Manilii Astronomicon,* 1655 (item 167).

Zinner Collection

Houzeau, 501; Lalande, p. 239

NUC: CSdS; CU; DLC; ICN; ICU; IEN; MdBJ; MA; MH; MiU; MnU; NjP; NN; NcD; OkU

---

114 MANILIUS, MARCUS, fl. Rome, ca. A.D. 9–14

Astronomicon.

Padua: Joseph Cominus, 1743

18 cm. 113 leaves. Illustrations, decorative woodcuts, and initial letters.

Zinner Collection

Lalande, p. 419

NUC: CSdS; ICU; INS; MiU; MH; NN; OkU; WU

PERSPECTIVA
HORARIA
SIVE DE HOROGRAPHIA
GNOMONICA TVM THEORETICA,
TVM PRACTICA LIBRI QVATVOR.

In quibus Gnomonices antiqui fines latiùs protenduntur: traditurque ratio,& delineatio Geometrica expeditiſſima non ſolùm communium, quæ radio directo vel vmbra pariter directa; ſed etiam aliorum nouæ inuentionis Solarium horariorum, quæ radio vel vmbra tum reflexis tum refractis horas, aliaque ad cœleſtium motuum notitiam pertinentia indicant.

In his verò præcipuam admirationem habet Thaumantias Catoptrica atque Dioptrica, id eſt reflexus, ac refractus à ſpeculo cylindrico ſolaris radius, omnes, qui in Sphæra cogitari poſſunt, circulos gnomonicè reddens Iridis modo ac ſpecie:

Lux quoque ſecundùm propriam naturam ſumpta ſuas ibi habet partes, vbi è principijs eius phyſicis ratio redditur reflexionum,ac refractionum eiuſdem. Conſequitur verò methodus certiſſima teleſcopium efficiendi non modò ſphæricum ſed etiam hyperbolicum atque ellipticum.

Autore R. P. F. EMANVELE MAIGNAN Toloſate, Ordinis Minimorum in Regio nationis Gallicanæ Romano S S. Trinitatis montis Pincij Cænobio Sacræ Theologiæ Profeſſore.

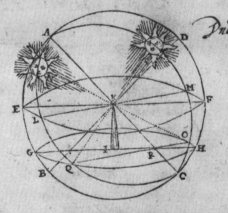

ROMAE.
Typis, & Expenſis Philippi Rubei.
M. DC. XXXXVIII.
Cum Licentia Superiorum.

---

111. Maignan, *Perspectiva Horaria* [Perspectives on sundials] (1648), title page (reduced)

111. Maignan, *Perspectiva Horaria* (1648) plate (reduced)

111. Maignan, *Perspectiva Horaria* (1648) frontispiece (reduced)

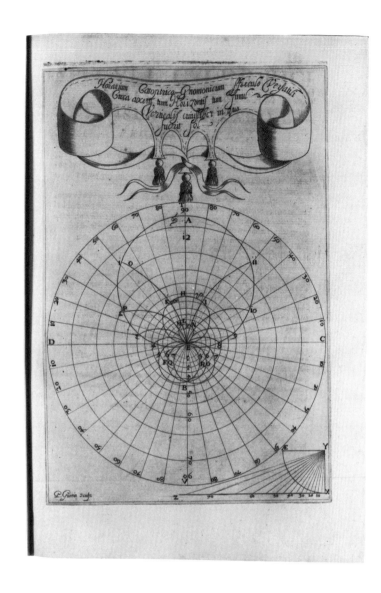

111. Maignan, *Perspectiva Horaria* (1648) (reduced)

111. Maignan, *Perspectiva Horaria* (1648) (reduced)

Marci Manilii astronomicon liber primus incipit

Armine diuinas artis & conscia fati
Sydera diuersos hominum uariantia casus:
Cælestis rationis opus deducere mundo
Aggredior:primusq3 nouis helicóa mouere
Cantibus: & uiridi nutantis uertice siluas.
Hospita sacra serens nulli memorata priorum
Nunc mihi tu cæsar patriæ princepsq3 paterq3 /
Qui regis augustis parentem legibus orbem /
Concessumq3 patri mundum deus ipse meteris /
Das animum uiresq3 facis ad tanta canenda.
Iam propiusq3 fauet mundus scrutantibus ipsum.
Et cupit ethereos per carmina pandere sensus /
Hoc sub pace uacat tantum iuuat ire per ipsum
Aera & immenso spaciantem uiuere cælo .
Signaq3 & aduersos stellarum noscere cursus /
Quod solum nouisse parum est :impensius ipsa
Scire iuuat magna penitus precordia mundi.
Queque reget generetq3 suis animalia signis
Cernere & in numerum phæbo modulante referre.
Bina mihi positis lucent altaria flammis /
Ad duo templa precor duplici circundatus aestu /
Carminis & rerum certa cum lege canentem /
Mundus & immenso uatem circum strepit orbe /
Vixq3 soluta suis immittit uerba figuris?
Quem primum interius licuit cognoscere terris
Munera cælestum quis enim condentibus illis
Clepsisset furto mundum quo cuncta reguntur?

Invocatio

facis. is breue.

clepsisset

112. Manilius, *Astronomicon* [Compendium on astronomy] (1471?) incipit

Anno · 1478 · die · 25 · Januarii · hora · 2 · noctis · Lune diei

Astro: magno Inf. pagi: ibidem regat corrige·

Advertendum est / corpora universi orbis inter se ordine quodam coniungi / ut
continentiae et contenta / loci ambitu. Terra etenim ab aqua / Aqua ab aere
aer ab igne / ignis a spera Lune / lune vero spera ab alia / continetur
spera / quo pacto usque ad ultimam licet progredi. veluti igitur minime
absonum videtur / in eodem universo ponere aliquod corpus ita contentum /
quod nullo modo ei locus continens alterius / ut Terra / Similiter In con-
veniens non erit / dare corpus aliquod / quod situ sit locus continens alterius / et quod nullo modo sit in loco / nec ab aliquo contentum / Infra / Ultima sphera esse aiunt / sive celum / quod primum mobile nuncupat /
supra quod empyreum existat / ut Theologi tradidere / ubi beatorum locus
est / preter quod / nec locus / nec motus / nec Tempus est. ut 2 de ce-
lo et mundo Aristo: scripsit: sacerdotum i sexto principi: 1o

Spere octo perhibentur a philosophis . s. stelliferum celum / saturnus / Iuppiter
mars / sol / venus / mercurius / et luna /

112. Manilius, *Astronomicon* (1471?) manuscript page at end of the volume

198

113. Manilius, *Astronomicon* (1655) title page

115 MARINONI, GIOVANNI JACOPO DE, 1676–1755

De Astronomica Specula Domestica et Organico Apparatu Astronomico

Vienna: Leopold J. Kaliwoda, 1745

36 cm. 236 pages. First edition. Bound in calf, one of the most exquisitely illustrated astronomical works ever printed. The copper-engraved plates are sharp, forty-three of them are folding. There are eighteen smaller plates and many vignettes, decorated initials, and borders.

This work is a catalogue of the great collection of astronomical instruments assembled in the Vienna Observatory.

Marinoni was born in Udine, Italy (the Austrian border area) and studied in Vienna. He was appointed Imperial Court Mathematician and in 1726 became Director of the Academy of Geometry and Military Science. He visited Bologna and later Paris to see astronomical instruments in use there before designing and building an observatory in Vienna.

Lalande, p. 426

NUC: DLC; DN-Ob; ICJ; IU; MB; MiU; NNE; WU

116 MAURO, MARCO, of Florence, Servite, 1493–1556

Annotationi sopra la lettione della spera del Sacro Bosco

Florence: L. Torrentino, 1550

23 cm. 219 pages. Many woodcut illustrations and diagrams in the text. Large woodcut illustration on title page.

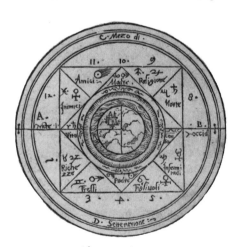

title-page vignette

Earlier editions appeared in 1537 and 1547.

Lalande, p. 69

NUC: CaBVaU; CLU; DFo; DLC; ICJ; ICU; IU; InU; MB: MH; MiU; NN; RPB; RPJCB; WU

117 MEMMO, GIOVANNI MARIA, d. 1553

Tre libri della sostanza et forma del mondo

Venice: G. de Farri, 1545

20 cm. 78 leaves. Many woodcut illustrations. Bound in contemporary limp vellum.

First and only edition of an astronomical cosmographical treatise.

NUC: ICN; MH; MiU; NN; OkU; WU

118 MERCATOR, NICOLAUS, 1619?–87

Institutionum Astronomicarum Libri Duo, de Motu Astrorum

London: William Godbid, for sale at Samuel Simpson, Cambridge, 1676

19 cm. 352 pages. Diagrams, tables. Modern half-calf binding. Provenance, title page: "A. Freeman." First edition.

Not to be confused with the famed Dutch geographer Gerardus Mercator, Nicolaus Mercator (originally Niklaus Kauffmann), born at Eutin, Schleswig-Holstein, was a mathematician and astronomer. He graduated from the University of Rostock and was appointed to its faculty of Philosophy in 1642. His tract on calendar improvement caught Cromwell's attention after which he went to England and resided there for nearly thirty years. He made his living in London as a tutor in mathematics. He was elected to the Royal Society in 1666 and came into contact with Newton. The two books of his *Institutiones Astronomicae* (1676) offered the student an excellent grounding in contemporary theory, and Newton used them to fill gaps in his rather shaky knowledge of planetary and lunar theory. Newton's lightly annotated copy is now at Trinity College, Cambridge (*DSB*, v. 9, pp. 310-2).

Lalande, p. 284

NUC: CLU-C; CSt; CU; CtY-M; DFo; DGU; DLC-P4; IU; MiU; NhD; PPL; OkU; RPB

DE

ASTRONOMICA
SPECULA

DOMESTICA

ET

ORGANICO

APPARATU ASTRONOMICO

LIBRI DUO

REGINÆ

DICATI

A JOANNE JACOBO MARINONIO

PATRICIO UTINENSI,

Cæfareo antehac, nunc Regio Mathematico & Confiliario;
Inclytorum Statuum Inferioris Auftriæ Mathematico,
Scientiarum Academiis Bononienfi & Neapolitanæ adfcripto.

Jo.Chrift.Winnikler.Sc.

VIENNÆ AUSTRIÆ M. DCC. XLV.
Excudebat LEOPOLDUS JOANNES KALIWODA.

115. Marinoni, *De Astronomica Specula Domestica* [Concerning the domestic astronomical studies]
(1745) title page (reduced)

115. Marinoni, *De Astronomica Specula Domestica* (1745)
interior view of observatory (reduced)

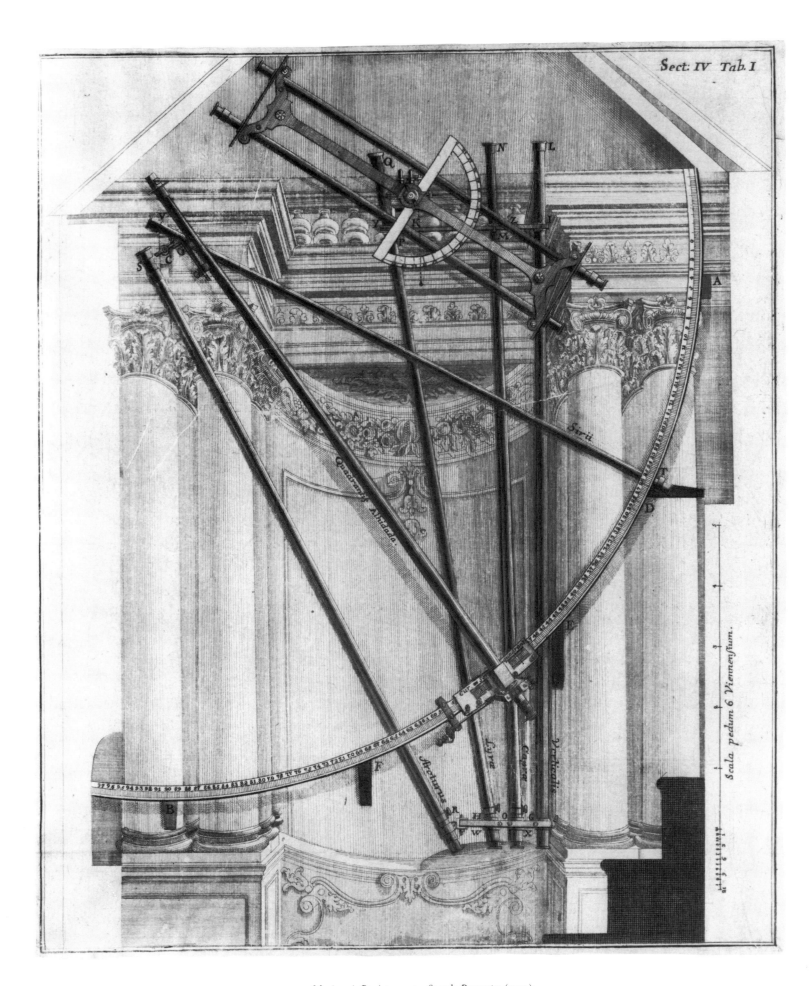

115. Marinoni, *De Astronomica Specula Domestica* (1745)
frontispiece telescopes (reduced)

115. Marinoni, *De Astronomica Specula Domestica* (1745)
frontispiece (reduced)

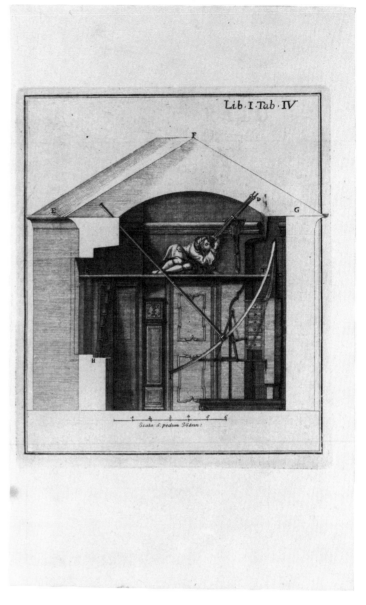

115. Marinoni, *De Astronomica Specula Domestica* (1745)
an astronomer at work (reduced)

Nomi de i Caratteri de i Pianeti, per chi non conoscessi quelli; & delli. 4. Elementi.

Elementi. 4.

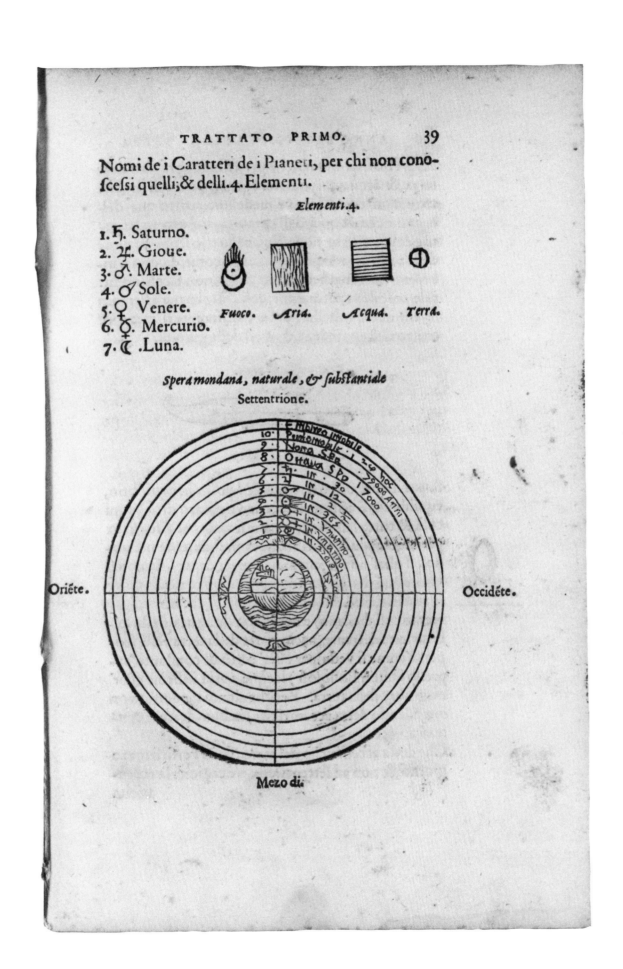

1. ♄. Saturno.
2. ♃. Gioue.
3. ♂. Marte.
4. ☉ Sole.
5. ♀. Venere.
6. ☿. Mercurio.
7. ☾. Luna.

Fuoco.   Aria.   Acqua.   Terra.

Spera mondana, naturale, & substantiale

Settentrione.

Oriéte.

Occidéte.

Mezo di.

116. Mauro, *Annotationi sopra la lettione della spera del Sacro Bosco*
[Annotations on the lessons of the sphere of Sacro Bosco] (1550)
earth-centered celestial sphere

TRE LIBRI

DELLA SOSTANZA ET FOR
ma del Mondo del Clarissimo M. Giouan
Maria Memo, Dottor & Caualiere.

Ne quali per modo di Dialogo si disputano molte acutissime questioni, & sono poi risolute con
le ragioni de i piu saui Philosophi, &
de i piu dotti Astrologi antichi.

Con i priuilegi del sommo Pontefice Paulo III. della Maestà Ce-
sarea, & dell'Illustrissimo Senato Venetiano per anni diece.

117. Memmo, *Tre libri della sostanzo et forma del mondo* [Three books on the substance
and form of the world] (1545) title page

NICOLAI MERCATORIS
Holfati, è Soc. Reg.
INSTITUTIONUM
ASTRONOMICARUM
LIBRI DUO,
DE MOTU
ASTRORUM
COMMUNI & PROPRIO,
Secundum Hypotheses Veterum
& Recentiorum præcipuas;
DEQVE
Hypotheseon ex observatis conftructione:
CUM
TABULIS TYCHONIANIS
Solaribus, Lunaribus, Lunæ-Solaribus,
Et *RUDOLPHINIS* Solis, Fixarum,
Et Quinque Errantium;
Earumque Usu Præceptis & Exemplis commonftrato.
QVIBUS ACCEDIT
APPENDIX
De iis, quæ Noviffimis temporibus
Cœlitus innotuerunt.

LONDINI,
Typis *Gulielmi Godbid,* fumtibus *Samuelis Simpfon*
Bibliopolæ Cantabrigienfis. 1676.

118. Mercator, *Institutionum Astronomicarum Libri Duo, de Motu Astrorum* [Astronomical fundamentals
on the movement of the stars in two books] (1676) title page

119 MICALORI, JACOMO, 1570–1645

Della sfera mondiale

Urbino: M. Mazzantini, 1626

20 cm. 152 pages. Woodcut illustrations.

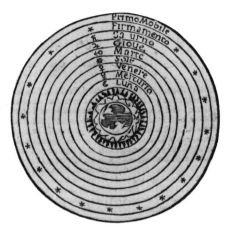

earth-centered celestial sphere

Little-known treatise on celestial orbs according to the Ptolemaic system.

NUC: MiU; OkU; RPJCB; WU

120 MISNER, AEGIDIUS

Beschreibunge des Cometen... Anno M.D.LXXII

Erfurt: Conrad Dreher, 1573

20 cm. 10 leaves. Provenance, recto fly leaf: "Hans Ludendorff"; his ex Libris is inside front cover. Bound with this title is Misner's *Elegia de Cometa.*

Zinner Collection

Lalande, p. 99; Zinner, 2636

NUC: CSdS

121 MISNER, AEGIDIUS

Elegia de Cometa... Anni M.D.LXXIII

Erfurt: Conrad Dreher, 1573

20 cm. 3 leaves. Bound with item 120.

Zinner Collection

Zinner, 2636

NUC: CSdS

122 MOLLER, ALBIN

Gründlicher und warer Bericht von dem newen Cometstern

Eisleben: J. Gaubisch, 1605

21 cm. 8 leaves. Illustrations.

Lalande, p. 143; Zinner, 4058

NUC: CSdS

123 MONTANARI, GEMINIANO, 1633–87

L'astrologia convinta di falso

Venice: F. Nicolini, 1685

23 cm. 158 pages. Marginalia, portrait of Montanari.

Montanari was born at Modena and was active in astronomy, geophysics, biology, and ballistics. One of his last works, *L'astrologia convinta di falso*, contains many autobiographical notes. At age twenty he was sent to Florence to study law. Later at Vienna he became interested in Galileo's ideas and acquired proficiency in mathematics and astronomy. After returning to Italy he began teaching these subjects at the University of Bologna in 1664 where he spent his most productive years. The volume of his work was enormous. He also fought battles against astrology throughout his life and succeeded in banning it from universities (*DSB*, v. 9, pp. 484f.).

Zinner Collection

NUC: DLC; ICU; NIC; NN

124 MONTANARI, GEMINIANO, 1633–87

La fiamma volante gran meteora

Bologna: Manolessi, 1676

21 cm. 48 leaves. Folding plate. Vignette on title page. Ex Libris Hans Ludendorff.

Zinner Collection

NUC: CSdS; DFo; NIC

DELLA
SFERA MONDIALE
DEL SIGNOR
IACOMO MICALORI
CANONICO D'VRBINO
LIBRI QVATTRO.

Ne' quali compendiofamente fi moftra quanto è neceffario
a generale intelligenza di Sfera : con alcune cofe cu-
riofe a tal materia appartenenti.

INCIEL

CON QVESTA

SI SPATIA.

IN VRBINO,

Appreffo Marc' Antonio Mazzantini. 1626.
CON LICENZA DE' SVPERIORL

6rgsris. ss+ggeb eirgsqeeb3r. Maemaee 1627

Beschreibunge des

Cometen/Welcher in dem Himli=
schen zeichen des Stiers mense Nouembri, Anno
M. D. LXXII. angefangen hat
zu erscheinen.

VNA CVM ELEGIA DE
eodem Cometa.

AVTORE M. AEGIDIO
MISNERO LIPSENSE.

IACTA EST ALEA.

Gedruckt zu Erffurdt / Durch
Conradum Dreher/ zum rothen Creutze / bey
Sanct Michel.

120. Misner, *Beschreibunge des Cometen* [Description of the comet] (1573) title page

Gründlicher vnd warer Bericht/
Von dem newen Cometstern / so in der
Lufft vnter dem Himmel gesehen / nach dem
Niedergang der Sonnen/ in October vnd
Novemb. des M. DC. IV. Jahrs.

Jderman zu getrewer Warnung / mit vleis beschrieben vnd an Tag gegeben / Durch

M. Albinum Mollerum von Straupitz/ in dem Marggraff-
thumb Nderlausitz/ alten Theologum vnd Astronomum.

Erstlich Gedruckt zu Eißleben durch Jacobum Gaubisch/
Jm M. DC. V. Jahr.

122. Moller, *Gründlicher und warer Bericht von dem newen Cometstern*
[Fundamental and true report concerning the new comet star] (1605)
title page with portrait of Moller

Trà la Pag. VIII., e IX.

123. Montanari, *L'astrologia convinta di falsi* [Astrology convicted of falseness]
(1685) portrait of Montanari

LA FIAMMA VOLANTE

GRAN METEORA

Veduta sopra l' Italia la sera de 31.
Marzo M.DC.LXXVI.

SPECVLAZIONI FISICHE, ET ASTRONOMICHE
Espresse dal Dott. GEMINIANO MONTANARI
Professore delle Scienze Matematiche nello
Studio di Bologna

IN VNA LETTERA

All' Illustriss. & Eccellentiss. Sig. il Sig. Marchese

FEDERICO GONZAGA

De Marchesi di Mantoua, Prencipe del S. R.
Imperio, Nobile Veneto, &c.

In BOLOGNA, Per li Manolessi.   M.DC.LXXVI.
Con licenza de' Superiori.

124. Montanari, *La fiamma volante gran meteora*
[The flaming, flying great meteor] (1676) title page

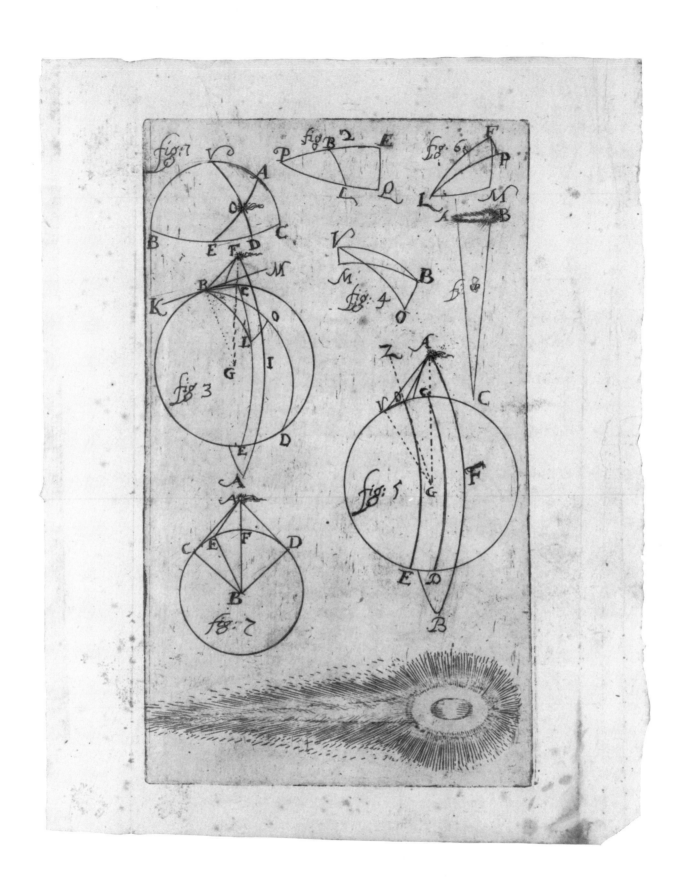

124. Montanari, *La fiamma volante gran meteora* (1676) diagram

125 MOXON, JOSEPH, 1627–1700

A Tutor to Astronomy and Geography

London: T. Roycroft, 1674

21 cm. 283 pages. Illustrations, full-calf binding. Provenance, inside back cover: "T. Collisgaw."

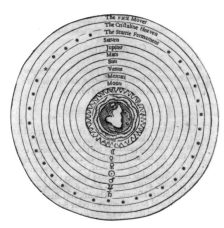

geocentric sphere

Moxon was a hydrographer and mathematician born at Wakefield, Yorkshire. Skilled in smithing, engraving, printing books and pictures, globe and map making, he operated a shop selling books, maps and instruments. He was elected a fellow of the Royal Society in 1678.

NUC: CU; CtY-M; DLC; FU; MH; MnU; NcD; NcU; RPJCB

126 MULERIUS, NICOLAUS, 1564–1630

Tabulae Frisicae Lunae-Solares

Alkmaar: J. Meester, 1611

24 cm. Quarto. 287 leaves. Illustrations, tables. Bound in modern full leather, gold lettering on spine. Author's signature page 8. First edition.

Mulerius, or sometimes Muliers, was a physician and mathematician best known for having edited the third edition of Copernicus's *De Revolutionibus Orbium Coelestium* (1617). Born at Bruges, Belgium, he received his doctor of medicine degree at the University of Leiden. He later became professor of medicine and mathematics at the University of Groningen where he also served as the librarian. He published several books in the field of astronomy including one on the astrolabe, ephemerides, lunar and solar tables, and one on Copernicus (*Iselin*, v. 5, p. 237).

Lalande, p. 155

NUC: CtU; DN-Ob; NNC; OU; OkU; WU

127 MÜLLER, JOHANN ULRICH

Der unbetrügliche Stünden-Weiser

Ulm: In Verlag Johann Conrad Wohler. Gedruckt durch Matthaeum Schmidt, Marchtall, 1702

18 cm. 333 leaves. Illustrations, tables, many copper-engraved plates, some folding. Title in red and black. Bound in tooled vellum over boards. Signature on title page. First edition. Later editions appeared in 1712 and 1715.

The author was a German mathematician and historian who lived at Ulm at the end of the seventeenth century. He is known for his books on mathematics and astronomy and for one on sundials (*Iselin*, v. 5, p. 220).

Zinner Collection

NUC: CSdS; ICJ; MH

128 NESS, CHRISTOPHER, 1621–1705

A Full and True Account of the Late Blazing-Star

London: J. Wilkins, 1680

18 cm. 8 pages. First edition.

Ness (or Nesse) was an English divine and a Calvinist dissenter. He was educated at Saint John's College, Cambridge, where he received B.A. and M.A. degrees.

NUC: MH

129 NESSTFELL, JOHANN GEORG, 1694–1762

Kurz-gefasste...Beschreibung der...Copernicanischen Planeten-Machine

Bamberg: G. A. Gertner, 1761

33 cm. 67 pages. Three copper-engraved plates, exquisite woodcuts.

Nesstfell studied the making of astronomical globes at Banz Monastery in Germany. Thereafter he designed and built planetariums including a Copernican model that brought him to the attention of Emperor Francis I, who appointed him Court Artificer (*Hofmechaniker*) in Vienna.

NUC: CSdS

A TUTOR TO
Aſtronomy and Geography.

Or an eaſie and ſpeedy way to know the USE of both the

GLOBES,
Cœleſtial and *Terreſtrial*.

In Six BOOKS.

The
1. Teaching the Rudiments of *Aſtronomy* and *Geography*.
2. { Shewing by *Aſtronomical* and *Geographical* Problemes.
3. { the Globes } Problemes in *Navigation*.
4. { the ſolution } *Aſtrological* Problemes.
5. { of } *Gnomonical* Problemes.
6. { *Trigonometrical* Problemes.

More fully and amply than hath yet been ſet forth, either by
Gemma Friſius, Metius, Hues, Wright, Blaew, or any others that have
taught the Uſe of the GLOBES: And that ſo Plainly and Metho-
dically, that the meaneſt Capacity may at firſt reading apprehend it, and
with a little practice grow expert in theſe Divine Sciences.
With an APPENDIX ſhewing the Uſe of the *Ptolomaick Sphere*.

***

The Third Edition Corrected and Enlarged.

***

By JOSEPH MOXON, *Hydrographer to the King's moſt Excellent Majeſty.*

Whereunto is added the Antient *Poetical ſtories of the Stars*: ſhewing
Reaſons why the ſeveral ſhapes and forms are pictured on the *Cœleſtial Globe.*

As alſo a Diſcourſe of the *Antiquity, Progreſs* and *Augmentation* of *Aſtronomy.*

***

Job XXVI. 7.13.

*He ſtretcheth out the North over the empty place, and hangeth the Earth upon nothing.
By his Spirit he hath garniſhed the Heavens: His hand hath framed the crooked Serpent.*

LONDON,

Printed by *Tho. Roycroft*, for *Joſeph Moxon*: and Sold at his Shop on
Ludgate-Hill, at the ſign of *Atlas*. MDCLXXIV. *1674*

126. Mulerius, *Tabulae Frisicae Lunae-Solares* [Lunar-solar Frisian tables] (1611) title page

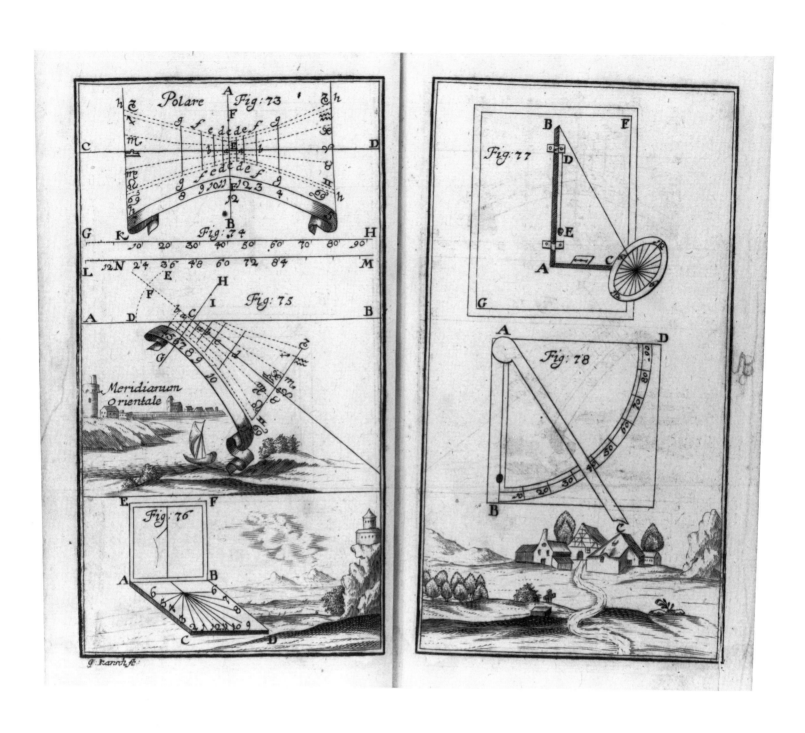

127. Müller, *Der unbetrügliche Stünden-Weiser*
[The unerring timekeeper] (1702) diagrams

218

A

Full and True ACCOUNT

Of the Late

BLAZING·STAR:

With some probable Prognosticks upon what may be its Effects.

1680.

A Blazing Star is called a *Comet* from the Latin word *Coma*, the Hair, because it seemeth to send forth Streamers of flaming Hair to those that behold it a far off. There be various Opinions of Authors concerning those *Comets*; some whereof are so improbable, that only to report them, is enough to refute them. As, 1. *Democritus* dreamed that *Comets* were the Souls of famous Men triumphing in Heaven. 2. *Thaddeus* thinketh that they are the Secrets of Nature, and (like the occult Quality of Philosophers) ought not to be enquired after. 3. *Paracelsus* supposeth that they are Fires carried about by Spirits which are conscious of their own Fates. 4. *Anaxagoras* imagines them to be a Conjunct Apparition of Planets; because when Planets come near together they seem to touch one another, and that Conjunction of 2 or 3 Lights into one, causeth the *Phænomenon*, or Appearance of a longer Star; which by varying its Place, varieth its Form also. 5. *Appianus* and *Prætorius* (both) acknowledge that *Comets* are Meteors, or Vapours exhaled, yet deny that they are inflamed, or set on fire in their own Bodily Matter, but only enlightned by the Refract Rays of the Sun and other Stars, both upon its Body and Tail. 6. But this last Opinion of *Aristotle* is most probable; that a *Comet* is a Fiery Meteor made up of Copious, Viscous and Fat Vapours, drawn up into the highest Region of the Air by the influence of the Sun and Stars; and then when it is ripened, taketh Fire, and shineth in the Figure of a Star, to

128. Ness, *A Full and True Account of the Late Blazing-Star* (1680) page one

130 NEWTON, SIR ISAAC, 1642–1727

Opera quae Exstant Omnia

London: J. Nichols, 1779–85

30 cm. 5 volumes. Copper-engraved plates (three folding), tables, diagrams. Bound in full calf. Two ex Libris: Lord Berwick and Franz Sondheimer.

This most famous edition of Newton's collected works was edited by Samuel Horsley. Manuscript inscription on the flyleaf of Volume one: "Dilecto suo filio E. T. M. Phillipps hoc volumina. E libris Thomae Parkinson, S.T.D. in avunculi memoriam amantissimi d.d. S.T.M.P. Dec. 16, 1830." A similar inscription appears in Volume five. Volume two has dedicatory Latin verse by Edmund Halley.

NUC: CLSU; CSmH; CU; DFo; DLC; DN-Ob; IaU; ICJ; MdAN; MdBP; MWiW-C; MiU; MoSW; NN; NWM; NjP; NjNbS; NcU; OCU; ODW; OO; OU; PBm; WU

131 NEWTON, SIR ISAAC, 1642–1727

Philosophiae Naturalis Principia Mathematica

Cambridge: n.p., 1713

26 cm. 260 leaves. One folding plate and numerous diagrams. Bound in full calf, paneled spine. Second edition, limited to 750 copies. Ex Libris Henry Poole Hepburn.

printer's vignette

Contains important preface by Cotes attacking the Cartesian philosophy, a second preface by Newton and extensive additions such as the chapters on the lunar theory of comets being much enlarged from the first edition.

NUC: CaBVaU; CLL; CLSU; CLU-C; CSt; CU; CtY; ICJ; ICU; IU; KU; MB; MBdAF; MCM; MH; MiU; MnU; NIC; NNC; NPV; NcRS; PPI; PU; TxU; UU; WaWW

132 NEWTON, JOHN, 1622–78

Astronomia Britannica Exhibiting the Doctrine of the Sphere

London: Printed for the Author by R. and W. Leybourn, 1657

20 cm. 169 leaves. Decorated initials. Diagrams and astronomical tables. Bound in full leather. Part I appeared in 1657. Parts II and III were printed in 1656. Marginalia. Provenance: Book I, verso of title page, "Thomas Benneworth, Ejus Liber, July 3d 1786"; recto of preliminary leaf 3, "Christopher Stothard's Book 1756."

title-page vignette

John Newton, mathematician and astronomer (unrelated to Sir Isaac Newton), was born at Oundle, Northamptonshire. He graduated from Saint Edmund Hall, Oxford, B.A. in 1641 and M.A. in 1642. He was the author of twenty-two books on mathematics and astronomy.

Lalande, p. 244

NUC: CLU-C; IU; MH; NNC; PPL; RPB; TxU

133 NOLTHIUS, ANDREAS, fl. 16th century

Observatio und Beschreibung des newen Cometen

Erfurt: S. Paul, 1573

21 cm. 10 leaves.

Zinner Collection

Zinner, 2637

NUC: CSdS

ISAACI NEWTONI

OPERA

QUÆ EXSTANT OMNIA.

COMMENTARIIS ILLUSTRABAT

SAMUEL HORSLEY, LL. D. R. S. S.

REVERENDO ADMODUM IN CHRISTO PATRI

ROBERTO EPISCOPO LONDINENSI A SACRIS.

LONDINI:

EXCUDEBAT JOANNES NICHOLS.

M DCC LXXIX.

130. Newton, I., *Opera* [Works] (1779–85) title page (reduced)

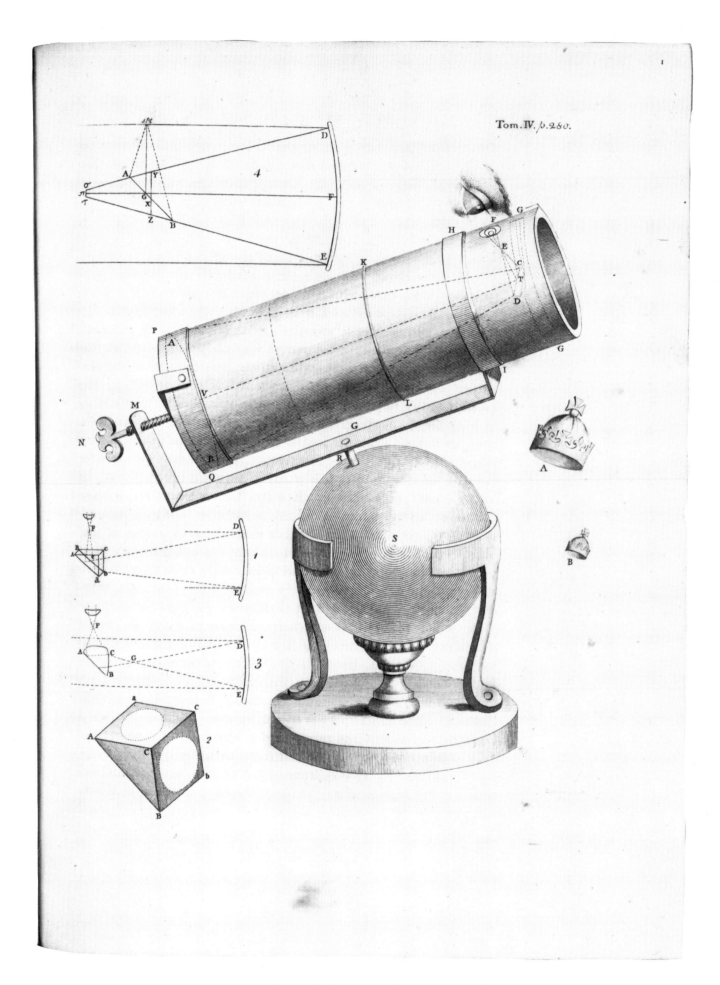

130. Newton, I., *Opera* (1779–85) telescope (reduced)

PHILOSOPHIÆ
NATURALIS
PRINCIPIA
MATHEMATICA.

AUCTORE
ISAACO NEWTONO,
Equite Aurato.

Editio Secunda Auctior et Emendatior.

CANTABRIGIÆ, MDCCXIII.

131. Newton, I., *Philosophiae Naturalis Principia Mathematica* [The mathematical principles of natural philosophy] (1713) title page

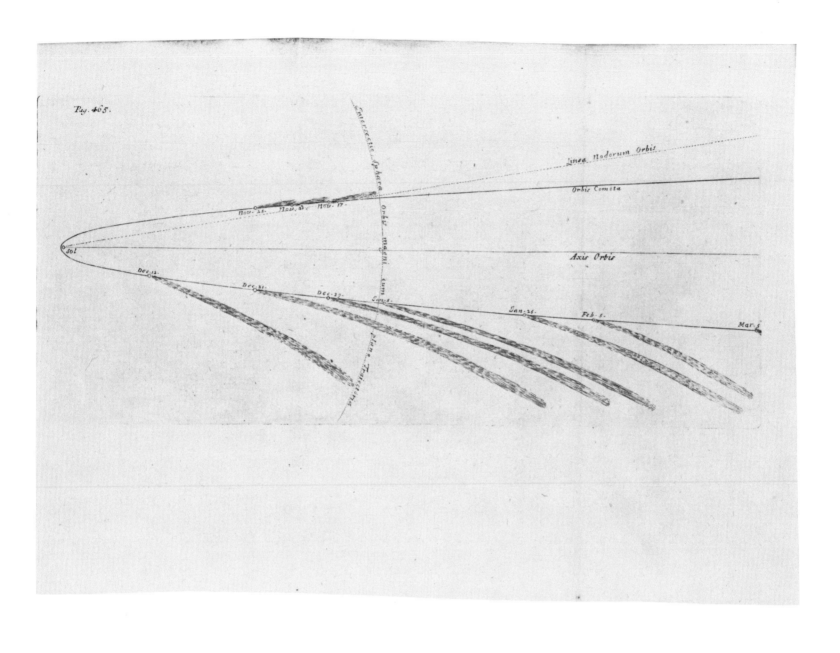

131. Newton, I., *Philosophiae Naturalis Principia Mathematica* (1713)
folding plate showing the path of a comet (reduced)

Astronomia
BRITANNICA,

Exhibiting

The Doctrine of the Sphere, and
Theory of the Planets Decimally
by Trigonometry, and by Tables.

Fitted for the Meridian of *LONDON*,
according to the *Copernican* Systeme
As it is illustrated by *Bullialdus*, and the easie way
of Calculation, lately published by
Doctor *WARD*.

By JOHN NEWTON, *M. A:*

LONDON,
Printed for the Author, by *R.* and *W. Leybourn*, and are to be
sold by *Thomas Pierrepoint*, at the Sun in St. *Pauls* Church-
yard, 1 6 5 7.

132. Newton, J., *Astronomia Britannica Exhibiting the Doctrine of the Sphere* (1657) title page

OBSERVATIO

vñd Beſchreibung des Ve=
wen Cometen/ ſo vmb das ende des 1572. vnd
noch in dieſem 73. Jar erſchienen/ Ge-
ſchehen vnd geſtellet/ Durch

Andream Nolthium Mathematicum.

Gedruckt zu Erffurdt/ zum bundten Lawen,
bey Sanct Paul.

133. Nolthius, *Observatio und Beschreibung des newen Cometen*
[Observation and description of the new comet] (1573) title page

134 NOSTRADAMUS, MICHAEL, 1503–66

The True Prophecies or Prognostications of Michael Nostradamus, Physician to Henry II. Francis II. and Charles IX. Kings of France, and One of the Best Astronomers that Ever Were. Translated and Commented by Theophilus de Garencières

London: Printed by Thomas Ratcliffe, and Nathaniel Thompson, and are to be sold by John Martin, at the Bell in St. Pauls Church-yard..., 1672

29 cm. Folio. 18 preliminary leaves, 522 pages. Title page printed in red and black. Decorated initials and headpieces. Although an English language version appeared in Antwerp in 1558, this is the first one published in England. Translator Theophilus de Garencières (1610–80) was a French physician who lived in England from 1636 until his death.

Nostradamus (or Michel de Notredame) was born at Saint-Rèmy in Provence. He studied medicine at the University of Montpellier where he came into bitter conflict with the faculty. He left there in 1532 leading the life of an itinerant physician until 1547 when he married a wealthy widow at Salon near Marseilles. Eight years later, claiming divine inspiration for his astrological forecasts, he published the first of his books of prophecies. They have been reprinted, translated, interpreted and commented upon in hundreds of editions for the titillation of kings and commoners alike ever since.

Although he earned both admiration and enmity already in his own time, the controversy over the credibility of his vague prognostications endures. Astronomers and many others judge him a charlatan. (*DSB*, v. 10, pp. 152–3).

Three professors of astronomy at San Diego State University objected to including Nostradamus in any catalogue of astronomical works. Of course, he was not an astronomer and he contributed nothing to astronomy. The works of other astrologers, however, are also listed in this catalogue. Many astronomers among the ancients, even as late as the sixteenth century, were concerned about the meaning of the stars and their influence on mankind. Kepler cast a horoscope for Count Albrecht von Wallenstein in ca. 1611 (Arthur Beer, *Kepler: Four Hundred Years*, Oxford: Pergamon Press, 1975, p. 449).

NUC: CLU-C; CSmH; CtY; DLC; IU; MiU; MWiW-C; NjN; N; NIC; NN; NNNAM; NPV; OCl; PPL; PU; TU; ViU.

---

135 *Observatio Viennensii Cometae*

Vienna?: 1742?

16 cm. 1 leaf. Holograph manuscript in Latin script on paper.

136 ORIGANUS, DAVID, 1558–1628

Annorum Priorum 30 Incipientium ab Anno Christi 1595, & Definentium in Annum 1624, Ephemerides Brandenburgicae Coelestium Motuum et Temporum

Frankfurt an der Oder: J. Eichhorn, 1609

26 cm. 566 leaves. Bound in hand-tooled vellum over boards.

Origanus (Tost) was professor of mathematics and Greek at the University of Frankfurt an der Oder beginning in 1586. Prior to that he was a professor at the University of Wroclaw.

Zinner Collection

Zinner, 4248

NUC: no copy

137 ORSINI, LATINO, 16th century

Trattato del radio latino

Rome: Marc' Antonio Moretti, 1586

18 cm. 128 pages. Second edition. Illustrations, diagrams. Vignette on title page. Bound in contemporary vellum over boards. Manuscript notes on front and back flyleaves.

Zinner Collection

NUC: CU; CtY; DFo; DLC

138 PERLACH, ANDREAS, ca. 1500–51

Commentaria Ephemeridum

Vienna: Egidius Aquila, 1551

21 cm. 111 leaves. Tables, diagrams. First and only edition of an early book on astronomy. Finely printed by one of Vienna's greatest typographers.

Perlach, teacher of astronomy at Vienna, published ephemerides for various years in the second quarter of the sixteenth century. His earliest ephemeridum that Lalande lists is for the year 1529.

Lalande, p. 73; Zinner, 2023

NUC: WaPS

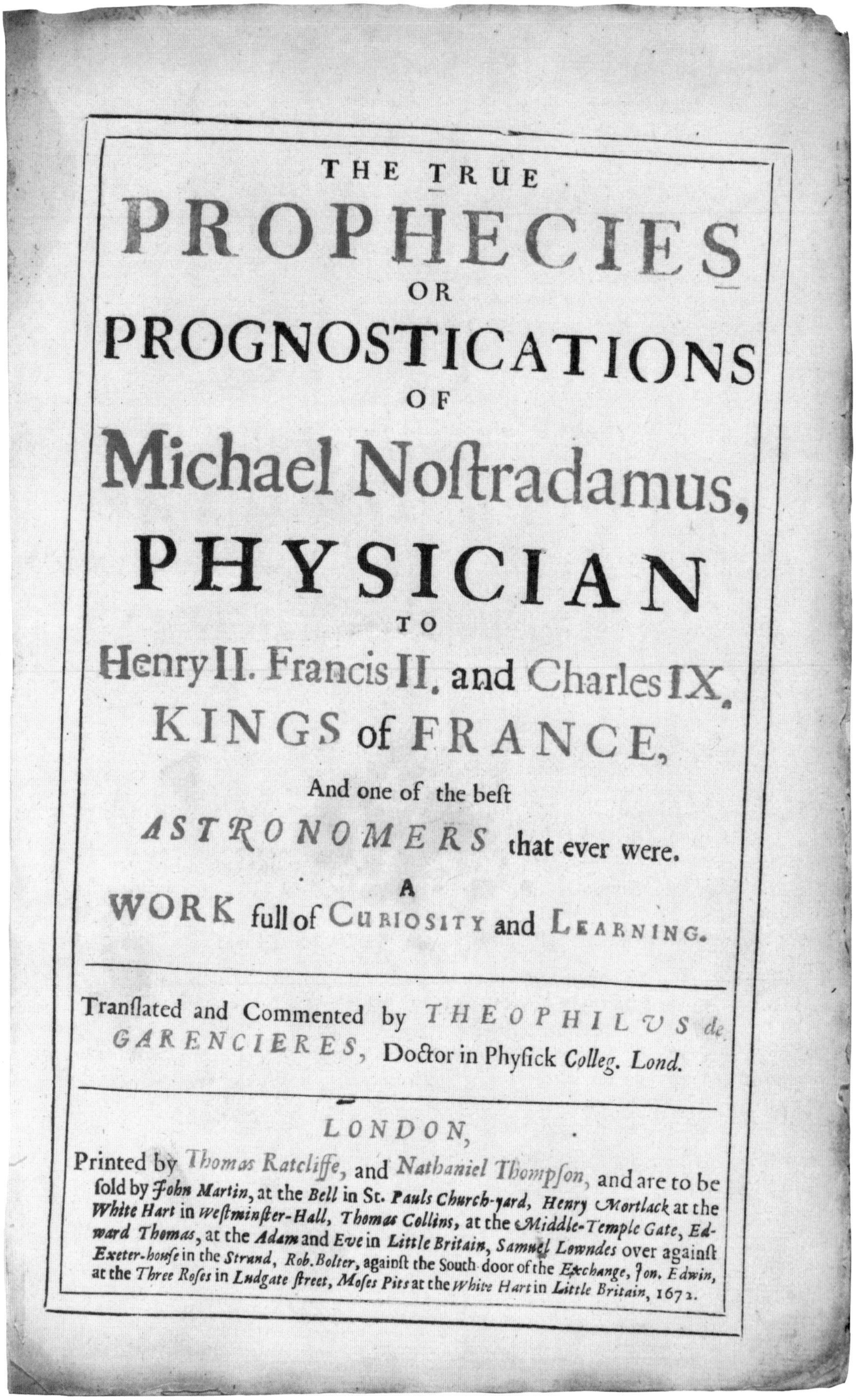

THE TRUE

PROPHECIES

OR

PROGNOSTICATIONS

OF

Michael Nostradamus,

PHYSICIAN

TO

Henry II. Francis II. and Charles IX.

KINGS of FRANCE,

And one of the best

ASTRONOMERS that ever were.

A

WORK full of CURIOSITY and LEARNING.

Translated and Commented by *THEOPHILVS de GARENCIERES*, Doctor in Physick *Colleg. Lond.*

LONDON,

Printed by *Thomas Ratcliffe*, and *Nathaniel Thompson*, and are to be sold by *John Martin*, at the *Bell* in St. *Pauls Church-yard*, *Henry Mortlack* at the *White Hart* in *Westminster-Hall*, *Thomas Collins*, at the *Middle-Temple Gate*, *Edward Thomas*, at the *Adam* and *Eve* in *Little Britain*, *Samuel Lowndes* over against *Exeter-house* in the *Strand*, *Rob. Bolter*, against the South-door of the *Exchange*, *Jon. Edwin*, at the *Three Roses* in *Ludgate street*, *Moses Pits* at the *White Hart* in *Little Britain*, 1672.

134. Nostradamus, *The True Prophecies or Prognostications* (1672) title page (reduced)

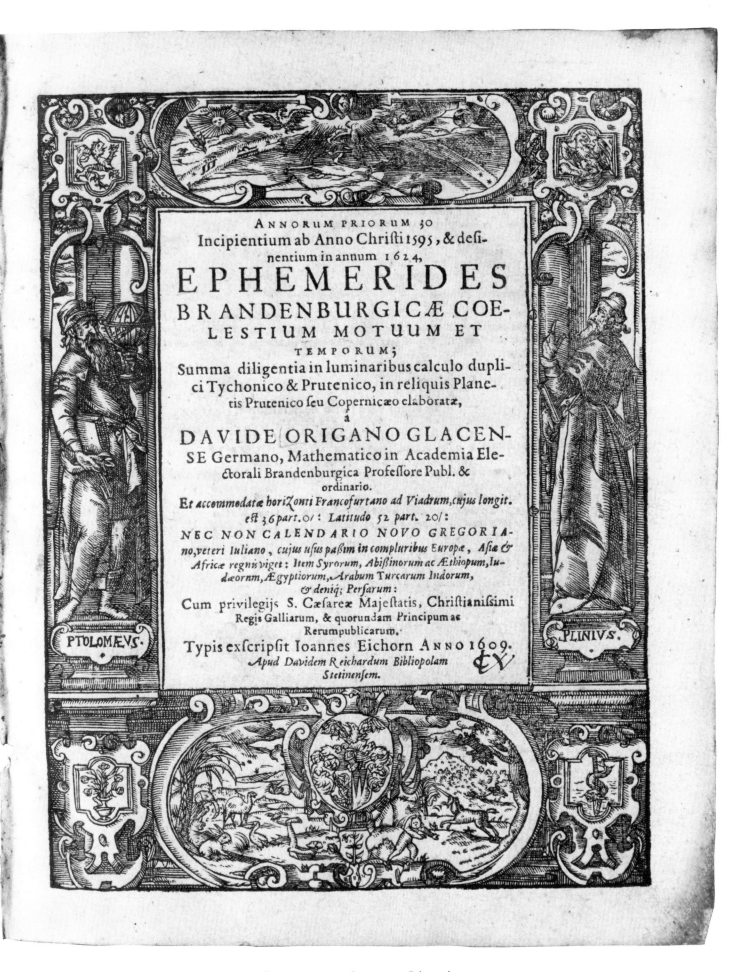

ANNORUM PRIORUM 30
Incipientium ab Anno Christi 1595, & defi-
nentium in annum 1624,
EPHEMERIDES
BRANDENBURGICÆ COE-
LESTIUM MOTUUM ET
TEMPORUM;
Summa diligentia in luminaribus calculo dupli-
ci Tychonico & Prutenico, in reliquis Plane-
tis Prutenico feu Copernicæo elaboratæ,
à
DAVIDE ORIGANO GLACEN-
SE Germano, Mathematico in Academia Ele-
ctorali Brandenburgica Professore Publ. &
ordinario.
Et accommodatæ horizonti Francofurtano ad Viadrum, cujus longit.
eft 36 part. 0/ : Latitudo 52 part. 20/ :
NEC NON CALENDARIO NOVO GREGORIA-
no, veteri Iuliano, cujus usus passim in compluribus Europæ, Asiæ &
Africæ regnis viget: Item Syrorum, Abissinorum ac Æthiopum, Iu-
dæornm, Ægyptiorum, Arabum Turcarum Indorum,
& deniq; Persarum:
Cum privilegijs S. Cæsareæ Majestatis, Christianissimi
Regis Galliarum, & quorundam Principum ac
Rerumpublicarum.
Typis exscripsit Ioannes Eichorn ANNO 1609.
Apud Davidem Reichardum Bibliopolam
Stetinensem.

PTOLOMÆVS.

PLINIVS.

136. Origanus, *Annorum Priorum 30...Ephemerides*
[Ephemerides for thirty prior years] (1609) title page

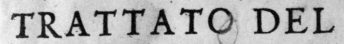

TRATTATO DEL
RADIO LATINO

Istrumento giustissimo & facile più d'ogni
altro per prendere qual si voglia mi-
sura, & positione di luogo, tanto
in Cielo come in Terra :

*Il quale, oltre alle operationi proprie sue, fà anco tutte
quelle della gran Regola di C. Tolomeo, & del
antico Radio Astronomico,*

Inuentato dall' Illustrissimo & Eccellentissimo
Signor Latino Orsini,

*Con li Commentarij del Reuerendo Padre Maestro Egnatio Danti
da Perugia, hoggi Vescouo di Alatri, & da esso di nuouo
ricorretto, & ampliato con molte nuoue operationi .*

CON LICENZA DE'SVPERIORI.

IN ROMA *Appresso Marc'Antonio Moretti, &*
Iacomo Brianzi. M. D. LXXXVI.

137. Orsini, *Trattato del radio latino* [Treatise concerning the plain radius] (1586) title page

AND. PERLACHII COMMENTA.

Typus Eclipseos Lu-
næ.

SEPTENTRIO.

SECVNDÆ PARTIS
commentariorum
finis.

138. Perlach, *Commentaria Ephemeridum* [Commentary on the ephemerides] (1551) diagram

139 PEURBACH, GEORG, 1423–61

Novae Theoricae Planetarum

Venice: D. Melchior Sessa, 1537

16 cm. 40 leaves. Woodcut diagram on title page and forty-one woodcuts in the text. Printer's device on verso of last leaf. Contemporary manuscript annotations in ink. A 1485 edition of this work appears in Sacro Bosco (item 156). Bound with Sacro Bosco, J., *Liber de Sphaera*, 1541 (item 161).

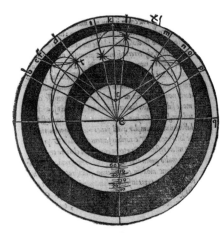

diagram

Peurbach (or Peuerbach) received his B.A. in 1488 and M.A. in 1453 from the University of Vienna after which he taught astronomy there. He traveled and lectured through Germany, France, and Italy, enjoying an international reputation. Emperor Frederick III appointed him Imperial Court Astrologer in 1457. His most famous student and associate was Regiomontanus (Johannes Müller von Königsberg, 1436–76). Peurbach's book *Theoricae Novae Planetarum* is an elementary but thorough textbook of planetary theory describing the solid sphere representations of Ptolemaic planetary models. Zinner states that fifty-six editions were published up to the middle of the seventeenth century (*DSB*, v. 15, pp. 473ff.).

NUC: Thirty-three editions, but no copy of this 1537 edition.

140 PEURBACH, GEORG, 1423–61

Theoricae Novae Planetarum

Paris: C. Wechel, 1543

17 cm. 64 leaves. Bound in contemporary limp vellum. Woodcut illustrations, diagrams, two folding plates. Provenance, title page: "Collegii Ballearii Monti Sion"(?).

Lalande, p. 62

NUC: NN; RPB

141 PICCOLOMINI, ALESSANDRO, 1508–78

De le stelle fisse

Venice: G. Varisco, 1570

21 cm. 125 leaves. Woodcut initials and diagrams; tables, star charts. Bound with item 142.

Piccolomini was a broadly educated Italian philosopher and writer on philosophy and science. In 1557 he was appointed archbishop of Patrasso and later of Siena.

NUC: CtY; DFo; DLC; MH; NIC; NcD; PPD; WU

142 PICCOLOMINI, ALESSANDRO, 1508–78.

La sfera del mondo

Venice: Giovanni Varisco, 1573

21 cm. 182 leaves. Marginalia. Bound in contemporary vellum over boards. Also bound with this title is his *De le stelle fisse*, 1570 (item 141).

Lalande, p. 97

NUC: CtY; DFo; DLC

interceptus. Sed motus accessus & recessus est arcus circuli parui inter caput Arietis mobilis & intersectionem æquatoris & circuli parui per medietatem circuli septentrionalem progrediendo. Hoc motu contingit ut stellæ fixæ uideantur nunc moueri uersus orientem, nunc uersus occidentem, nunc motu ueloci, nunc motu tardo. Nam cum fuerit caput Arietis mobilis in quartis parui circuli ab æqua-

Theorica ultima octauæ Sphæræ.

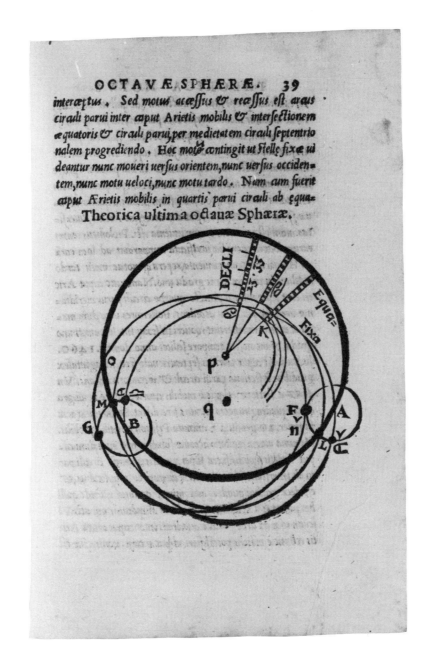

139. Peurbach, *Novae Theoricae Planetarum* [New theories of the planets] (1537) diagram

233

THEORI·
CAE NOVAE PLANE-
TARVM GEORGII PVR-
bachij fœliter incipiunt.

FIGVRA NOVEM SPHAERA-
rum & elementorum ordinem designans.

A. *Terra.*
B. *Aqua*
C. *Aer*
D. *Ignis.*
E. *Luna*
F. *Mercurius*
G. *Venus*
H. *Sol*
I. *Mars*
K. *Iuppiter*
L. *Saturnus*
M. *firmametũ*
N. *zodiacus*
nonæ sphæræ

PARISIIS.
Apud Chriſtianum Wechelum ſub ſcuto Baſilienſi in
uico Iacobæo: & ſub Pegaſo in uico Bellouacenſi.
An. M. D. XLIII.

Collegii Balearis Montis ſion.

140. Peurbach, *Theoricae Novae Planetarum* [New theory of the planets] (1543)
title page with geocentric celestial sphere

tres orbes duo centra tenent. Nam superficies conuexa
supremi & concaua infimi idem centrum habent, quod
est mundi centrum. Vnde tota sphæra solis, sicut & alterius cuiuscunque planetæ tota sphæra concentrica mundo
dicitur esse. Sed superficies concaua supremi atque conuexa infimi una cum utriusque superficiebus medij, unum
aliud, quod centrum eccentri dicitur, habent.

THEORICA TRIVM OR-
bium Solis.

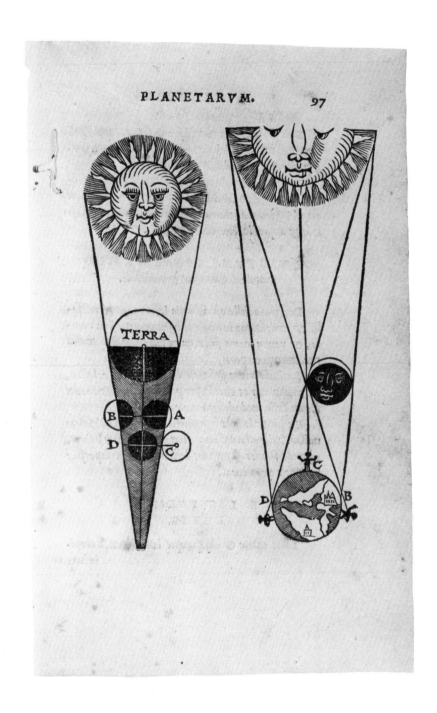

140. Peurbach, *Theoricae Novae Planetarum* (1543)
diagram of an eclipse

DE LE STELLE FISSE
LIBRO VNO,

DOVE DI TVTTE LE XLVIII IMMAGIN CELESTI

minutiſſimamente ſi tratta; & non ſolo le fauole loro ordinatamen-
te ſi narra, ma ancora le figure di ciaſcheduna n'apparon coſi
manifeſte, & diſtintamente diſpoſte & formate, come à
punto per il Ciel ſi diſtendono:

ET OLTRE A QVESTO CI SON TAVOLE, CON

nuoua inuention fabricate, con le lor dichiarationi, coſi facili & chiare,
che per il mezo di quelle & de le figure inſiememente, potra cia
ſcheduno, con marauiglioſa ageuolezza, in ogni tempo de
l'anno, à qual ſi ſia hora di notte, conoſcere non
ſolo le dette immagin nel Cielo, ma qual
ſi voglia ſtella di quelle.

CON PRIVILEGIO.

IN VENETIA

Per Giouanni Variſco, & compagni.   M D LXX.

141. Piccolomini, *De le stelle fisse* [Concerning the fixed stars] (1570) title page

hanno d'hauere li corpi celesti nel gouernare in parte co i monimenti, & co i lumi loro queste cose qua giù da basso. Et quantunque sia molto vniuersalmente allegato, & creduto questo decuplo auanzo degli elementi tra di loro; nientedimanco, come tal oppenione sia falsa, & come s'habbia da intender questo auanzo decuplo, & come lo prende Aristotile, ho dichiarato assai à lungo nel già detto mio libro, della grandezza dell'Acqua, & della Terra? doue io pruouo apertamente esser maggiore questa di quella.

In tal guisa adunque, come habbiamo dichiarato, si diuide essencialmente, & sostantialmente tutta questa gran machina del Mondo; come si può vedere, & imaginare in questa figura.

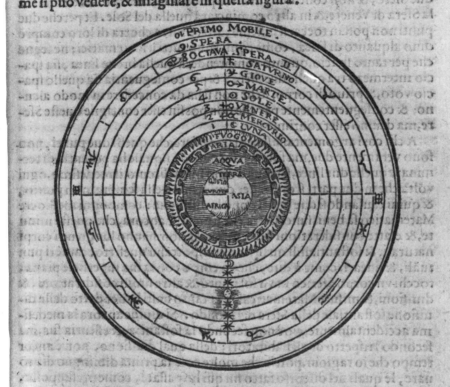

Che le Sfere, nelle quali si è diuiso l'vniuerso, non sono continue tra di loro, ma contigue; & come questo s'intenda. Capo IIII.

HAbbiamo da notare ancora intorno all'ordine & sito delle dette Sfere, che le non sono continuate tra di loro, quantunque si tocchino l'vna l'altra senz'alcun mezo. Percioche quando fusse questo, bisognarebbe,

C 3

142. Piccolomini, *La sfera del mondo* [The sphere of the world] (1573) geocentric sphere

238

143 PLINIUS SECUNDUS, GAIUS, A.D. 23–79

Naturalis Historiae

Venice: Rainald Novimagio Alamani, 1483

32 cm. 354 leaves. Rubricated throughout. Initial letters and paragraph marks in red, a few with scrollwork. Old half leather, gilt-ruled, and a blind-stamped backstrip with gilt lettering and ornaments. Manuscript notes in three different hands and three signatures at the end of the errata.

The first printed edition appeared at Venice in 1469. Seven more editions appeared before this 1483 edition.
 Known as Pliny the Elder, the author was a well-educated Roman who served the empire in Africa, Germany, and Spain. His *Natural History* is an encyclopedia of knowledge about the world in the first century A.D.

NUC: CU; CU-S; CtY; DLC; ICN; IU; KU; MBM; MH; MH-A; NcU; TxU

Goff: BMedL; FolgSL; HarvCL; HEHL; LC; LC(T); McGUL; NewL; NLM; SoMethUL; UKanL; UNCal; WArtGL; YUL

144 PLINIUS SECUNDUS, GAIUS, A.D. 23–79

The Historie of the World. Translated into English by Philemon Holland

London: Adam Islip, 1601

34 cm. 720 leaves. Two volumes bound in one. First English edition. Marginalia. Vignette on title page and decorated initials throughout. Manuscript signature on title page.

Wormser Collection, San Diego State University Library

NUC: CLU-C; CSmH; CSt; CU; CtY; DDO; DFo; DLC; IaU; ICJ; ICN; KyU; MeB; MdAN; MB; MH-A; MWA; MiU; MnU; NIC; NNNAM; NPV; NjP; NcD-MC; NcU; OC; OCl; OrU; PBL; ViU; WU

145 PRAETORIUS, JOHANNES (i.e., HANS SCHULTZE), 1630–80

De Suspecta Poli Declinatione, et Eccentricitate Firmamenti vel Ruina Coeli

Leipzig: Christian Michael, 1675

20 cm. 239 pages. First edition. Text in German and Latin.

Attack on astrologers in the light of the Copernican system.

Lalande, p. 283

NUC: NN

146 PTOLEMAEUS, CLAUDIUS, ca. A.D. 100–ca. 170

Omnia quae Extant Opera

Basel: Heinrich Petri, 1551

32 cm. 264 leaves. Fine printer's device on title and colophon. Two large folding woodcut plates. Numerous woodcut geometrical figures and diagrams, some full page. Old vellum. Marginalia.

constellation

Edited by Erasmus Oswald Schreckenfuchs (1511–97), an Austrian who studied at Ingolstadt, Leipzig and Basel. He later taught mathematics at Tübingen and Freiburg.
 A large section is heavily annotated in an old hand. Many corrections. It might be assumed this copy was owned by a knowledgeable scientist, probably German. Inside the front cover is the engraved ex libris of Aytoun of Inchdairnie. Aytoun is the name of an old Scottish family. Inchdairnie is in Fifeshire, eastern Scotland. The best known Aytoun in recent times was poet William Edmondstoune Aytoun (1813–65). Perhaps he or his father Roger Aytoun placed his bookplate in this volume.
 Ptolemy was the greatest astronomer of Greco-Roman times but knowledge about his life is meager. He was a Greek or a Hellenized Egyptian who lived at Alexandria. His major work, the *Almagest* (a title from Arabic words meaning mathematical or astronomical compilations), is a manual covering the whole of mathematical astronomy as the ancients conceived it. It provides a theoretical basis for their system of the universe by placing an immovable earth at its center with the sun, planets, and stars revolving around it. That "Ptolemaic system" was generally accepted until the sixteenth century when it was displaced by the Copernican system (*DSB*, v. 11, pp. 186–206).

Lalande, p. 71; Zinner, 2026

NUC: CtU; ICJ; IEN; MiU; MnU; NIC; NjP; OkU; PPM; RPB; TxU; WU

*Provenance: "Sum Hortensij/1630", i.e. Martin Hortensius (1605–1639), Dutch astronomer, Copernican; p.269 ref. "D. Lansbergius", i.e. Philips van Lansbergen (1561–1632); p.334, ref. "nova stella", Sept./Oct. 1633
R.S. Westman 8/5/97

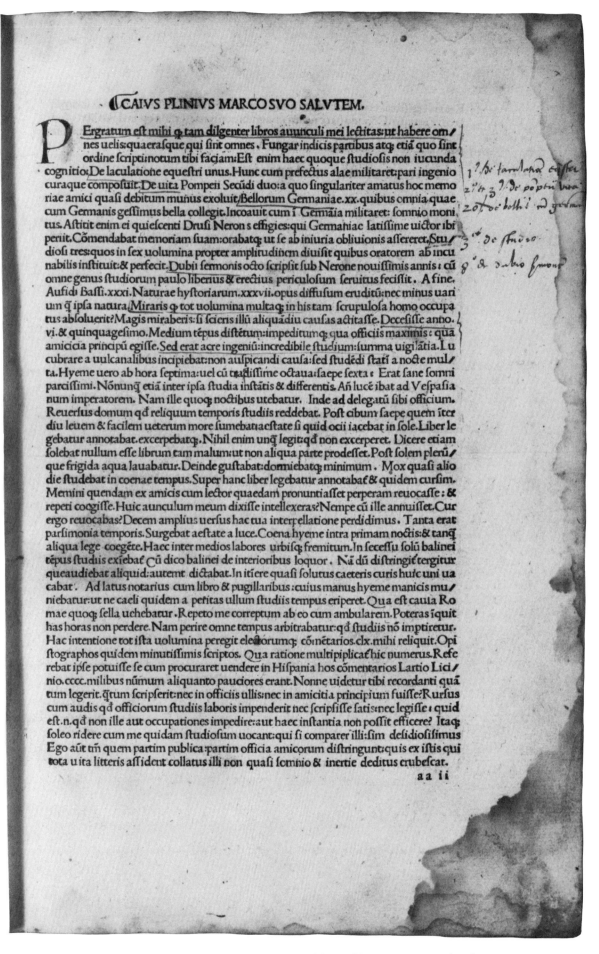

¶CAIVS PLINIVS MARCO SVO SALVTEM.

PErgratum est mihi q̃ tam diligenter libros auunculi mei lectitas:ut habere om/
nes uelis:quaerasque qui sint omnes. Fungar indicis partibus atq; etiã quo sint
ordine scripti:notum tibi faciam:Est enim haec quoque studiosis non iucunda
cognitio:De laculatiõe equestri unus.Hunc cum prefectus alae militaret:pari ingenio
curaque composuit.De uita Pompeii Secũdi duo:a quo singulariter amatus hoc memo
riae amici quasi debitum munus exoluit/Bellorum Germaniae.xx.quibus omnia quae
cum Germanis gessimus bella collegit.Incoauit cum i Germãia militaret: somnio moni
tus.Astitit enim ei quiescenti Drusi Neron s effigies:qui Germaniae latissime uictor ibi
periit.Cõmendabat memoriam suam:orabatq; ut se ab iniuria obliuionis assereret.Stu/
diosi tres:quos in sex uolumina propter amplitudinẽ diuisit quibus oratorem ab incu
nabilis instituit:& perfecit.Dubii sermonis octo scripsit sub Nerone nouissimis annis : cũ
omne genus studiorum paulo liberius & erectius periculosum seruitus fecisit. A fine.
Aufidi Bassi.xxxi.Naturae hystoriarum.xxxvii.opus diffusum eruditũ:nec minus uari
um q̃ ipsa natura.Miraris q̃ tot uolumina multaq; in his tam scrupulosa homo occupa
tus absoluerit?Magis miraberis:si scieris illũ aliquãdiu causas actitasse. Decessisse anno.
vi.& quinquagesimo. Medium tẽpus distẽtum:impeditumq; qua officiis maximis : qua
amicicia principũ egisse. Sed erat acre ingeniũ:incredibile studium:summa uigilãtia.Lu
cubrare a uulcanalibus incipiebat:non auspicandi causa:sed studẽdi statĩ a nocte mul/
ta.Hyeme uero ab hora septima:uel cũ tardissime octaua:saepe sexta. Erat sane somni
parcissimi.Nõnunq; etiã inter ipsa studia instãtis & differentis.Añ luce ibat ad Vespasia
num imperatorem. Nam ille quoq; noctibus utebatur. Inde ad delegatũ sibi officium.
Reuersus domum qd̃ reliquum temporis studiis reddebat. Post cibum saepe quem iter
diu leuem & facilem ueterum more sumebat:aestate si quid ocii iacebat in sole.Liber le
gebatur annotabat.excerpebatq;.Nihil enim unq̃ legit:qd̃ non excerperet. Dicere etiã
solebat nullum esse librum tam malum:ut non aliqua parte prodesset.Post solem plerũ/
que frigida aqua lauabatur.Deinde gustabat:dormiebatq; minimum. Mox quasi alio
die studebat in coenae tempus.Super hanc liber legebatur annotabat & quidem cursim.
Memini quendam ex amicis cum lector quaedã pronuntiasset perperam reuocasse : &
repeti coegisse.Huic aunculum meum dixisse intellexeras?Nempe cũ ille annuisset.Cur
ergo reuocabas?Decem amplius uersus hac tua interpellatione perdidimus. Tanta erat
parsimonia temporis.Surgebat aestate a luce.Coena hyeme intra primam noctis:& tanq̃
aliqua lege coegẽte.Haec inter medios labores urbisq; fremitum.In secessu solũ balinei
tẽpus studiis exiebat cũ dico balinei de interioribus loquor. Nã dũ distringit̃ tergitur
queaudiebat aliquid:autemt dictabat.In itiere quasi solutus caeteris curis huic uni ua
cabat. Ad latus notarius cum libro & pugillaribus:cuius manus hyeme manicis mu/
niebatur:ut ne caeli quidem a petitas ullum studiis tempus eriperet.Qua est cauia Ro
mae quoq; sella uchebatur.Repeto me correptum ab eo cum ambularem.Poteras iquit
has horas non perdere.Nam perire omne tempus arbitrabatur:qd̃ studiis nõ imptiretur.
Hac intentione tot ista uolumina peregit electorumq; cõmetarios.clx.mihi reliquit.Opi
stographos quidem minutissimis scriptos. Qua ratione multipiplicat̃ hic numerus.Refe
rebat ipse potuisse se cum procuraret uendere in Hispania hos cõmentarios Lartio Lici/
nio.cccc.milibus nũmum aliquanto pauciores erant.Nonne uidetur tibi recordanti quã
tum legerit.q̃tum scripserit:nec in officiis ullis:nec in amicitia principium fuisse?Rursus
cum audis qd̃ officiorum studiis laboris impenderit nec scripsisse satis:nec legisse. quid
est.n.qd̃ non ille aut occupationes impedire:aut haec instantia non possit efficere? Itaq;
soleo ridere cum me quidam studiosum uocant:qui si comparer illi:sim desidiosissimus
Ego aũt tñ quem partim publica:partim officia amicorum distringunt:quis ex istis qui
tota uita litteris assident collatus illi non quasi somnio & inertie deditus erubescat.

aa ii

143. Plinius, *Naturalis Historiae* [History of the world] (1483) incipit (reduced)

THE
HISTORIE
OF THE WORLD.

Commonly called,

THE NATVRALL HISTORIE OF
C. PLINIVS SECVNDVS.

Translated into English by PHILEMON HOLLAND
Doctor in Physicke.

The first Tome.

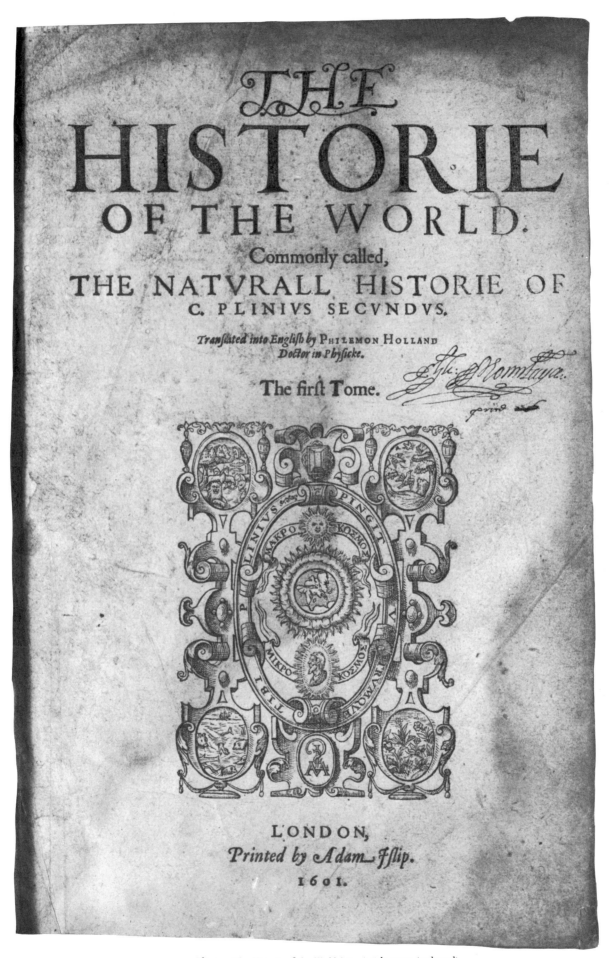

LONDON,
Printed by Adam Islip.
1601.

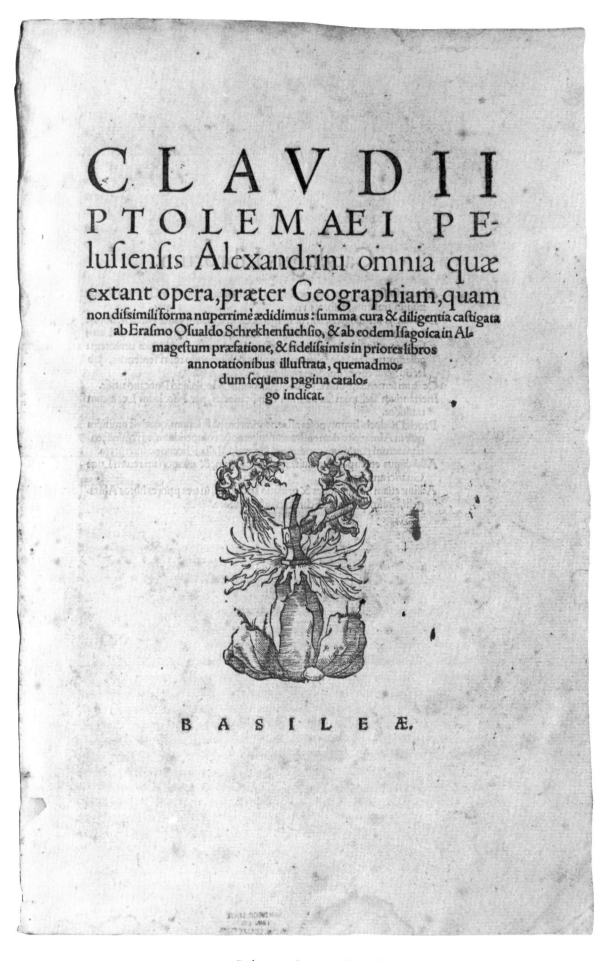

CLAVDII
PTOLEMAEI PE-
lusiensis Alexandrini omnia quæ
extant opera, præter Geographiam, quam
non dissimili forma nuperrimè ædidimus : summa cura & diligentia castigata
ab Erasmo Osualdo Schrekhenfuchsio, & ab eodem Isagoica in Al=
magestum præfatione, & fidelissimis in priores libros
annotationibus illustrata, quemadmo=
dum sequens pagina catalo=
go indicat.

BASILEÆ.

146. Ptolemaeus, *Omnia quae Extant Opera*
[All the existing works] (1551) title page (reduced)

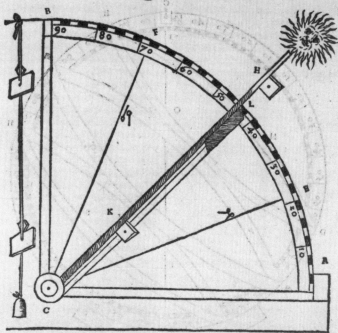

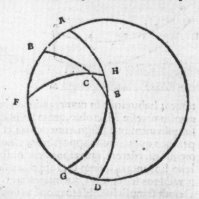

ctura & uſu huius quadrantis. Nunc ſequi-

tur alterum inſtrumentum, quo ueteres ma
thematici uſi ſunt in indagãdis æquinoctijs
à quibus pendet annui temporis cognitio,
nec non in indagandis ſolſtitijs. Cuius ſtru
ctura ſic ſe habet : præparetur primùm duo
circuli æquales & mediocres magnitudine,
quorum ſuperficies diligentiſſimè ſint præ
paratæ, hoc eſt, ad normam politæ, alter ſit
pro meridiano & diuidat in 360. partes æ-
quales, ſicut eſt circulus A B D G in hac figura, alter uerò referat planũ æquatoris, & ſit
circulus A Q P. Et cùm aliquãdo hoc ſequẽ-

ti inſtrumẽto obſeruetur ingreſſus Solis in
pũcta ſolſtitialia, poſſunt etiam duo tropi-
ci adiũgi, quemadmodũ ſunt minores duo
circuli B N Ɔ tropicus æſtiualis, & H R S tropicus brumalis, qui æquè ſunt diligẽter po
liendi ac ſuperiores duo: hij quatuor circuli
adaptentur meridiano ad angulos rectos,
nõ ſecus ac in ſphæra materiali coluris, quo
facto, fabricetur ſedes inſtrumẽti ad formã
F T G Y H cuius pars F T G ſit excauata, ut queat
at in ea uolui, hoc eſt, eleuari & deprimi, po
ſtremò adiungatur perpendiculum I R K in
puncto uertitis I ut ſit uolubile. Et cum uolueris eo uti, ponito ſuper planũ L M, ſuper
lineam meridianã L V, quod planũ ſit per-
pendiculare ad horizontale planum: ſic ſi-
tuato inſtrumento directè ad planum meri
diani, eleuetur circulus meridionalis à pun
cto T uerus G ſecundũ quantitatẽ comple-
menti polaris altitudinis loci tui, aut nume
ra à puncto A uerſus C polarem: altitudinẽ
& demitte perpendiculum à uerticali puncto, quo facto, obſerues circa æquinoctiũ,
& cum tota ſuperficies æquatoris ſuperior
A P Q illuminabitur, ac concauitas eius fuerit tota obumbrata circa æquinoctium uer-
nale, dicas eo tempore Solem eſſe in ipſo æ
quinoctio, & ſic agẽdũ eſt etiã in reliẽ pun
cto ẽquinoctiali. De ſolſtitijs nõ eſt alia ratio
niſi quòd

ctangulo B N X circumscribitur 360 . ipsa uerò linea B X talium 8 . 3 . qualium est B N quæ rectum angulum subtendit 120 . qualium igitur est B X linea 2 . 39 . & semidiame

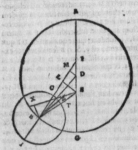

ter excentrici 60 . talium etiam erit B N epicycli semidiameter 39 . 30 . proximè , quare proportio etiam semidiametri excentrici ad semidiametrum epicycli proportio est quam 60 . habent ad 39 . 30 .

De emendatione periodicorum motuum Martis. Cap. IX.

Sed gratia etiam emendationis periodicorum motuum unam cœpimus de priscis obseruationibus , qua declaratur quòd anno 13 , secundum Dionissium Capricornionis 05 , stella Martis matutina cernebat boreali Scorpionis incumbere fronti, est tempus obseruationis in anno 52 . à morte Alexandri. hoc est, annis 476 . à Nabonassaro, Athir secundū Aegyptios die 20 . sequente 21 . in mane . In quo tempore medium motum Solis inuenimus Capricorni gradus obtinentem 23 , 54 . Fixa uerò quæ est in boreali fronte Scorpionis à nobis obseruata est, etiam distas à Scorpione gradibus 6 . 10 . Quoniam igitur anni 409 . qui fuerunt ab obseruatione usq̃ ad Antoninum, progressus fixarum facit gradus quatuor, & 5 . sexagesimas proximè, fixa (quam diximus) in tempore illius obseruationis 2 . 15 . gradus Scorpionis obtinuisse debet, totidem ergo etiam stella Martis obtinuisse similiter, quoniam etiam tempore nostro, id est, in principio Antoniniani imperii, maxima longitudo Martis 25 . 30 . Cancri gradus obtinebat debet in tempore obseruationis 21 . 25 . obtinuisse, patet

igitur quòd stella quidem apparens 100 , gradibus , & sexagesimis 50 , tunc à maxima longitudine distabat . Medius uerò motus ☉ ab eadem longitudine maxima gradib. 182 . 19 . ab apposita autem minima quæ longitudine 2 . 29 .

				Tempore
♂	23	54	♑	Ptolemæi
☉	25	30	♋	Ptolemæi
♂	21	85	♋	Priscorum
Differen.	4	5	In	annis 409
✱	6	20	♏	Ptolemæi
✱	2	15	♏	Priscorum
Different.	4	5	In	409. annis

54 grad. 4. M.5. adijciantur.

¶ His ita suppositis, sit A B G, centrum epicycli, deferens excentricus, cuius centrum D, & diameter A D G. In qua zodiaci centrum sit E, maioris autem excentricitatis sit E, & descripto in centro B epicyclo I T, protrahantur F B I, & D B & M B I nec, & à puncto F ad lineam D B ducatur perpendicularis F C, & supponatur stellam esse in T puncto epicycli, & coniuncta linea B T, trahatur à puncto B ipsi æquidistans linea E L à qua uidelicet per ea, quæ iam demonstrata sunt, medius motus Solis erit coniunctaq̃ linea E T, ducantur ad ipsam à punctis D, & B perpendiculares D M, & B N, & similiter à puncto D ad lineam B N perpendicularis, D X, ut figura D M N X rectangulum parallelogramum siat. Quoniam igitur medius motus apparentis motus stellæ à maxima longitudine talium est partium 100 . & sexagesimarū 50 . qualium quatuor recti sunt 360 . angulus uerò medius motus Solis G E L 2.19 . earundem erit etiam angulus T E L, hoc est , angulus B T E talium 81 . 39 . qualium quatuor recti sunt 360 . qualium uerò duo recti sunt 360 . taliū 163 . 18 . qua re arcus etiam lineæ B N talium est 163 . 18 . qualium est circulus, qui rectangulo B T N circumscribitur 360 . ipsa uerò linea B N talium 118 . 43 . qualium est T B, quæ rectum angulum subtendit 120 . quare qualium est B T semidiameter epicycli 39 . 30 . & E D quæ est inter centra 2 . talium 163 . 18 . qualium uerò centra 2 . talium 163 . 18 . qualium uerò duo recti sunt 360 . taliū 201 . 40 . ac ideo, qui deinceps angulus D E M 158 . 20 . earundem , erit etiam arcus D M talium 159 . 30 . qualiū est circulus qui

qui D E M rectangulo circumscribitur 360 . ipsa uerò linea D M talium 117 . 52 . qualium est D E quæ rectum angulum subtendit 120 . quare qualium est D B linea 2 . & B N 39 . 5 . talium etiam erit D M, hoc est , N X 5 . 54 . et reliqua B X talium 8 . 3 . qualium est B D semidiameter excetrici 60 . quare qualium est

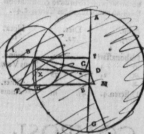

B D, quæ rectum angulum subtendit 120 . talium etiam erit B X 66 . 18 . & arcus suus talium 67 . 4 . proximè, qualium est circulus, qui rectangulo B D X circumscribitur 360 . & angulus igitur B D X talium est 67 . 4 . qualium duo recti 360 . totus uerò B M 247 . 4 . est autem etiā E D M angulus 21 . 40 . earundem , propterea quòd D E M angulus demonstratus est esse 158 . 20 . & reliquus igitur B D E angulus 225 . 24 . esse colligitur, & qui deinceps est angulus B D A 134 . 36 . similiter, quare arcus etiam F C talium est 134 . 36 . qualium est circulus qui rectangulo D F C circumscribitur 360 . & arcus D C 45 . 24 . reliquorum ad semicirculum; chordæ igitur etiam suæ F C quidē talium erit 110 . 42 . qualium est D F, quæ rectum angulum subtendit 120 . D C uerò 46 . 18 . earundem , quare qualium est D F linea 2 . & D B semidiameter excentrici 60 . talium F C erit 5 . 32 . & D C 2 . 19 . & reliqua chorda C B 57 . 41 . ideo etiam B F quæ rectum angulum subtendit

57 . 57 . proximè earundem à qualium igitur B F 110 . talium F C quidem erit 11 . 28 . & arcus suus 10 . 58 . talium qualium est circulus, qui rectangulo B C F circumscribitur 360 . quare angulus etiam F B D talium est 10 . 58 . qualium duo recti sunt 360 . sed erat etiam angulus B D A 134 . 36 . earundem , totus igitur B F A angulus earundē est 145 . 34 . qualium uerò quatuor recti sunt 360 . talium est 72 . 47 . quare medius (secundum longitudinem stellæ motus, hoc est , à centrum epicycli distabat in tempore obseruationis proposita à maxima longitudine gradibus 72 . 47 . & propterea 4 . 12 . Libræ gradus obtinebat, uerum quoniam etiam G E L angulus 2 . 19 . earundem supponitur , qui iam duobus rectis semicirculi A B G æqualis est, reliquus igitur A F B mediæ longitudinis angulo, & I B T inæqualitatis, hoc est , angulo medius motus stellæ in epicyclo habebimus reliquum igitur angulum I B T 109 . 41 . earundem. Quare in eadem obseruationis tempore stella distabat à maxima epicycli longitudine dictos inæqualitatis grad. 109 . 41 . qui nobis erant inueniendi.

¶ Sed demonstratum etiam fuit quod in tempore tertiæ oppositionis distabat secundum inæqualitatem ab eadem maxima epicycli longitudine gradib. 171 . 16 . addidit ergo in interiecto (inter obseruationes) tempore (quod quidem 410 . Aegyptiacos annos & dies 231 . 40 . proximè continet) post 192 . integros circulos, addidit inquam grad. 61 . 41 . quanta fermè additione inuenimus per tabulas quas de medijs motibus ipsius conscripsimus, ab ipsis enim diurnus nobis motus constitutus est, diuisâ multitudine graduum quæ per circulos & additionem colligitur in dies , qui inter duas obseruationes fuisse colliguntur.

Anni.	Dies.	Horæ
410.	231.	8.

Periodicas ♂ conuersiones 192. complectuntur.

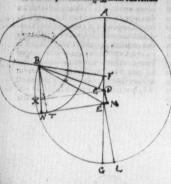

147 RAO, CESARE

I meteori

Venice: Giovanni Varisco, 1582

21 cm. 183 leaves. Decorated initials. Marginalia, contemporary vellum over boards. First and only edition. The colophon is dated 1581.

NUC: AzU; DFo; MB; MBdAF; MH; MiU; NNE; NcD; OkU; WU

148 RASCH, JOHANN

Practica mit vil guter erinderung gestellet

Munich: Adam Berg, 1583

20 cm. 4 leaves. Bound in modern gold-tooled leather.

Astrological forecast for the year 1583 when the planets Mars and Venus ruled.

Zinner, 3103

NUC: CSdS

149 RAY, JOHN, 1627–1705

The Wisdom of God Manifested in the Works of the Creation... The Heavenly Bodies, Elements, Meteors

London: Samuel Smith, 1692

18 cm. Two volumes bound in one. Old calf. Second edition, very much enlarged.

Norland Collection, San Diego State University Library

NUC: CaBVaU; DLC; NcU; NjP; TxU

150 REGIUS, HENRICUS, 1598–1679

Philosophia Naturalis

Amsterdam: L. Elzevir, 1654

21 cm. 490 pages. Illustrations, diagrams. Bound in modern half calf. Second edition. Pages 82–141 are on astronomy.

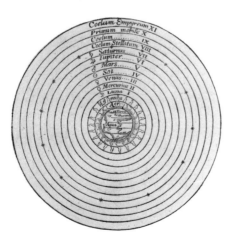

a geocentric sphere

Regius was an enthusiastic follower of Descartes and his physiological ideas. He carried on a long correspondence with him from Utrecht.

Norland Collection, San Diego State University Library

NUC: CU; DNLM; MB; MH; MiU; NjP; NIC; NNE; PU

151 RINGELBERGH, JOACHIM STERCK VAN, 1499?–1536?

Institutiones Astronomicae

Venice: D. Melchior Sessa, 1535

16 cm. 55 leaves. Printer's device on title page and verso of last leaf. Woodcut border around first page of text and one woodcut diagram in text. Bound with Sacro Bosco, J., *Liber de Sphaera*, 1541 (item 161).

printer's vignette

Educated at the University of Louvain, Ringelbergh (or Ringelberg) taught philosophy and mathematics at various cities in Germany and France.

NUC: CSt; ICN; MiD; MiU; NIC; TxU

152 RIVARD, DOMINIQUE FRANÇOIS, 1697–1778

Traité de la sphère

Paris: Jean Desaint, 1743

20 cm. 160 pages. Bound in contemporary calf with item 153. Three folding engraved plates, tables. Second edition revised, corrected, and enlarged.

Houzeau, 2407

NUC: ICJ; MH; PP

I METEORI
DI CESARE RAO
DI ALESSANO
CITTÀ DI TERRA
D'OTRANTO.

I QVALI CONTENGONO QVANTO
intorno a tal materia si puo desiderare.

Ridotti a tanta ageuolezza, che da qual si voglia, ogni
poco ne gli studi essercitato, potranno facil-
mente e con prestezza esser intesi.

Con la Tauola de i Capitoli, e delle materie, che in essi si contengono.

COL PRIVILEGIO.

IN VENETIA, Appresso Giouanni Varisco,
& Compagni. M D LXXXII.

147. Rao, *I meteori* [The meteors] (1582) title page

Practica/

Mit vil guter erinderung/Gestellet durch Jo-
han, Rasch zu Wienn in Osterreich/
auff das Jar

M. D. LXXXIII.

Herrschend Planeten diß Jars/
Mars.   Venus.
♂   ♀

Getruckt zu München/bey Adam Berg.

148. Rasch, *Practica mit vil guter erinderung gestellet* [Handbook introducing
many good admonitions] (1583) title page

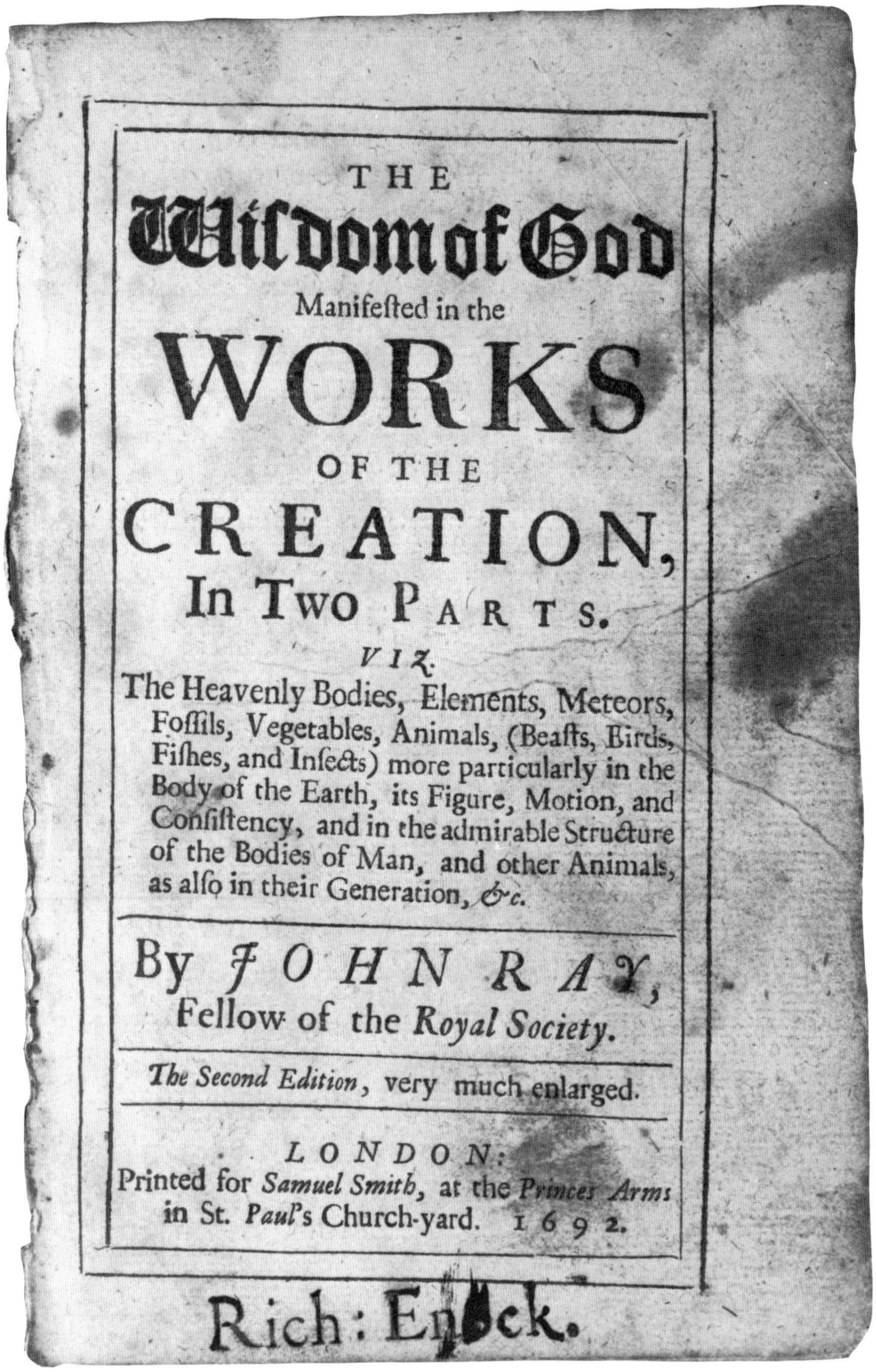

THE

Wisdom of God

Manifested in the

WORKS

OF THE

CREATION,

In Two Parts.

VIZ.

The Heavenly Bodies, Elements, Meteors,
Fossils, Vegetables, Animals, (Beasts, Birds,
Fishes, and Insects) more particularly in the
Body of the Earth, its Figure, Motion, and
Consistency, and in the admirable Structure
of the Bodies of Man, and other Animals,
as also in their Generation, &c.

By *JOHN RAY,*
Fellow of the *Royal Society.*

The Second Edition, very much enlarged.

LONDON:
Printed for *Samuel Smith,* at the *Princes Arms*
in St. *Paul's* Church-yard. 1692.

Rich: Enock.

149. Ray, *The Wisdom of God Manifested in the Works of the Creation* (1692) title page

HENRICI REGII

ULTRAJECTINI

PHILOSOPHIA
NATURALIS.

EDITIO SECUNDA,

Priore multò locupletior, & emendatior.

AMSTELODAMI,
Apud Ludovicum Elzevirium.
cIɔ Iɔc LIV.

1654

150. Regius, *Philosophia Naturalis* [Natural Philosophy] (1654) title page

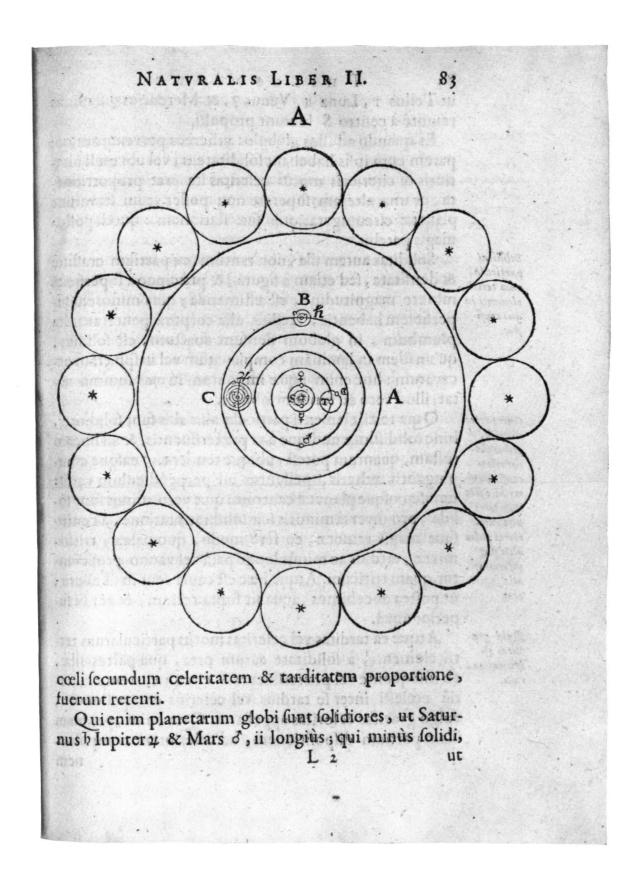

cœli secundum celeritatem & tarditatem proportione,
fuerunt retenti.

Qui enim planetarum globi sunt solidiores, ut Saturnus ♄ Iupiter ♃ & Mars ♂, ii longiùs; qui minùs solidi,

L 2   ut

150. Regius, *Philosophia Naturalis* (1654) a diagram

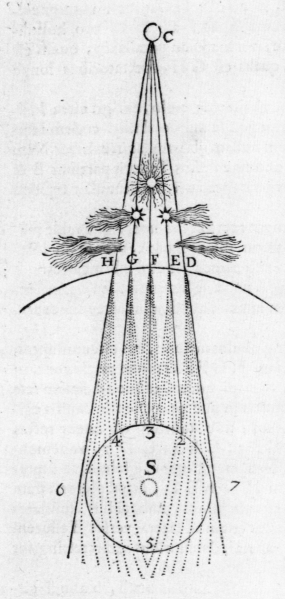

cilliores C H 4,
vel C D 2, cau-
dam ejus repræ-
fentantes : Vel
apparet undique
comatus feu rofe-
us, ut in 3, per ra-
dios directos &
fortes C E 3,
cometæ caput, &
C G 3 ab unâ
parte, ac C E 3
ab alterâ , & ita
undique in reli-
quis circumftan-
tibus partibus re-
fractos , & debi-
liores, comam ex-
hibentes: Vel fo-
la ejus cauda in-
ftar trabis appa-
ret , ut in parte
orbitæ 5, per fo-
los radios debilio-
res & refractos
C D 2 5 , vel
C H 4 5; quia ra-
dii directi C H 6,
vel C D 7, vel ulli
alii directi, ad fpe-

ctatoris oculum , in circuitûs parte 5 exiftentem , per-
venire non poffunt.

Caufa, cur cometa , in parte orbitæ Telluris 4 aut 2
visus,

150. Regius, *Philosophia Naturalis* (1654) calculation concerning a comet

CANDIDE ET GENEROSE.

HENRICVS REGIVS ULTRAJECTINVS, MEDICVS, ET PHILOSOPHVS,
ET IN PATRIA ACADEMIA MEDICINÆ PROFESSOR .

150. Regius, *Philosophia Naturalis* (1654) portrait of Regius

IOACHI
MI RINGELBERGII
Antuerpiani Inſtitutionum
Aſtronomicarum
Liber Primus.

Quid inter Aſtronomiam Aſtrolo-
giamq́; interſit.   Cap. I.

VNDI Naturam ambi-
tumq́; tractaturus , perinde
quaſi è ſublimi cœli uertice
terrę globum deſpiciens, opti-
mo iure admirari uideor , quos in medio orbe
anguſtiore ſpatio labores cæteri inueniant.
Plinius formicam humile animal haud paruo
cōnatu extollit , uermium ſcilicet induſtriam.
Maro apes traditurus, duces ſtrenuos pollice-
tur, pręlia, mores gentium populorumq́,. Quaſi
magni quicquam in eo ſit , quod antiquitas
omnis punctum ac centrum nuncupauit. Hic
cœli uaſtitas aperitur. Hic ea luſtrabimus,

A iiij

TRAITÉ
DE LA
SPHERE,

Par M. RIVARD, *Profeſſeur de Philoſophie en
l'Univerſité de Paris, au Collége de Beauvais.*

SECONDE EDITION,

Revue, corrigée & augmentée par l'Auteur, dans laquelle
on a ajouté un TRAITÉ DU CALENDRIER.

Le prix eſt de 36 ſols pour les deux Traités en feuilleſt.

A PARIS,

Chez JEAN DESAINT & CHARLES SAILLANT, Libraires
rue S. Jean-de-Beauvais, vis-à-vis du College.

M. DCC. XLIII.

Avec Approbation & Privilege du Roi.

152. Rivard, *Traité de la sphère* [Treatise of the sphere] (1743) title page

Pl. 3.

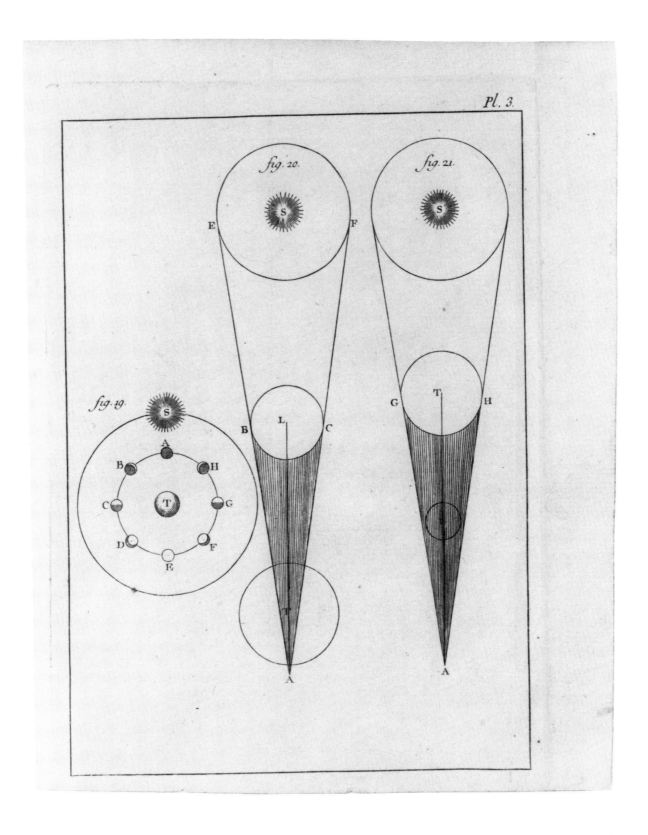

152. Rivard, *Traité de la sphère* (1743) diagram of eclipses

153 RIVARD, DOMINIQUE FRANÇOIS, 1697–1778

Traité du calendrier

Paris: Jean Desaint, 1744

20 cm. 91 pages. Tables. Bound with his *Traité de la sphère*, 1743 (item 152) in contemporary calf. Second edition revised and enlarged.

Houzeau, 2407

NUC: MH; PP

154 ROGERS, JOHN, M.D.

A Dissertation on the Knowledge of the Ancients in Astronomy

London: J. & J. Rivington, 1755

20 cm. 134 pages. Illustrations, three folding copper-engraved plates. Inscription by author on flyleaf: "To the Right Hon.ble Lord Willoughby of Parham—by ye Author." First and only edition.

Lalande, p. 457

NUC: CSt; OCU; OkU; PPL

155 ROST, JOHANN LEONHARD, 1688–1727

Der aufrichtige Astronomus

Nürnberg: B.P.C. Monath, 1727

24 cm. 192 leaves. Illustrations, tables, marginalia, fourteen folding plates. Bound in vellum over boards.

Mathematician Rost was born at Nürnberg. First educated at the gymnasium there, he later began making astronomical observations before moving on to Altdorf, Leipzig, and Jena, where he studied mathematics and physics. In 1712 he returned to Nürnberg and joined Wurzelbau in his astronomical observations. In 1723 he was admitted to the Prussian Society of the Sciences, Berlin. In 1724 he discovered an eight-day difference between the Protestant and the Gregorian Easter. He was the author of forty-seven works, most of them on astronomical subjects, many on eclipses (*Iselin*, v. 5, pp. 1238–9).

Zinner Collection

Lalande, p. 383

NUC: CSdS; DLC; MiU; OkU; WU

156 SACRO BOSCO, JOANNES DE, ca. 1200–56?

Sphaera Mundi

Venice: Erhard Ratdolt, 1485

20 cm. 58 leaves. Illustrations, diagrams, some partly colored. The first printed book to use multicolored diagrams. Marginalia. Incipit: Noviciis Adolfscentibus: ad Astronomicam.

Impreſſum eſt hoc opuſculum mira arte & diligentia Erhardi Ratdolt Auguſtenſis. Anno ſalutiferę incarnationis. 1485.

detail from the colophon

Known to the English as John of Holywood, Sacro Bosco (or Sacrobosco, or Sacro Busto, which is *holy wood* in Latin), an English medieval monk and astronomer, was born at Holywood, Yorkshire. He died at Paris in 1256 (or 1244?). Very little is known about his life. English biographers maintain he was educated at Oxford. In about 1220 he went to Paris and was admitted to the university there in 1221. He was soon elected professor of mathematics. By 1231 he was the outstanding mathematician and astronomer of his time. His fame rests on his *De Sphaera* written in about 1220. It was based on Ptolemy and his Arabic commentaries placing the earth at the center of the celestial sphere. It was accepted as the fundamental astronomy text first at the University of Paris, then throughout Europe until as late as the seventeenth century (*DSB*, v. 12, pp. 60-3).

Also contained in the text of this work are Peurbach *Theoricae Novae Planetarum* beginning on the verso of the leaf 18, and *Disputatio* by Regiomotanus beginning the recto of leaf 45.

Zinner Collection

Houzeau, 478

NUC: CSdS; CtY-M; DCU; DLC; ICN; IU; MCM; MWiW; MBMu; MnU; NN; NcU; RPJCB; ViU

Goff: AmBML; BPJ; BPubL; BurL; ChL; CUAL; HDH; HEHL; JCBL; LC; LeUL(H); MFArtL; MMu(P)L; NewL; NYPL; OFE; PH; PML; RSS; UIllL; UKanL; UMin(B)L; UNCaL; UVa(Mc)L; WArtGL; YU(M)L

Der Aufrichtige ASTRONOMVS.

Welcher
von verschiedenen, so wol zur
DOCTRINA SPHAERICA
als
zur Bewegung der COMETEN
und zu den
OBSERVATIONIBVS ASTRONOMICIS
gehörigen Materien, einen ausführlichen Unterricht ertheilet.
Dabey er ferner auf eine-überaus deutliche Art lehret:
Wie man die
ECLIPSES PRIMI SATELLITIS JOVIS
durch blosses Addiren erforschen;
Deßgleichen alle
Mond- und Sonnen-Finsternisse
biß auf das Jahr 1750, ohne einige Rechnung,
Nur durch Circkel und Lineal
sehr genau anzeigen soll.
Zu weitern Aufnehmen der höchst-nützlichen
ASTRONOMIE,
an das Licht gestellet und durch viele Figuren begreiflicher gemacht,
von
Johann Leonhard Rost/
der Königl. Preußischen Societaet der Wissenschafften, Mitgliede.

***

Nürnberg.
Bey Peter Conrad Monath, 1727.

155. Rost, *Der aufrichtige Astronomus* [The properly established astronomer] (1727) title page

155. Rost, *Der aufrichtige Astronomus* (1727) fanciful frontispiece

156. Sacro Bosco, *Sphaera Mundi* [The sphere of the world] (1485) frontispiece

THEORICAE NOVAE PLANETARVM GEORGII
PVRBACHII ASTRONOMI CELEBRATISS. DE Sole

Ol babet tres orbes a se iuicẽ omni
q̃ cʒ diuifos atcʒ fibi cõtiguos quorũ
fupremus ƀm fupficiem conuexã ẽ
mũdo cõcentricus: ƀm cõcauã autẽ
eccentricus. Infimus uero ƀm con/
cauã cõcentricus : fed ƀm conuexã
eccentric⁹. Terti⁹autẽ in botũ me/
dio locat⁹ tam ƀm fupficiẽ fuã con/
uexã q̃ cʒ cõcauã eft mũdo eccentric⁹
Dicit autẽ mũdo concentric⁹ orbis

THEORICA SOLIS.

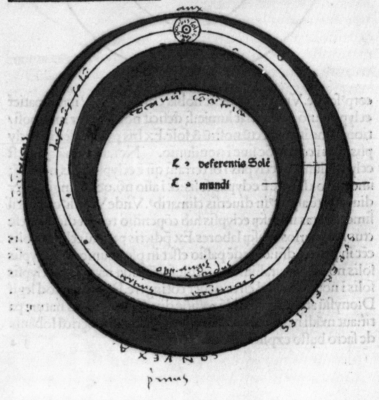

---

156. Sacro Bosco, *Sphaera Mundi* (1485) text by Peurbach
diagram of the "sun's orbit"; diagram of the poles

Eccentricus

cui⁹centrū ē centrū mūdi. Eccentric⁹uero cui⁹ centrū est aliud a
centro mūdi. Duo itaꝗ primi sūt eccentrici ꓢm quid: & uocāt
orbes augē solis deferentes. Ad motū eni eorū aux solis uariaᵵ
Tertius uero est eccentric⁹simpliciter:& uocaᵵ orbis solē defe/
rens.ad motū eni eius corp⁹solare infixū sibi moueᵵ.Hi tres or
bes duo·centra tenēt. Nā supficies cōuexa suprēmi & concaua
infimi idē centrū habent qð est mūdi centrū.Vnde tota sphēra
solis sicut & alterius cuiuscūꝗ planetē tota sphēra concentrica
mnndo diciᵵ esse.Sed superficies concaua suprēmi atꝗ conue/
xa infimi una cū utrisꝗ superficiebus medii unū aliud.qð cen/
trum eccentrici diciᵵ.habent.   Mouenᵵ autē orbes deferētes

de motibꝫ
istorꝫ t᷑ orbiū ⊙

THEORICA AXIVM ET POLORVM.

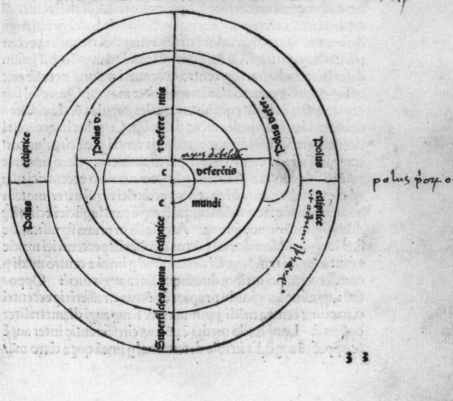

polus ꝑꝙ orbiū

33

Seĉdʒ Ŝ ſbaʒ

firmãnĥ

Polus

Axis

Polus

Sphęra aūt duplicit diui/
dit ƒm ſubſtātiā &ƒm acci/
dēs. Scōm ſubſtātiā i ſphę/
ras noué ſcʒ ſphęrā nonā: ą
ꝑmꝰ motꝰ: ſiue primū mo/
bile dicit. & i ſphęrā ſtella
rū fixaʒ ą firmamētū nūcu
pat: & i ſeptē ſphęras ſeptē planetarū: quarū quędā ſūt maiores
quędam minores: ƒm ꝙ plus accedunt uel recedūt a firmamēto
Vnde inter illas ſphęra Saturni maxima eſt. Sphęra uero lunę
minima: ꝓut in ſequenti figuratione continetur.

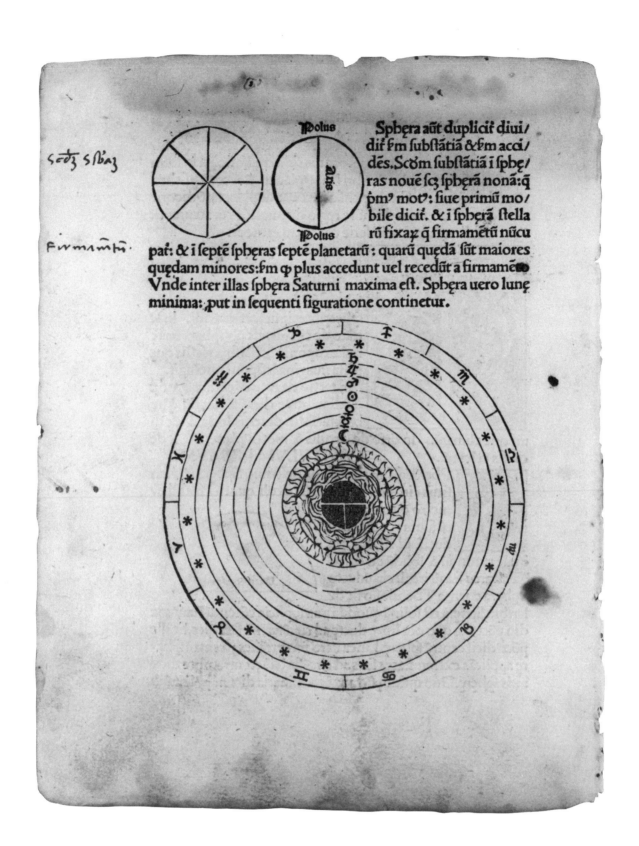

156. Sacro Bosco, *Sphaera Mundi* (1485) geocentric celestial sphere

157 SACRO BOSCO, JOANNES DE, ca. 1200–56?

Sphaera Mundi

Venice: Octavius Scotus, 1490

22 cm. 43 leaves. Illustrations (woodcuts) some colored. Bound in contemporary vellum over boards. Marginalia. Ex Libris: Eric Sexton, Lord Hyde.

SPHAERA
MVNDI
ICIS
DE
SACRO   BUSTO.
A.D. 1490.

cover title

NUC: CSt; CtY; DFo; DLC; ICN; ICU; IU; InU; MB; MH; MnU; NN; NNC; NNE; NNJ; NjP; OU; PBm

Goff: AELow; BMawrCL; BPubL; BurL; CDH; ColUL; CPhL; HarvCL; HDH; HEHL; IS(-); JCreL; LC; McGU(O)L; MFArtL; MMu(P)L; NewL; NYPL; OhStUL; PML; StanUL; TGM; UESocL; UMin(B)L; UOkL; WArtGL; YU(M)L

158 SACRO BOSCO, JOANNES DE, ca. 1200–56?

Textus de Sphaera

Paris: Simon Colin, 1527

32 cm. 35 leaves. Woodcut illustrations. Marginalia.

The first appearance of this Paris edition was 1500. It was reprinted eight times up to 1538.

Houzeau, 582; Lalande lists other Paris editions, but not 1527.

NUC: MH

159 SACRO BOSCO, JOANNES DE, ca. 1200–56?

Liber de Sphaera

Venice: F. Bindoni, 1537

15 cm. 31 leaves. Woodcut illustrations and diagrams. Manuscript inscription on title page: "Nocet empta dolore Voluptas."

NUC: NcD

160 SACRO BOSCO, JOANNES DE, ca. 1200–56?

Sphera volgare novamente tradotta con molte notande

Venice: B. Zanetti, 1537

21 cm. 56 leaves. Diagrams, tables. Bound in modern half vellum over boards. First Italian edition.

Houzeau, 598; Lalande, p. 56

NUC: AzU; CSmH; CtY-M; DFo; DLC; DN; IU; MH; MiU; MnU; NN; NNC; NNE; NNH; NcD; OkU; RPJCB; ViW

161 SACRO BOSCO, JOANNES DE, ca. 1200–56?

Liber de Sphaera

Venice: D. Melchior Sessa, 1541

16 cm. 32 leaves. Illustrations, much marginalia. Forty-four woodcuts, woodcut initials, printer's device on verso of last leaf. Bound with this work are four contemporary titles: Ringelbergh (item 151), Peurbach (item 139), Apianus (item 6), and Glareanus (item 74) entered elsewhere in this catalogue.

NUC: MiU

directe oppositus solis i firmaměto. Vnde cū in plenilunio luna fuerit i capite uel i cauda draconis sub nadir solis: tunc terra iterponet soli & lunae: & conus umbre terre cadet sup corpus lunae. Vnde cū luna lumē nō heat nisi a sole: i rei ueritate deficit a lumine. Et est eclypsis generalis i oi terra si fuerit i capite uel cauda draconis directe. Particularis uero eclypsis si fuerit ppe uel ifra metas determinatas eclypsi. Et sp i plenilunio uel circa cōtigit eclypsis. Vnde cū i qilibet oppōne hoc e i plenilunio nō sit luna i capite uel cauda draconis nec opposita nadir solis: nō e necesse i quolibet plenilunio pati eclypsim: ut patet i psěti figura q subsequě. Cū aut fuerit luna i capite uel cauda draconis: uel ppe metas supradictas: & i cōiūctiōe cū sole: tūc corps lunae iterponet iter aspectū nřm & corps solare. Vnde obūbrabit nobis claritate solis: & ita sol patiet eclypsim: nō qa deficiat lumine: sed deficit nobis pp iterpositiōe lunae iter aspectū nřm & sole. Ex his patet q nō sp e eclypsis solis i cōiūctione siue i nouilunio. Notādū et q quādo e eclypsis lunae: e eclypsis i oi terra: sed quādo e eclypsis solis nequaq imo i uno climate e eclypsis solis: & i alio nō: qd cōtigit pp diuersitate aspectus i diuersis climatibus. Vnde Virgilius elegantissime naturas utriusq eclypsis sub cōpēdio tetigit dicēs. Defectus lunae uarios solisq labores. Ex pdictis patet q cū eclypsis solis esset i passione domini: illa passio eět i plenilunio: illa eclypsis solis nō fuit nālis: imo miraculosa cōtraria naturae: qa eclypsis solis i nouilunio uel circa dbet cōtigere. Propter qd legit: Dionysiū ariopagitā i eādē passione dixisse: Aut deus naturae patiť: aut mūdi machina dissoluet.

Opusculum sphaericum Ioannis de sacro busto explicitum est.

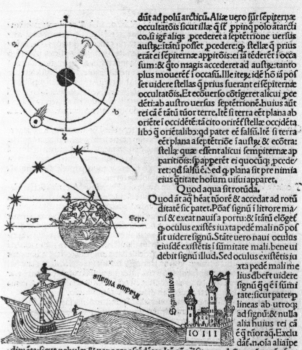

dūt ad polū arcticū. Aliae uero sūt sepiternae occultatōis sicut illae q sř ppinq polo ātarcico. si igř aliqs pcederet a septētrione uersus austř: itāu posset pcedere: q stellae q prius erāt ei sepiternae appitōis: ei iā těderēt i occasum: & qto magis accederet ad austř: tanto plus mouerēt i occasū. Ille iteř idē nō iā posset uidere stellas q prius fuerant ei sepiternae occultatōis. Et ecōuerso cōtigeret alicui pcedēti: ab austro uersus septētrionē. huius aut rei cā e tātū tūor terre. Ite si terra eět plana ab oriēte i occidētē: tā cito orirēt stellae occidētalibs q oriētalibs: qd patet eě falsū. Ite si terra eět plana a septētriōe i austř. & ecōtra: stellae quae essent alicui sempiternae apparitōis: sp apperēt ei quocūq pcederet: qd falsū e. Sed q plana sit pre nimia eius qtitate hoiū uisui apparet.

Quod aqua sit rotūda. Quod āt aq heat tūore & accedat ad rotūditate sic patet. Pōat signū i littore māris & exeat nauis a portu: & itāu elōget q oculus existens iuxta pedē mali nō possit uidere signū. Stāte uero naui oculus eiusdē existētis i sūmitate mali. bene ui debit signū illud. Sed oculus existētis iuxta pedē mali melius debet uidere signū q qi i sūmitate: sicut patet p lineas ab utroq ad signū: & nulla alia huius rei cā qnūoraq. Exclu dat. n. oia aliaipe dimēta: sicut nebulae & uapores ascēdētes. Ite cū aq sit corps hōgeneū: totū cū ptibs eiusdē erit rōis: sed ptes aq: sicut i guttulis & roribs herbaž accidit: rotūda naturalě apperūt formā: ergo & totū cuius sř ptes. Quod terra sit centř mūdi. Quod āt terra sit i medio firmamēti sita sic patet. Existētibs i supficie těrrae stellae apparēt eiusdē qtitatis siue sint i medio caeli: siue iuxta ortū: siue iuxta occasū: & hoc quia terra eqlř distat ab eis. Si. n. terra magis accederet ad firmamētū i una pte q in alia: aliqs existens i illa pte supficiei těrrae q magis accederet ad firmamē tū nō uideret caeli medietatě: sed hoc e cōtra Ptolaemeū & oēs phōs dicentes q

157. Sacro Bosco, *Sphaera Mundi* (1490) (reduced)

SPHAERAE mundi compendium foeliciter inchoat.

Nouiciis adolescétibus: ad astronomicá rep.capessendá aditú ipetrátibus: p breui
rectoq; tramite a uulgari uestigio semoto: Ioánis de sacro busto sphæricú opus
culú una cú additóibus nónullis lfa A sparsim ubi iterserté sint signatis: Cótra
q; cremonésia i plane tag; theoricas delyramenta Ioánis de móteregio disputa
ões trá acuratií.q; utilis : Nec nó Georgii purbachii: i eorúdé motus planetag; ac
curatis.theorica: dicatú opus: utili serie cótextú: fausto sidere ichoat.

Ractatum de sphæra q̃tuor capitulis distiguimus:
Dicturi primo cópositióe sphæræ qd sit sphæra:
qd eius centg;: qd axis sphæræ: qd sit polus mundi:
quot st sphæræ: & q̃ sit forma múdi. In scdo de cir
culis ex qbus sphæra materialis cóponit & illa sup
cælestis q p istá imaginat cóponi itelligit. In tertio
de ortu & occasu signog;: & de diuersitate dieg; &
noctiú: quæ sit habitantibus in diuersis locis: & de
diuisione climatum. In quarto de circulis & moti
bus planætarum: & de causis eclipsium.

DE diffóe sphæræ & de qbusdá pricipiis suppoñ
dis & sphæræ cópóne & comoditate Capi.primú.

ON est i ptáte nfa cælos sursú adire:circulos & gradus eog; uisu cerne
re:eosq; reuoluere undecúq;: & quádo placuerit.q̃ pterita i illis sunt:
haud hó pót itueri:nec hois ætas sufficeret expectare q̃ futura sút: &
q̃ psetia fiút dú uiuit hó cúcta nemo uidere pót. Núc alibi dies é:alibi
nox:uni sol orit uel stella q̃dá:alteri occidit:nec oíbus ieé locis qs simul pót.aliq̃
bus sphæra se demfat recta:aliqbus obliq̃ multipharie.Quas ob res bonú & có
modú est artificialé sphærá hfe:q̃ manibus ad libitú uolui: & scdm cóem situ &
pté cóspici possit: & oés eius gradus & circulos pcipi salté oportui:q̃ mediante
ueluti exéplo psetia pterita & futura & cá; naturalis sút sphæræ cæli facile itelli
gere ualeeus. Ad méoriá igt cóuertamus ea q̃ de circulis & púctis dicút atq; zo
diaci i scdo ca.huius: & ad similitudiné decimæ:nonæ uel octauæ sphæræ silf
fabricemus:prio ut moris é ex circiolis ex subtili metallo uel ligno idoneo i sua
rotúditate & stribus bene æquádo & firmádo duos circulos magnos se ortho/
gonalf secátes sup púcta q̃ polog; sút. Atq; circulú aliú p æqnoctiali ab ipsis po
lis æqdistáté. Silf & duos tropicos: & duos circulos arcticú & antarcticú i suis st
tib2.Atq; zoná zodiaci biptitá p ecliptica & i.xii.signa q̃ gradib2 i ecliptica signa
tis & suis noíb2 scdm ordiné sint signita: & unáquáq; q̃rta æqnoctialis a coluro
i colug; i gradus.xc.separabimus. Sitq; q̃rtæ zodiaci silf ptitæ:ita ut colurus unus
tráseat p duo solstitia & polos zodiaci:alter p duo púcta æqnoctií. His.viii.circu
lis bene firmatis & suis noíb2 & gradib2 distictis: scisq; duob2 rotúdis foramib2
i duob2 locis diametralf oppositis: ubi duo circuli coluri se secát: sint uere púcta
polog; ipíus sphæræ: axé rotúdá ex serro rectissimá p illa duxerimus ex utra g

a ii

mabat. Hinc motum ſequuntur omnes ſphæræ inferiores in motibus ſuis:ita ut reſpectu huius eclipticæ mobilis ſint auges deferentium & declinationes earum ſemper inuariabiles.

Theorica ultima octauæ ſphæræ.

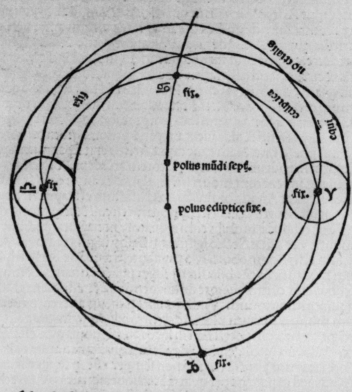

Hoc quoqʒ ſideralis ſcientie ſingulare opuſculum Impreſſum eſt Venetiis mandato & expenſis nobilis uiri Octauiani ſcoti ciuis modoetienſis Anno Salutis M.cccc.lxxxx.quarto nonas octobris.

ɑ◦TEXTVS DE SPHAERA IOAN-
NIS DE SACROBOSCO: INTRODVCTORIA ADDITIONE
(quantū neceſſarium eſt)commentarióқҙ,ad vtilitatem ſtudentiũ phi-
loſophiæ Pariſienſis Academiæ illuſtratus.Cum cõpoſitione Annuli
aſtronomici Boneti Latenſis:Et Geometria Euclidis Megarenſis.

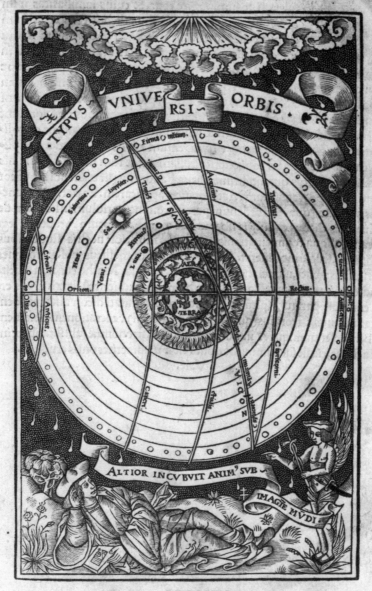

PARISIIS
Vænit apud Simonem Colinæum.
1527

158. Sacro Bosco, *Textus de Sphaera* [Text of the sphere] (1527) title page (reduced)

158. Sacro Bosco, *Textus de Sphaera* (1527) frontispiece (reduced)

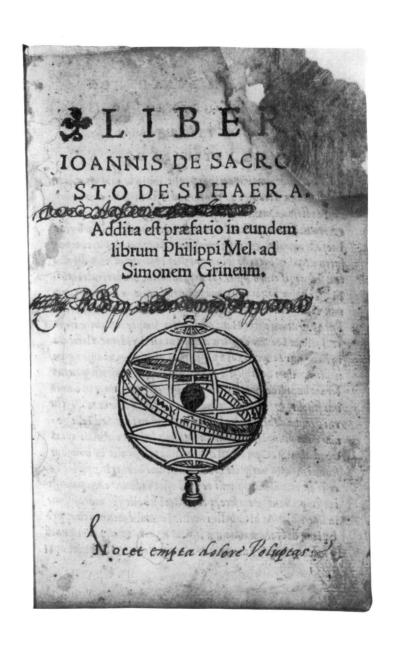

159. Sacro Bosco, *Liber de Sphaera* [The book of the sphere] (1537) title page

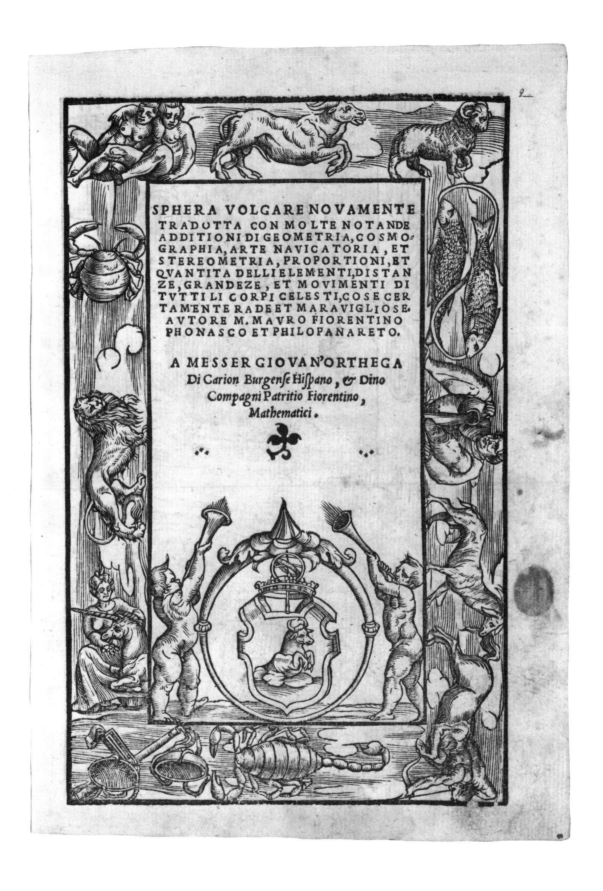

SPHERA VOLGARE NOVAMENTE
TRADOTTA CON MOLTE NOTANDE
ADDITIONI DI GEOMETRIA, COSMO=
GRAPHIA, ARTE NAVICATORIA, ET
STEREOMETRIA, PROPORTIONI, ET
QVANTITA DELLI ELEMENTI, DISTAN
ZE, GRANDEZE, ET MOVIMENTI DI
TVTTI LI CORPI CELESTI, COSE CER
TAMENTE RADE ET MARAVIGLIOSE.
AVTORE M. MAVRO FIORENTINO
PHONASCO ET PHILOPANARETO.

A MESSER GIOVAN'ORTHEGA
Di Carion Burgense Hispano, & Dino
Compagni Patritio Fiorentino,
Mathematici.

160. Sacro Bosco, *Sphera volgare novamente tradotta con molte notande*
[The common sphere newly translated with many notations] (1537) title page

160. Sacro Bosco, *Sphera volgare novamente tradotta con molte notande* (1537) frontispiece

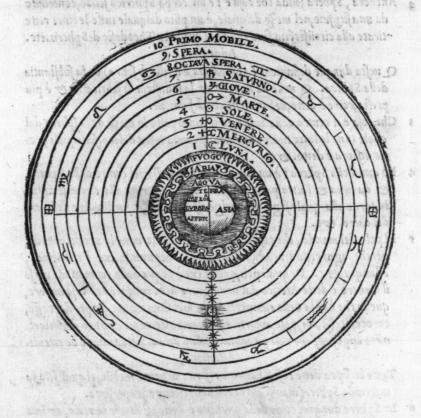

Figura della Sphera Substantiale.

O uer o dell'aggregato, di tutte le Sphere celesti, &
elementari, ò uero orbi, & c.

160. Sacro Bosco, *Sphera volgare novamente tradotta con molte notande* (1537)
a geocentric celestial sphere

162 SACRO BOSCO, JOANNES DE, ca. 1200–56?

De Anni Ratione

Wittenberg: V. Creuzer, 1545

17 cm. 67 leaves. Bound in contemporary hand-tooled vellum over boards with his *Libellus de Sphaera*, 1549 (item 163).

Zinner Collection

Zinner, 1881

NUC: NN; NNC

163 SACRO BOSCO, JOANNES DE, ca. 1200–56?

Libellus de Sphaera... cum Praefatione Philippi Melanthonis

Wittenberg: V. Creuzer, 1549

17 cm. 66 leaves. Illustrations, diagrams. Bound in contemporary hand-tooled vellum over boards with item 162.

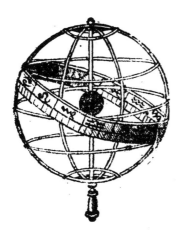

title-page vignette

Zinner Collection

Lalande, p. 68; Zinner, 1881

NUC: DLC; MiU; NN; RPJCB

164 SACRO BOSCO, JOANNES DE, ca. 1200–56?

Sphaera. Addita sunt quaedam Explanationem

Venice: F. Rampazeto, 1564

17 cm. 32 leaves. Woodcut illustrations, diagrams. Marginalia.

NUC: no copy

165 SACRO BOSCO, JOANNES DE, ca. 1200–56?

Sphaera. Emendatiore... Opera & studio Franconis Burgersdicii

Leiden: B. & A. Elzevir, 1626

16 cm. 60 leaves. Bound in contemporary limp vellum. Woodcut diagrams, tables, marginalia, volvelle.

a small volvelle

Houzeau, 596; Lalande, p. 188

NUC: DLC; MB; MCM; PHC

166 SALUSBURY, THOMAS, d. 1666

Mathematical Collections and Translations

London: Printed by William Leybourn, 1661

36 cm. 352 leaves. Bound in modern three-quarter brown morocco. Fine text engravings and diagrams, decorative initials, and ornaments. Provenance, title page: Thomas Desaguliers 1752" (1725?–80). Bound with this work is Fatio de Duillier, N., *Navigation Improv'd*, 1728 (item 49).

This book is famous because it contains the first and, until 1953, the only English translation of Galileo's epoch-making work, *Dialogue Concerning the Two Chief World Systems*.

The Library also owns the Zeitlin facsimile reprint of 1967.

NUC: CaBVaU; CSt; CU; CtY; DFo; DLC; ICJ; NIC; NNC; NcD; PPAmP

suas duas lineas. Et secundum hanc acceptionem, stel=
læ, quæ sunt iuxta polos extra zodiacum, dicuntur
esse in signis.

Item intelligatur corpus quoddam, cuius basis
sit.signum, secundum quod nunc ultimo accipimus

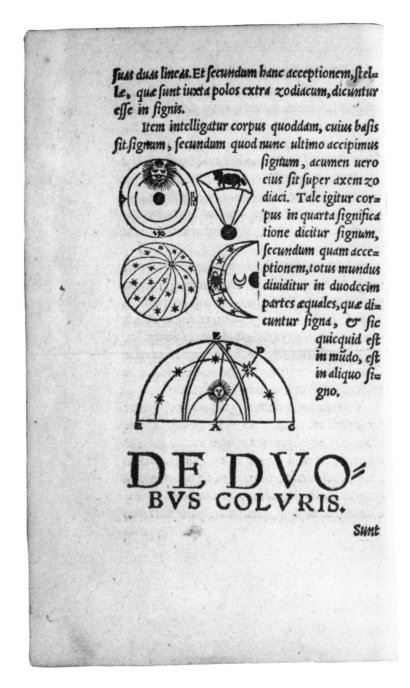

signum, acumen uero
eius sit super axem zo
diaci. Tale igitur cor=
pus in quarta significa
tione dicitur signum,
secundum quam acce=
ptionem, totus mundus
diuiditur in duodecim
partes æquales, quæ di=
cuntur signa, et sic
quicquid est
in mũdo, est
in aliquo si=
gno.

DE DVO=
BVS COLVRIS.

Sunt

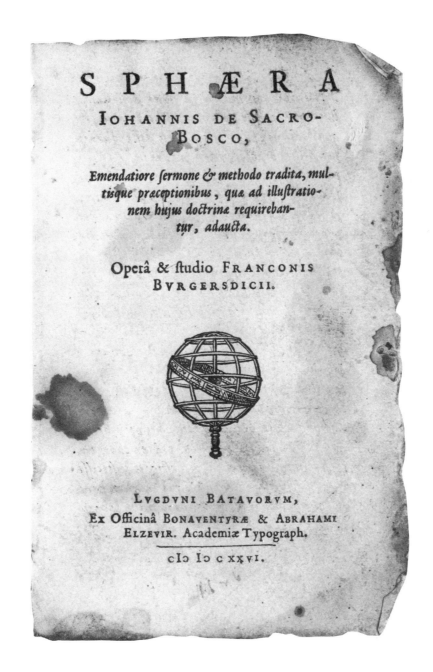

SPHÆRA

IOHANNIS DE SACRO-
BOSCO,

Emendatiore sermone & methodo tradita, mul-
tisque præceptionibus, quæ ad illustratio-
nem hujus doctrinæ requireban-
tur, adaucta.

Operâ & studio FRANCONIS
BVRGERSDICII.

LVGDVNI BATAVORVM,
Ex Officinâ BONAVENTYRÆ & ABRAHAMI
ELZEVIR. Academiæ Typograph.
cIɔ Iɔ c xxvi.

165. Sacro Bosco, *Sphaera. Emendatiore* [The sphere corrected] (1626) title page

& Mercurius, pari celeritate moventur cum
Sole. Luna circumvolvitur spatio dierum 27,
horarum 7, min. 43, sec. 7.

*Supra omnes hosce orbes mobiles, est immobilis, sedes
beatorum, quam cælum empyreum, & cum Apostolo,
cælum tertium, Theologi appellant. Itaque universa
mundi moles, constat quindecim corporibus; quatuor
scilicet elementis, septem orbibus Planetarum, cælo
stellato, qui octavus orbis est, orbe nono, & decimo
sive primo mobili, & cælo empyreo. Horum seriem ex-
hibet figura subjecta.*

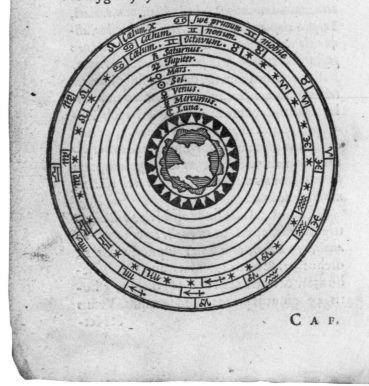

C A P.

165. Sacro Bosco, *Sphaera. Emendatiore* (1626) a geocentric celestial sphere

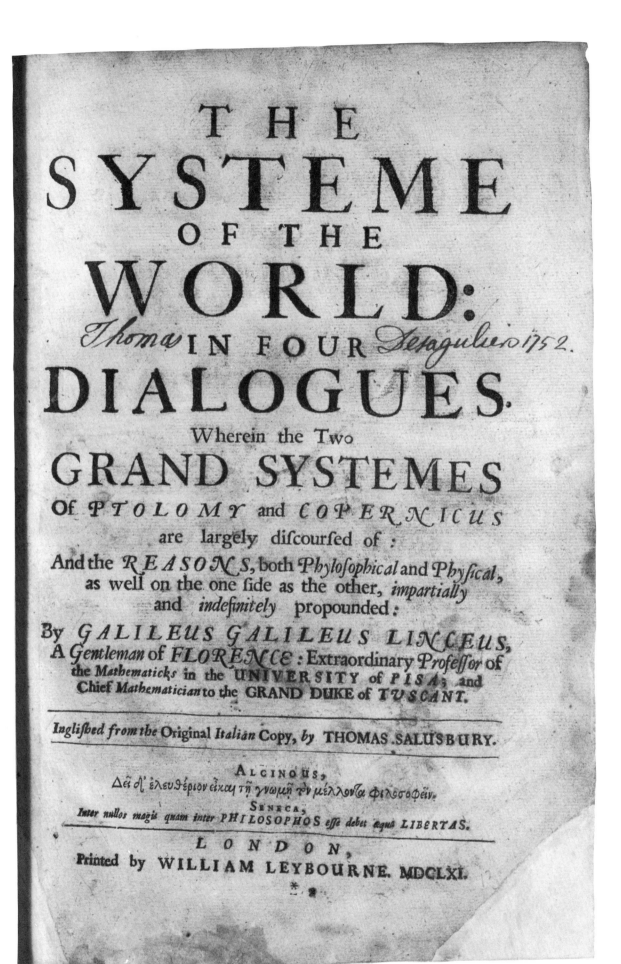

THE
SYSTEME
OF THE
WORLD:
Thomas IN FOUR *Desagulier 1752.*
DIALOGUES.

Wherein the Two
GRAND SYSTEMES
Of *PTOLOMY* and *COPERNICUS*
are largely difcourfed of :
And the *REASONS*, both *Phylofophical* and *Phyfical*,
as well on the one fide as the other, *impartially*
and *indefinitely* propounded :
By *GALILEUS GALILEUS LINCEUS*,
A *Gentleman* of *FLORENCE* : Extraordinary *Profeffor* of
the *Mathematicks* in the UNIVERSITY of *PISA*; and
Chief *Mathematician* to the GRAND DUKE of *TUSCANY*.

Inglifhed from the Original Italian Copy, by THOMAS SALUSBURY.

ALCINOUS,
Δεῖ δἲ ἐλευθέριον εἶκαι τῇ γνωμῇ τὸν μέλλοντα φιλοσοφεῖν.
SENECA,
Inter nullos magis quam inter PHILOSOPHOS *effe debet æquâ* LIBERTAS.

LONDON,
Printed by WILLIAM LEYBOURNE. MDCLXI.
✱✱

166. Salusbury, *Mathematical Collections and Translations* (1661) title page (reduced)

MATHEMATICAL
COLLECTIONS
AND
TRANSLATIONS:
THE FIRST
TOME.
IN TWO PARTS.

THE FIRST PART;

Containing,

I. GALILEUS GALILEUS His SYSTEM of the WORLD.

II. GALILEUS His EPISTLE to the GRAND DUTCHESSE MOTHER, concerning the Authority of Holy SCRIPTURE in Philosophical Controversies.

III. JOHANNES KEPLERUS His Reconcilings of SCRIPTURE Texts, &c.

IV. DIDACUS à STUNICA His Reconcilings of SCRIPTURE Texts, &c.

V. P. A. FOSCARINUS His Epistle to Father FANTONUS, reconciling the Authority of SCRIPTURE, and Judgments of Divines alledged against this SYSTEM.

By THOMAS SALUSBURY, Esq.

LONDON,
Printed by WILLIAM LEYBOURN, MDCLXI.

166. Salusbury, *Mathematical Collections and Translations* (1661)
title page of part one (reduced)

GALILÆUS
Galilæus Lyncæus,
HIS
SYSTEME
OF THE
WORLD.

The First Dialogue.

INTERLOCUTORS.

SALVIATUS, SAGREDUS, and SIMPLICIUS.

SALVIATUS.

T was our yesterdayes resolution, and a-
greement, that we should to day discourse
the most distinctly, and particularly we
could possible, of the natural reasons, and
their efficacy that have been hitherto alledged on the one or other part; by the
maintainers of the Positions, *Aristotelian*,
and *Ptolomaique*; and by the followers
of the *Copernican Systeme*: And because

Copernicus reputeth the Earth a Globe like to a Planet.

Copernicus placing the Earth among the moveable Bodies of Heaven, comes to constitute a Globe for the same like to a Planet; it
would be good that we began our disputation with the examination of what, and how great the energy of the *Peripateticks* ar-
guments is, when they demonstrate, that this *Hypothesis* is impos-
sible

A

167 SCALIGER, JOSEPH, 1540–1609

Castigationes et Notae in M. Manilii Astronomicon

Strasbourg: J. J. Bockenhoffer, 1655

22 cm. 462 pages. This work is bound with its subject, Manilius, M., *Astronomicon*, 1655 (item 113).

One of the most learned critics of the sixteenth century, Scaliger was born at Aachen and began his studies at Bordeaux. Soon after he went to Paris where he attended the university, achieving wide renown as a brilliant scholar. His fame was such that the Leiden Academy offered him an honorary professorship, which he accepted and held for sixteen years.

Scaliger was not large in stature. He had fiery eyes. His erudition was extraordinary. His writings were numerous and treated on philosophy, mathematics, literature, and history (*Iselin*, v. 6, pp. 199–200).

Lalande, p. 239

NUC: MH

168 SCHICKARD, WILHELM, 1592–1635

Astroscopium

Stuttgart: J. Klos, 1698

14 cm. 112 pages. Illustrations.

Schickard was appointed professor of Hebrew and mathematics at the University of Tübingen in 1619. His little book on astronomy, *Astroscopium*, was first published in 1623 and reissued in numerous later editions. Besides engraving his own copperplates for his books and maps, he built musical instruments, quadrants, and sundials. (Zinner, *Astronomische Instrumente*, pp. 500–1).

Zinner Collection

Lalande, p. 335

NUC: CSdS

169 SCHILLER, JULIUS, d. 1627

Coelum Stellatum Christianum

Augsburg: A. Aperger, 1627

31 × 37 cm. 134 pages. Copper-engraved frontispiece, plates, star charts. First and only edition.

Arabic names of the stars

Schiller was an Augustinian monk at Augsburg who substituted the names of Christian saints for pagan Greek names of the constellations on his star charts. "Not one astronomer adopted them" (Lalande, p. 190).

Zinner Collection

Lalande, p. 190; Zinner, 5078

NUC: DLC

170 SCHÖNER, JOHANN, 1477–1547.

De Usu Globi Astriferi

Antwerp: n.p., 1548

17 cm. 5 leaves. Woodcut illustration on title page and fine woodcut initial on verso of second leaf. Bound with Gemma Frisius, R., *De Principiis Astronomiae et Cosmographiae* (item 72).

Lalande, p. 67

NUC: DLC; NN

WILHELMI SCHICKARDI,
Linguarum Orientalium, nec non
Matheseos apud Tubingenses
Professoris publici,

ASTROSCO-
PIUM,

Pro facillima Stellarum co-
gnitione excogitatum, & Com-
mentariolo illustra-
tum;

Nunc denuò in usum Reipu-
blicæ Literariæ locupletius re-
cnsum:
Accurante
WILHELMO SCHICKARDO
Juniore.

Stutgardiæ & Lipsiæ,
apud JOH. HEREBORD KLOSIUM.
M DC XCIIX.

168. Schickard, *Astroscopium* [Collection of knowledge on the stars] (1698)
frontispiece and title page

169. Schiller, *Coelum Stellatum Christianum* [Christian starry heaven]
(1627) added title page (reduced)

170. Schöner, *De Usu Globi Astriferi* [Concerning the use
of astronomical globes] (1548) title page

171 SCHWALBE, JOHANNES, preses; Respondens,
KASPAR FREYER

Disputatio Physico-Astronomica. De Novis Stellis

Wittenberg: Salomon Auerbach, 1627

19 cm. 6 leaves.

Zinner Collection

Zinner, 5079

NUC: CSdS

172 *La Science naturelle*

Paris: André Cailleau, 1724

16 cm. 459 pages.

Zinner Collection

NUC: MdBJ; NcD

173 SELNECCER, NICOLAUS, 1530–92

Nachricht über Herrn D. Nicolai Selnecceri

Zeitz: Friedeman Hetstaedt, 1680

19 cm. 8 leaves.

Curious little tract reprinting Selneccer's *Passio.
Christliche kurtze und tröstliche Erklärung*, Leipzig, 1580.
It chronicles the sinfulness of the times and declares
that new comets appearing in the heavens are bad
omens of God's displeasure and warns that the
world is surely coming to an end.

Selneccer was an ardent Lutheran reformer
who had studied theology at Wittenberg under
Luther's main collaborator, Philipp Melanchthon
(1497–1560). Like many participants in the Reformation movement he was interested in new knowledge
in the natural sciences. In this pamphlet reference is
made to Regiomontanus (1436–76), Stöffler (items
180–82), Tycho Brahe (items 28–9), and other
astronomers, but it has little significance for the history of astronomy.

Zinner Collection

NUC: no copy

174 SEMLER, CHRISTIAN GOTTLIEB, 1715–82

*Vollständige Beschreibung von dem neuen Cometen des
1742sten Jahres*

Halle: Rengerische Buchladen, 1742

18 cm. 99 leaves. Engraved frontispiece. This work is
bound with Wiedeburg, J., *Astronomisches Bedenken*, 1744
(item 207).

Zinner Collection

Lalande lists a similar title by the same author.

NUC: ICU; MH; NN

175 SHADEK, NICOLAUS DE?, fl. first half of the sixteenth century

[Kalender]

Kraków: M. Scharffenberger, 1531

18 cm. 2 unnumbered leaves. Fragment of a larger work.
Table. Colophon on recto of second leaf.

Shadek was an astronomer at the University of
Kraków where he published a series of annual
ephemerides from 1519 to 1532.

Zinner Collection

Zinner, 1467

NUC: no copy

176 SOUCIET, ETIENNE, 1671–1744

Observations mathématiques, astronomiques

Paris: Rollin Libraire, 1729–32

26 cm. Three volumes in one. Illustrations, folding copper-
engraved plates. Contemporary vellum over boards.

Zinner Collection

Lalande, p. 388

NUC: CSdS; CU; CtU; DN-Ob; ICJ; MH; MSaE; MiU;
NN; NNC; NWM; NjP; OkU; PPiD; RPB

177 SPERLING, JOHANN, 1603–58, preses;
Respondens, THOMAS SCHARNOW

Disputatio Physica de Stellis

Wittenberg: Michael Wendt, 1643

19 cm. 6 leaves.

Sperling was professor of physics at the University of
Wittenberg beginning in 1634.

Zinner Collection

Lalande, p. 216

NUC: CSdS

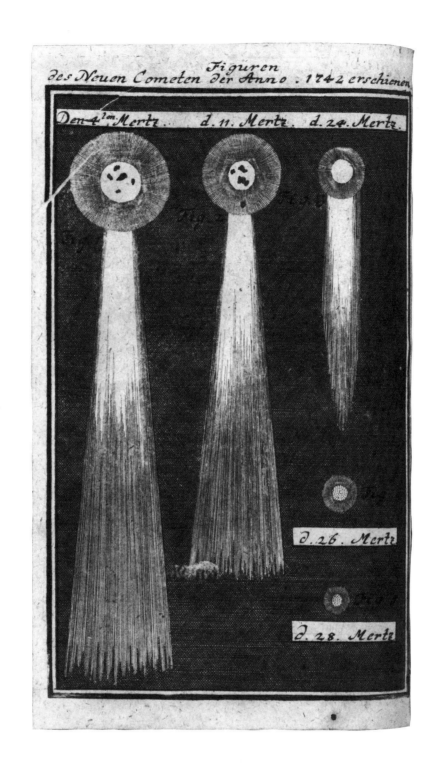

174. Semler, *Vollständige Beschreibung von dem neuen Cometen des 1742sten Jahres*
[Complete description of the new comet of the year 1742] (1742) frontispiece
depicting comet on different dates

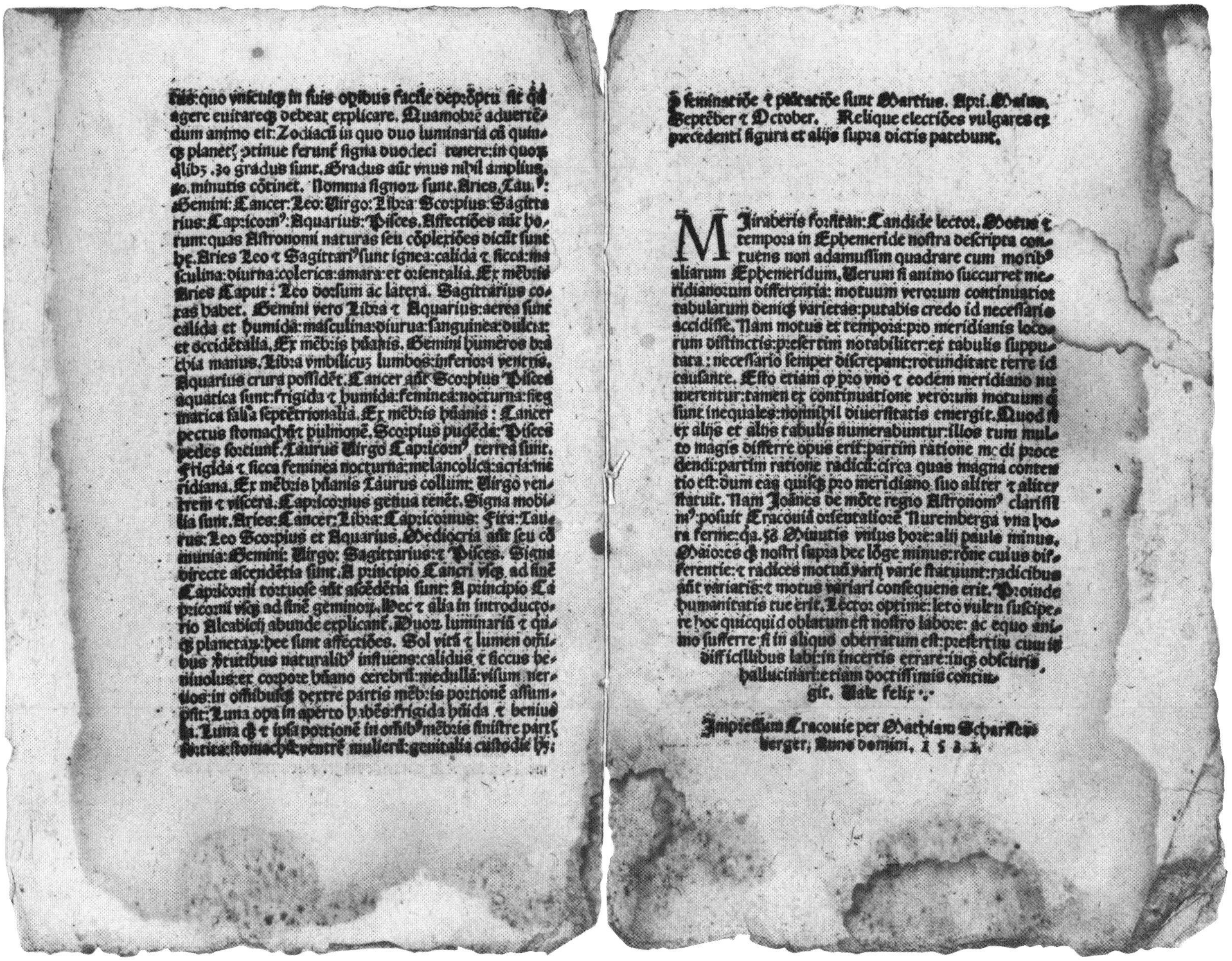

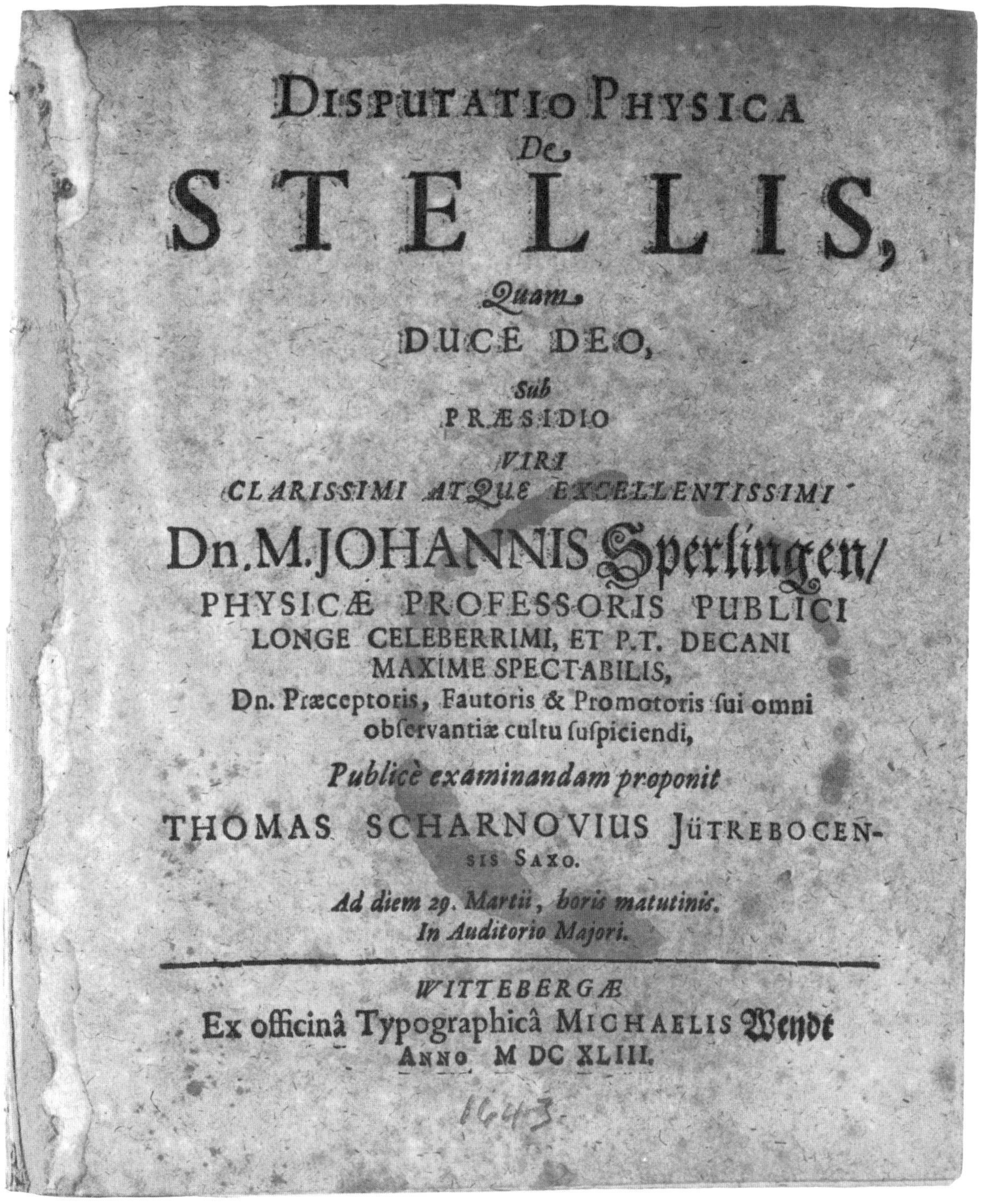

DISPUTATIO PHYSICA
De
STELLIS,
Quam
DUCE DEO,
Sub
PRÆSIDIO
VIRI
CLARISSIMI ATQUE EXCELLENTISSIMI
Dn. M. JOHANNIS Sperlingen/
PHYSICÆ PROFESSORIS PUBLICI
LONGE CELEBERRIMI, ET P.T. DECANI
MAXIME SPECTABILIS,
Dn. Præceptoris, Fautoris & Promotoris sui omni
observantiæ cultu suspiciendi,
Publicè examinandam proponit
THOMAS SCHARNOVIUS JÜTREBOCENSIS SAXO.
Ad diem 29. Martii, horis matutinis.
In Auditorio Majori.

WITTEBERGÆ
Ex officinâ Typographicâ MICHAELIS Wendt
ANNO M DC XLIII.

1643

177. Sperling, *Disputatio Physica de Stellis*
[Physical disputation concerning the stars] (1643) title page

178 STADIUS, JOHANNES, 1527–79

Ephemeris 1564–1573

n.p.: n.p., 1564?

21 cm. 140 leaves. Illustrations. Bound in vellum.

Stadius was a famous sixteenth-century mathematician. He was born at Loenhout in Brabant and studied the humanities and mathematics at the University of Louvain. He advanced so rapidly in his mathematical studies that he early prepared and published several editions of ephemerides covering successive years from 1554 up to 1606. His first ephemerides, prepared for the bishop of Liège, followed the *Alfonsine Tables* (item 3). Later he was called to France where he prepared prognostications on the future for officials at the French court. He wrote many astrological and astronomical tracts before his death at Paris (*Iselin*, v. 6, p. 546). Subsequent astronomers cited his tables, along with those of Leovitius (item 106) and others, to prove the Copernican theory (*Zinner*, pp. 37–8).

Zinner Collection

NUC: no copy

179 STENGEL, JOHANN PETERSON

Gnomonica Universalis

Ulm: D. Bartholomae, 1710.

17 cm. 178 leaves. Frontispiece. 110 plates. Illustrations of sundials. Two manuscript pages laid in. Provenance, front fly leaf: "H. Francke 1877."

Originally published in 1675 at Augsburg. Six more editions appeared up to 1755.

Zinner Collection

Houzeau, 962

NUC: no copy

180 STÖFFLER, JOHANN, 1452–1531

Almanach Nova Plurimis Annis Venturis

Venice?: n.p., 1504?

21 cm. 159 leaves. Ephemerides 1519–30, this appears to be a fragment from one of Stöffler's many editions of ephemerides.

Educated at Ingolstadt, Stöffler became professor of mathematics at the University of Tübingen in 1511. He was best known for his *Ephemerides*, which continued the ephemerides of Regiomontanus, and for his *Calendarium Magnum Romanum*. Philipp Melanchthon was one of his pupils.

Zinner Collection

Lalande, p. 31

NUC: DFo; MH

181 STÖFFLER, JOHANN, 1452–1531

Calendarium Romanum

Oppenheim: J. Köbel, 1518.

22 cm. 4-leaf fragment. Printed in red and black.

Zinner Collection

Lalande, p. 39; Zinner, 1101

NUC: CU; DLC; InU; MB; MH; MWA; MWiW-C; NNC; NcD; TxU

182 STÖFFLER, JOHANN, 1452–1531

Elucidatio Fabricae Ususque Astrolabii

Oppenheim: Jacob Köbel, 1524

32 cm. 88 leaves. Thirty-five woodcuts. Historiated initials and printer's devices.

The first edition was published in 1513. Up to 1619 six additional editions appeared.

Houzeau, 3231; Lalande, p. 44; Zinner, 1270

NUC: CtY; MH; NN; NcD-MC; OkU

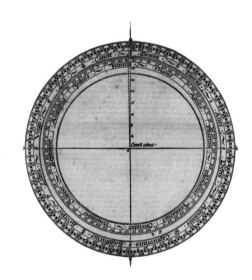

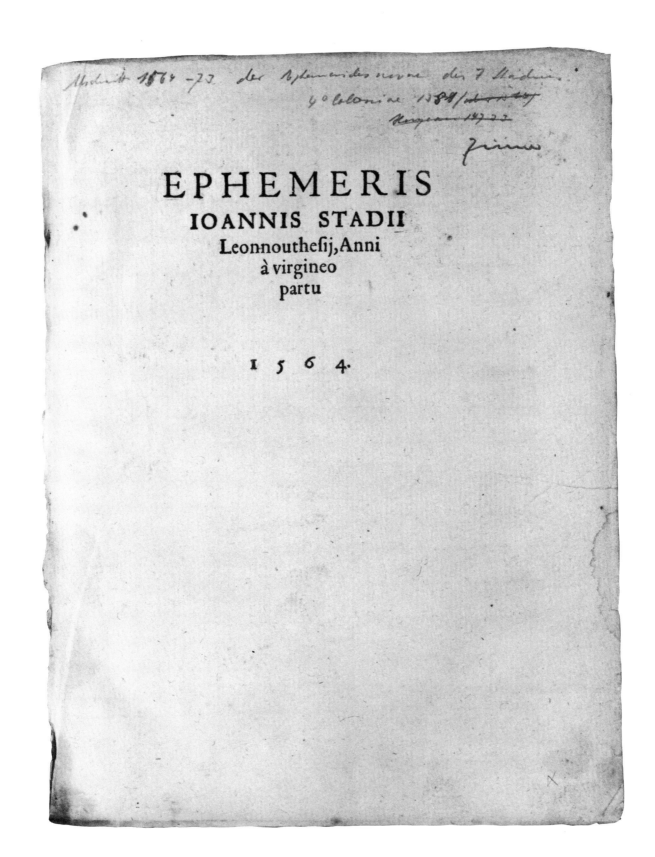

EPHEMERIS

IOANNIS STADII
Leonnouthesij, Anni
à virgineo
partu

1 5 6 4.

178. Stadius, *Ephemeris 1564-1573* (1564?) title page

179. Stengel, *Gnomonica Universalis* [The entire art of making sundials] (1710) frontispiece

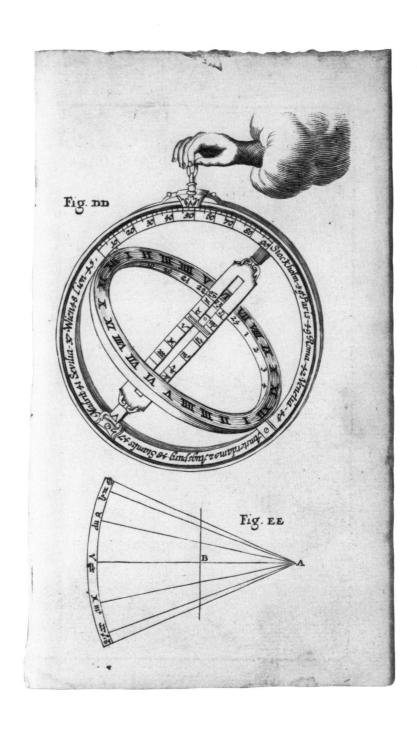

179. Stengel, *Gnomonica Universalis* (1710) diagram

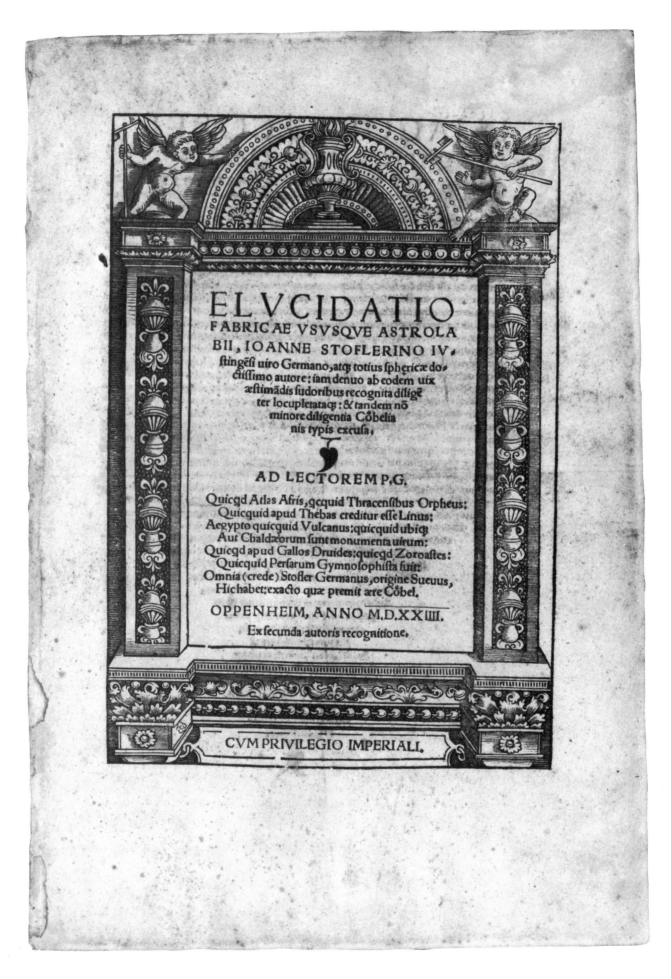

ELVCIDATIO
FABRICAE VSVSQVE ASTROLA
BII, IOANNE STOFLERINO IV,
stingēsi uiro Germano, atꝗ totius sphęricæ do,
ctissimo autore: iam denuo ab eodem uix
æstimādis sudoribus recognita dilige
ter locupletatacꝗ: & tandem nō
minore diligentia Cóbelia
nis typis excusa,

AD LECTOREM P.G.

Quicꝗd Atlas Afris, ꝗcquid Thracensibus Orpheus:
Quicquid apud Thebas creditur esse Linus:
Aegypto quicquid Vulcanus: quicquid ubiꝗ
Aut Chaldæorum sunt monumenta uirum:
Quicꝗd apud Gallos Druides: quicꝗd Zoroastes:
Quicquid Persarum Gymnosophista fuit:
Omnia (crede) Stofler Germanus, origine Sueuus,
Hic habet: exacto quæ premit ære Cóbel.

OPPENHEIM, ANNO M.D.XXIIII.
Ex secunda autoris recognitione,

CVM PRIVILEGIO IMPERIALI,

182. Stöffler, *Elucidatio Fabricae Ususque Astrolabii* [Elucidation on the manufacture
and use of the astrolabe] (1524) title page (reduced)

SECVNDA PARS DE

Propositio. LXI. secunde partis.

Oco non mutato/vbi primum steteris/ altitudinis coram positæ mensurā comphendere. ¶ Si hoc idem quod in antecedēte ppositione determinauimus, non mouendo te de loco, sed firmato pede absoluere uolueris, hoc pacto opare. ¶ Sume astrolabiū, & subleuato eo cōtra altitudinē mediclíniū torquēdo coaptabis, qusq p utrūcq foramē tabellæ summitatē altitudinis uideas, tūc si linea Fiduciæ ceciderit sup latus umbræ rectæ uel extensæ, denotat, qp altitudo rei maior est spatio intercepto inter basim aut radicē altitudinis & mediū pedis tui; & in quanta pportione se habent, 12, ab ista puncta quæ abscindit linea Fiduciæ; in tanta se habebit altitudo rei ad spatium inter te & ipsam, addita quantitate staturæ tuæ, ut supra admonuimus. ¶ Et practicatur sic. Numerę punctorum rectorę p lineam fiduciæ abscisorę serua, deinde metire spatium, quod intercipitur inter radicē altitudinis rei mensurandæ & pedem tuum, aliqua mensura tibi nota, puta p pedes uel passꝰ &c. & multiplicentur per 12. & productū diuidatur per numerum punctorum supra seruatum; et quod ex diuisione exierit, erit altitudo rei: addita quantitate staturæ tuæ. ¶ Verbi gratia, sit altitudo, b, c, mensuranda, spatiū a radice altitudinis ad pedem meum, c, d 5, passuum: statura uero, d, e, duorę passuū. Puncta scalæ umbræ rectæ tacta ab Alhidada, 6, duco spatiū, 5, passuū in 12 & pcreo, 60, q̃ diuido p, 6, pūcta recta, et habeo, 10, passus, qbus addo staturā duorū passuū, & colligo, 12, passus concludo igitur altitudinē ppositā habere, 12, passus.

Huius demōstrationis hāc cape figurā.

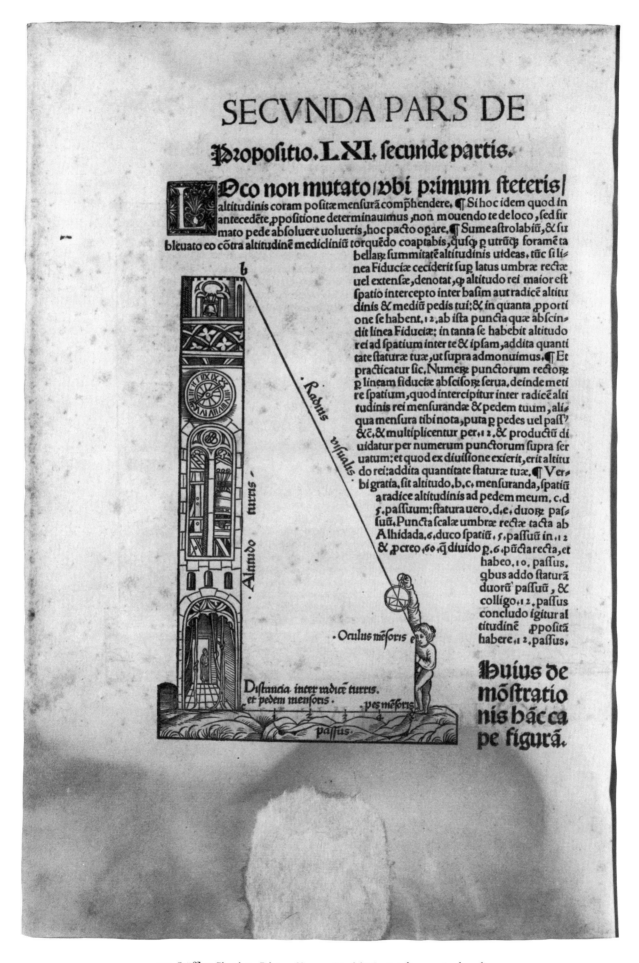

182. Stöffler, *Elucidatio Fabricae Ususque Astrolabii* (1524) diagram (reduced)

SECVNDA PARS·

182. Stöffler, *Elucidatio Fabricae Ususque Astrolabii* (1524) diagram (reduced)

AD IMPRESSOREM GEO/
RIVS SIMLER·

QVam Côbel apparet formofus in ære character,
Et Iuftingenfis per monumenta uiri,
Sic per te uiuit Stofler, tu nomen ab illo
Ducis, & artifices monftrat uterç labor.
Atç opere æternum duo nunc uiuetis in uno,
Ilia uel Codro terç, quaterç crepant,

OPPENHEIM IN AEDIBVS IACOBI COBELII,
MENSE MARTIO. ANNO RESTITVTAE
SALVTIS HVMANAE M.D.XXIIII.

182. Stöffler, *Elucidatio Fabricae Ususque Astrolabii* (1524) colophon (reduced)

183 STRAUCH, AEGIDIUS, 1632–82

Astrognosia

Wittenberg: T. Mevii & E. Schumacher, 1668

14 cm. 208 pages. Illustrations. Second edition.

Strauch was professor at the University of Wittenberg. His *Astrognosia* may be described as an astronomical textbook with astrological trimmings (Thorndike, L., *A History of Magic and Experimental Science*, New York: Macmillan, 1958, v. 7, p. 313).

Zinner Collection

Houzeau, 2919 (first edition 1659 was followed by others, the last 1722); Lalande, p. 272

NUC: CSdS; ICJ; NNUT

184 STRAUCH, AEGIDIUS, 1632–82

Von...dem jetzigen neuen Wunder-Sternen

Gdánsk: David-Friderich Rhete, 1681?

19 cm. 28 pages.

NUC: no copy

185 THEODORICUS WINSHEMIUS, SEBASTIANUS

Novae Quaestiones Sphaerae

Wittenberg: J. Crato, 1564

16 cm. 165 leaves. Illustrations, three folding plates, tables, diagrams. Bound in modern half vellum. First edition.

Theodoricus was a professor at the University of Wittenberg.

Lalande, p. 89; Zinner, 2356

NUC: WU

186 THOMAS, CORBINIANUS, 1694–1767

Firmamentum Firmianum

Augsburg: Merz & Mayr, 1731

17 × 22 cm. 111 leaves. Illustrations, eighty-four copper-engraved plates, many folding, tables.

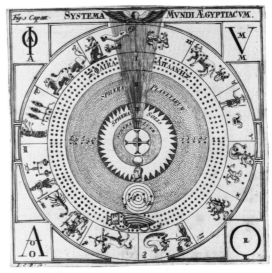

Egyptian cosmology

Thomas was a Benedictine monk and professor of mathematics at the University of Salzburg beginning in 1721.

Zinner Collection

Lalande, p. 392

NUC: CSdS; ICU; NNC; WU

187 TRIEGLER, JOANNES GEORGIUS

Sphaera. Das ist ein kurtzes Astronomisches Tractätlein

Leipzig: Joh. Herman, 1614

19 cm. 97 leaves. Illustrations. First edition. A second edition appeared in 1622.

Zinner Collection

Lalande, p. 162; Zinner, 4487

NUC: CSdS

Non cuivis contingit adire Corinthum.

ÆGIDII STRAUCHII,
PROFESS. WITTEB.
ASTROGNOSIA,
SYNOPTICE ET ME-
THODICE,
IN
USUM GYMNASIORUM
& *ACADEMIARUM*
ADORNATA.
ADDITA SUNT
ASTERISMORUM
ET PLANETARUM
SCHEMATA,
ÆREIS LAMINIS
EXPRESSA.
EDITIO SECUNDA, PRIORI
MULTO AUCTIOR.

WITTEBERGÆ,
Sumptibus Hæred. D. TOBIÆ MEVII, &
ELERDI SCHUMACHERI,
Literis MATTHÆI HENCKELII,
ANNO M. DC. LXIIX.

183. Strauch, *Astrognosia* [Star knowledge] (1668) title page and a folding frontispiece

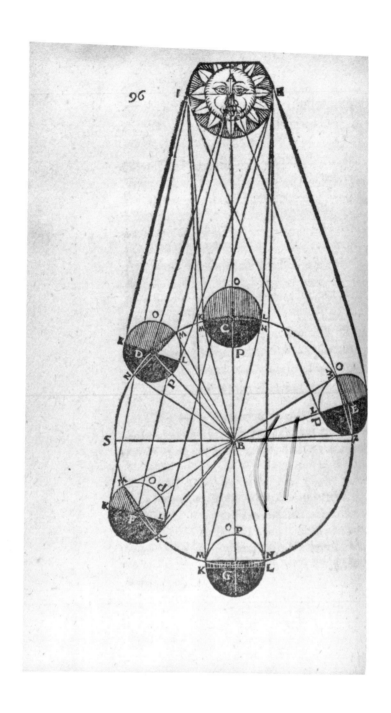

185. Theodoricus, *Novae Quaestiones Sphaerae* [New questions on the sphere] (1564) diagram

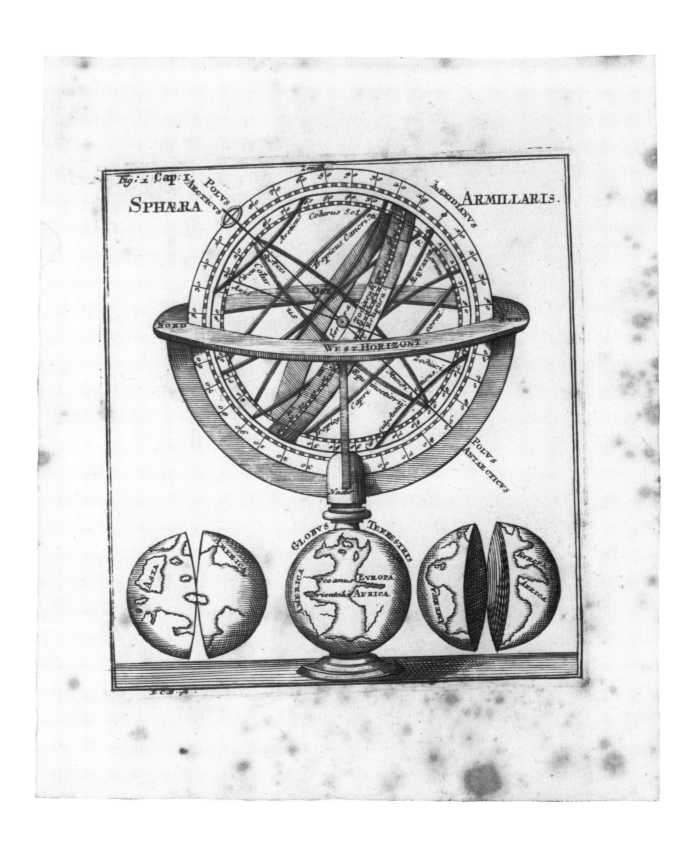

186. Thomas, *Firmamentum Firmianum* [The orb of the fixed stars] (1731)
an armillary

186. Thomas, *Firmamentum Firmianum* (1731) folding frontispiece (reduced)

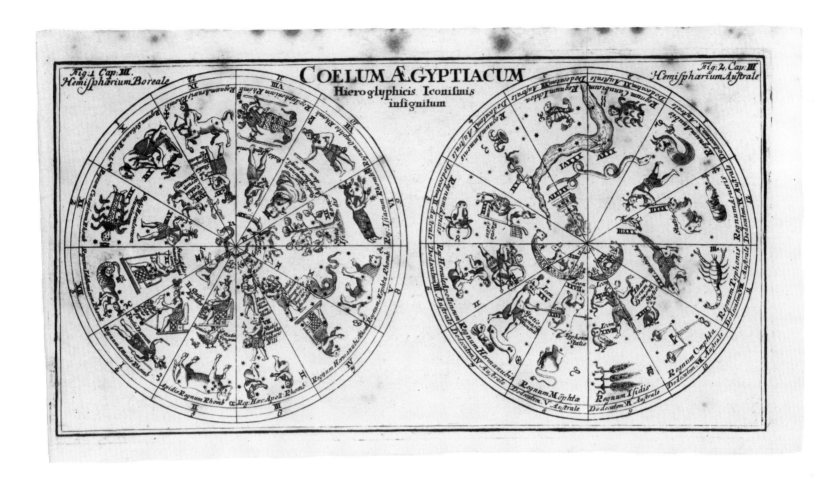

186. Thomas, *Firmamentum Firmianum* (1731) folding plate of the Egyptian star map (reduced)

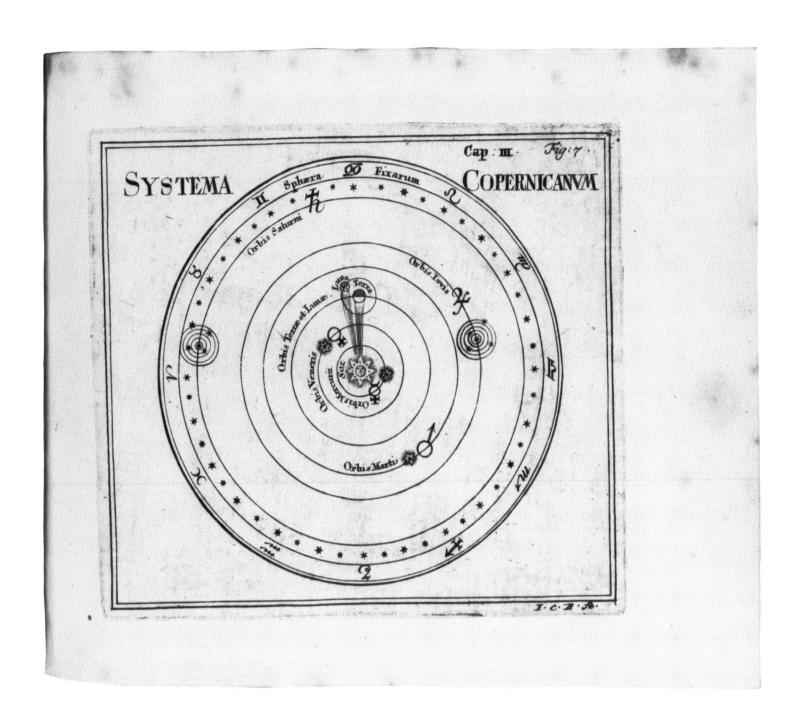

186. Thomas, *Firmamentum Firmianum* (1731) Copernican celestial sphere

187. Triegler, *Sphaera. Das ist ein kurtzes Astronomisches Tractätlein*
[Sphere. That is a short astronomical treatise] (1614) portrait of Triegler

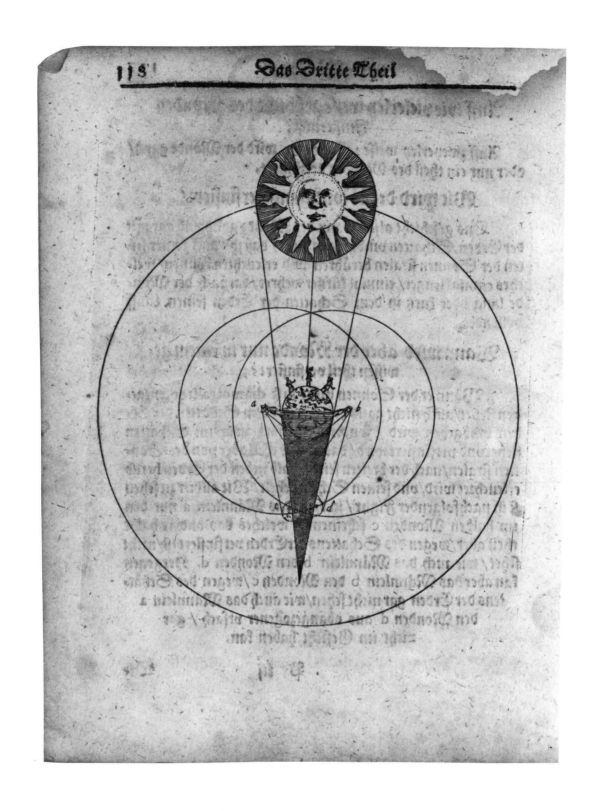

187. Triegler, *Sphaera. Das ist ein kurtzes Astronomisches Tractätlein* (1614)
diagram of an eclipse

188 *Typus Globi Astriferi*

Antwerp: J. Grapheus, 1548

17 cm. 27 leaves. Marginalia. Woodcut illustration on title page, historiated initial at head of chapter one, vignettes on third and last two leaves. Bound with Gemma Frisius, R., *De Principiis Astronomiae et Cosmographiae* (item 72).

Zinner Collection

NUC: no copy

vignette from the colophon

189 *Unterschiedliche Beschreibung und Bedeutunge... des... Wunder Cometen*

n.p.: n.p., 1681

19 cm. 46 pages.

NUC: MH

190 VAREN, BERNHARD, 1622–50

Geographia Generalis

Amsterdam: L. Elzevir, 1650

14 cm. 415 leaves. Illustrations. First edition.

Varen studied mathematics and medicine, receiving his M.D. from the University of Leiden in 1649. His best known work, *Geographia Generalis*, was first published in 1650. It became the standard geographic text for a century. Newton revised parts of it for an edition later published in England (*DSB*, v. 13, p. 583). See item 190.

Lalande, p. 358.

NUC: CU-S; CtY; DLC; ICJ; IEN; IU; LNT; LU; MiD; NN; NjP; OrU; PPL; PU; WU

191 VAREN, BERNHARD, 1622–50

Geographia Generalis... ab Isaaco Newton Editio Secunda Auctior & Emendatior

Cambridge: John Hayes, 1681

19 cm. 544 pages. Title page printed in red and black. Five folding engraved plates. Full leather. Second edition of the Newton revision, which first appeared at Cambridge in 1672. Provenance, title page: "Jo. Gilbert."

NUC: AzU; CaBVaU; CLU-C; CtY; DFo; DLC; IU; KU; MH; NN; NjR; NcD; PPL; PU

192 VERBIEST, FERDINAND, 1623–88

Astronomia Europaea sub Imperatore Tartaro Sinico

Dillingen: J. C. Bencard, 1687

21 cm. 126 pages. Illustrations, folding plate.

Verbiest was a Flemish Jesuit who went to China as a missionary in 1659, where he learned all he could about Chinese astronomy. He died in China in 1688. Besides his *Astronomia Europaea*, he wrote some twenty books in Chinese.

Zinner Collection

Houzeau, 294; Lalande, p. 318

NUC: CSdS; MiU; NN; PPiD

193 VIRLING, GEORG SAMUEL

Der wackere Stab des Herren...durch den...Cometen.

Erfurt: Benjamin Hempel, 1681

19 cm. 26 leaves. Two folding plates.

NUC: ICN; NNC

188. *Typus Globi Astriferi* [Figure of an astronomical globe] (1548) title page

Unterschiedliche
Beschreibung = und Bedeu=
tungen/
So wohl der COMETEN ins Gemein/
Als insonderheit
Des bißanhero nicht sonder grosses Entsetzen
erschienenen/und weit und breit
observirten
Wunder=Cometen/
Mit Fleiß zusammen getragen/
und
Gedruckt im Jahr 1681.

189. *Unterschiedliche Beschreibung und Bedeutunge…des…Wunder Cometen*
[Discriminating description and meanings of the miraculous comet] (1681) title page

190. Varen, *Geographia Generalis* [General geography] (1650) title page

BERNHARDI VARENI

Med. D.

GEOGRAPHIA

GENERALIS,

In qua Affectiones Generales Telluris
EXPLICANTUR,

Summâ curâ quam plurimis in locis Emendata, &
XXXIII Schematibus Novis, Ære incisis, unà cum
Tabb. aliquot quæ desiderabantur Aucta & Illustrata.

Ab ISAACO NEWTON Math. Prof. Lucasi-
ano apud CANTABRIGIENSES.

Editio Secunda Auctior & Emendatior.

CANTABRIGIÆ,
Ex Officina *Joann. Hayes,* Celeberrimæ Academiæ Typographi,
Sumptibus *Henrici Dickinson* Bibliopolæ. MDCLXXXI.

191. Varen, *Geographia Generalis* (1681) title page

ASTRONOMIA EUROPÆA

SVB IMPERATORE
TARTARO SINICO
Cám Hý
APPELLATO
EX UMBRA IN LUCEM REVOCATA
à

R.P. FERDINANDO

VERBIEST

FLANDRO-BELGA
E SOCIETATE JESU
Academiæ Aftronomicæ in Regia PeKinenfi
PRÆFECTO
Cum Privilegio Cæfareo, & facultate Superiorum.

DILINGÆ,
Typis & Sumptibus, JOANNIS CASPARI BENCARD,
Bibliopolæ Academici.
Per JOANNEM FEDERLE.
ANNO M. DC. LXXXVII.

192. Verbiest, *Astronomia Europaea sub Imperatore Tartaro Sinico* [European astronomy under the Tartar emperor of China] (1687) title page

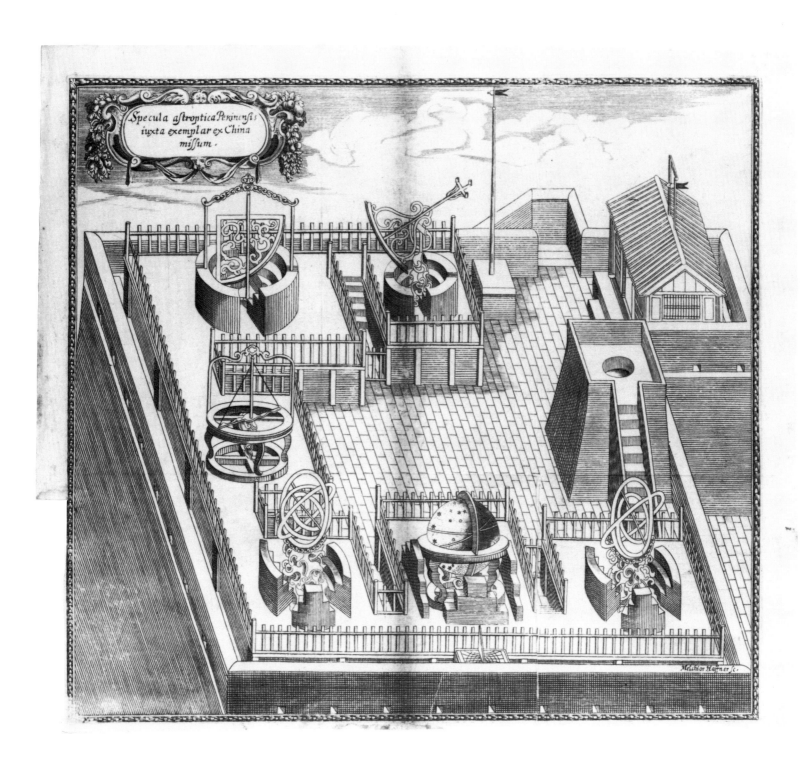

Specula astroptica Pekinensis iuxta exemplar ex China missum.

Melchior Hafner sc.

192. Verbiest, *Astronomia Europaea sub Imperatore Tartaro Sinico* (1687)
view of astronomical observatory at Beijing (reduced)

193. Virling, *Der wackere Stab des Herren…durch den…Cometen* [The watchful sceptre
of the Lord through the comet] (1681)

193. Virling, *Der wackere Stab des Herren…durch den…Cometen* (1681)
depiction of comets passing through several constellations

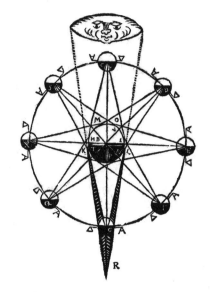

194 VOIGT, JOHANN HEINRICH, 1613–91

Astrologische Mittel-Strasse

Stade: Caspar Holwein, 1670?

19 cm. 48 pages. Woodcut headpiece.

Zinner Collection

NUC: no copy

195 *Von den Cometen*

Halle: n.p., 1769

18 cm. 51 leaves. Tables, vignettes. Bound with Wiedeburg, J. *Astronomisches Bedenken*, 1744 (item 207).

Zinner Collection

Lalande, p. 514

NUC: no copy

Weigel was educated at the University of Leipzig where he received a Master's degree. He was professor of mathematics at the Univeristy of Jena from 1753 until his death. He erected an observatory with four towers and built astronomical instruments.

Zinner Collection

NUC: ICN; NNC

196 WATTS, ISAAC, 1674–1748

The Knowledge of the Heavens

London: T. Longman, 1752

21 cm. 247 pages. Six folding plates. Page 62 misnumbered 29. Fifth edition corrected.

The first edition appeared in 1726. Watts was a popular hymn writer and religious dissenter.

NUC: IU; MB; MH; PMA; PP

198 WEIGEL, ERHARD, 1625–99

Fortsetzung des Himmels-Zeigers. Der Bedeutung...des ungemeinen Cometen

Jena: J. Bielcke, 1681

21 cm. 63 leaves. Illustrations, folding plate, decorative initials. Bound with item 199.

Another copy bound with item 203 has sixty-one leaves and lacks the folding plate.

Zinner Collection

NUC: no copy

197 WEIGEL, ERHARD, 1625–99

Fortsetzung des Himels Spiegels...Grosse Comet

Jena: J. Meyers, 1681

21 cm. 79 leaves. Illustration, one folding plate, decorative initials. bound with item 203.

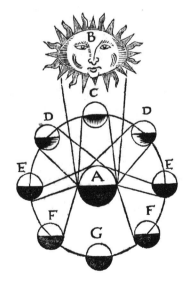

199 WEIGEL, ERHARD, 1625–99

Himmels-Zeiger der Bedeutung bey Erscheinung des ungemeinen Cometen

Jena: J. Bielcke, 1681

20 cm. 53 leaves. Illustrations. Bound with his *Fortsetzung des Himmels-Zeigers*, 1681 (item 198).

Zinner Collection

Lalande, p. 303

NUC: NNC

194. Voigt, *Astrologische Mittel-Strasse* [Astrological method] (1670?) title page

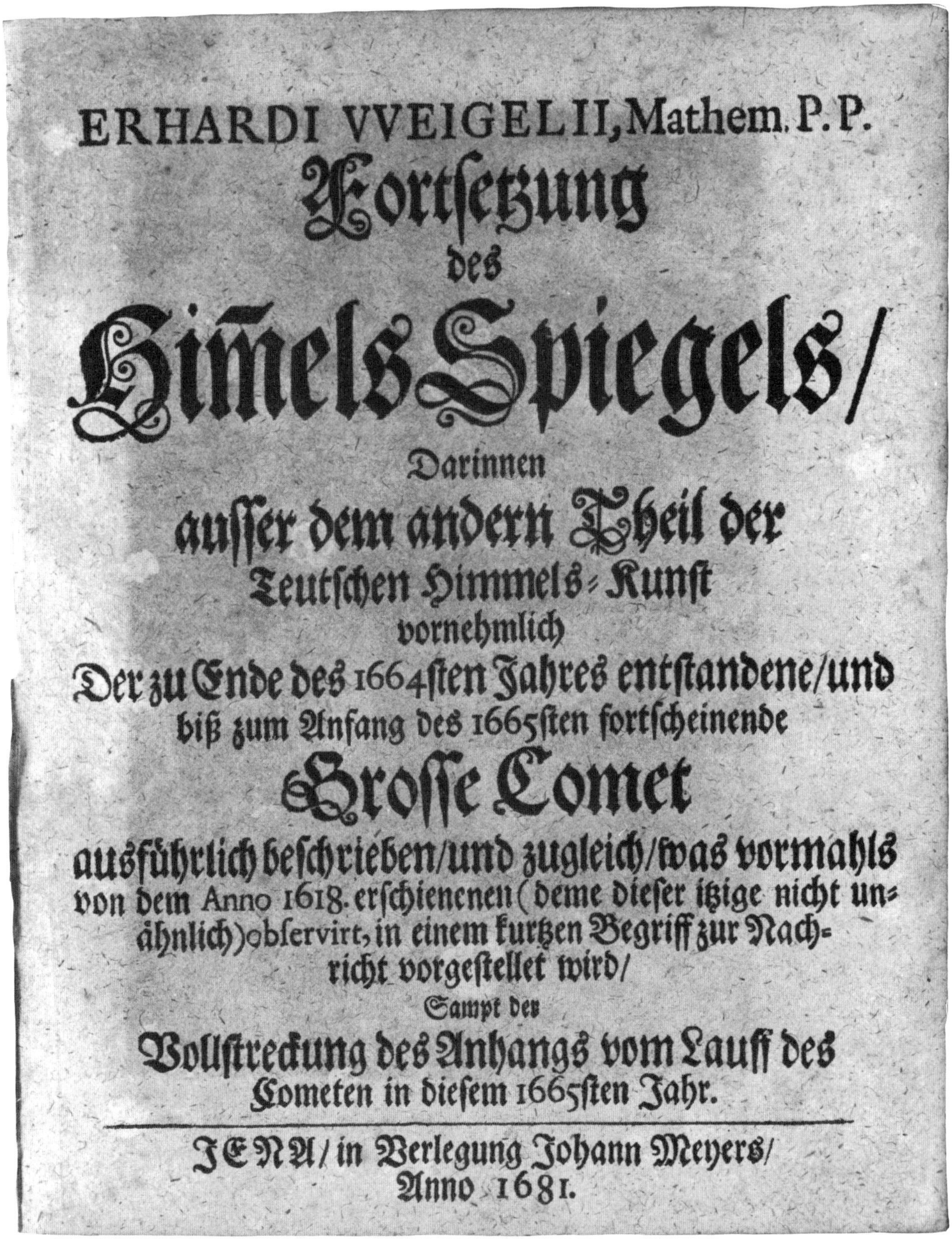

ERHARDI VVEIGELII, Mathem. P. P.

Fortsetzung
des
Himels Spiegels/

Darinnen

auffer dem andern Theil der
Teutschen Himmels-Kunst
vornehmlich

Der zu Ende des 1664sten Jahres entstandene/und
biß zum Anfang des 1665sten fortscheinende

Grosse Comet

ausführlich beschrieben/und zugleich/was vormahls
von dem Anno 1618. erschienenen (deme dieser itzige nicht un-
ähnlich) observirt, in einem kurtzen Begriff zur Nachricht vorgestellet wird/

Sampt der

Vollstreckung des Anhangs vom Lauff des
Cometen in diesem 1665sten Jahr.

JENA/ in Verlegung Johann Meyers/
Anno 1681.

197. Weigel, *Fortsetzung des Hiñels Spiegels…Grosse Comet* [Continuation of the mirror
of the heavens…Great Comet] (1681) title page

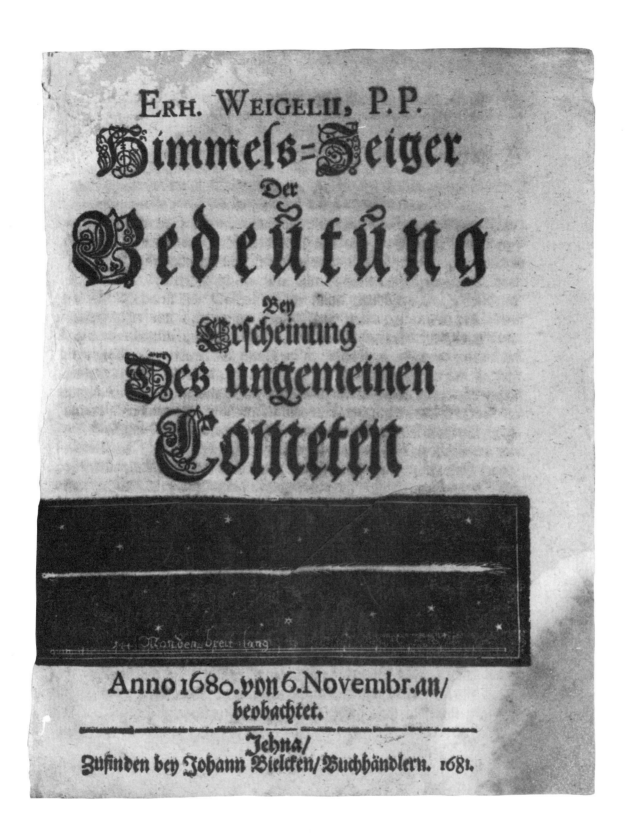

199. Weigel, *Himmels-Zeiger der Bedeutung bey Erscheinung des ungemeinen Cometen*
[The meaning of the sign in the heavens, the extraordinary comet] (1681)
title page showing the path of the comet

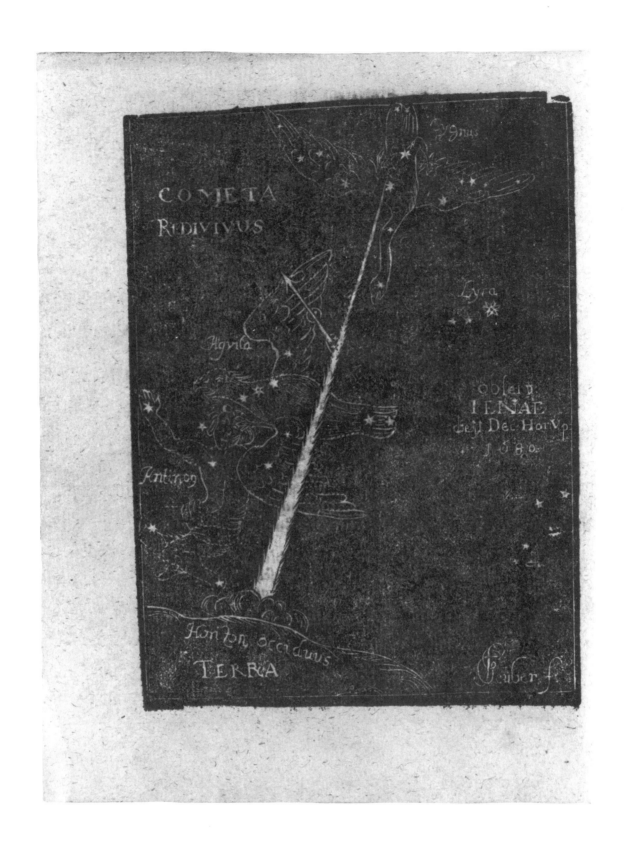

199. Weigel, *Himmels-Zeiger der Bedeutung bey Erscheinung des ungemeinen Cometen* (1681)
folding map showing the path of a comet

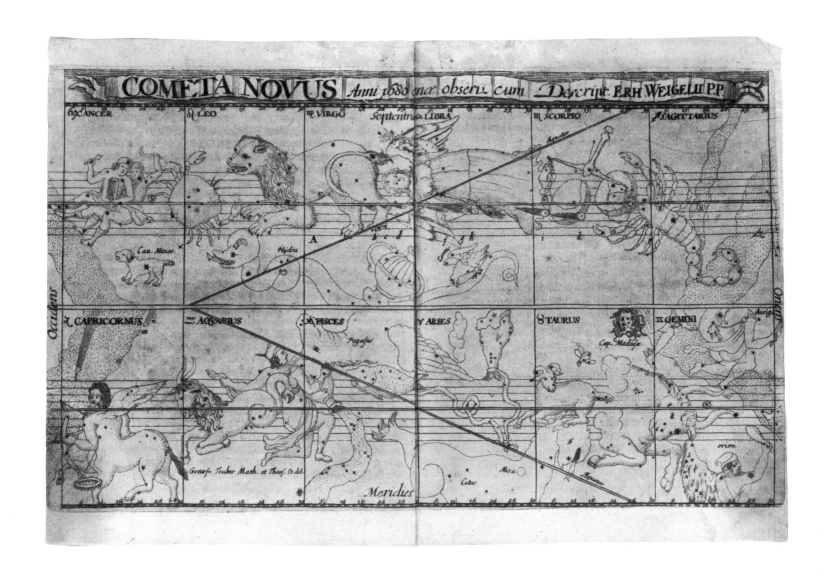

199. Weigel, *Himmels-Zeiger der Bedeutung bey Erscheinung des ungemeinen Cometen* (1681)
folding map showing the comet of 1680 (reduced)

200 WEIGEL, ERHARD, 1625–99

Kurtze Beschreibung der verbesserten Himmels- und Erd-Globen

Jena: J. Meyers, 1681

20 cm. 8 leaves. Folding plate.

Zinner Collection

NUC: CSdS; NNC

201 WEIGEL, ERHARD, 1625–99

Specimen Deliberationis Mathematicae

Jena: J. Bielcke, 1685

21 cm. 16 leaves. Four folding plates. Bound with item 203.

Zinner Collection

NUC: no copy

202 WEIGEL, ERHARD, 1625–99

Speculum Uranicum... Comet

Jena: J. Meyers, 1681

21 cm. 65 leaves. Illustrations, three plates, tables, decorative initials. Bound with item 203.

Zinner Collection

NUC: NNC

203 WEIGEL, ERHARD, 1625–99

Unmassgebliche mathematische Vorschläge

Jena: J. Bielcke, 1682

21 cm. 28 leaves. Decorative initials. Bound with this work are his: *Der durch angestellte Prob...den kleinsten Kindern...der Lateinischen Sprach...zugewehnen*, Jena, 1684; *Die bereiteste Execution des...Vorschlags...entworfen*, Jena, 1685; *Specimen Deliberationis Mathematicae*, Jena, 1685 (item 20); *Von der Würckung des Bemuths...des neuen Cometen*, Jena, 1684 (item 204); *Speculum Uranicum...Comet*, Jena, 1681 (item 202); *Fortsetzung des Himmels-Spiegels...zu Ende des 1664...biss zum Anfang des 1665sten fortscheinende Grosse Comet*, Jena, 1681; and *Fortsetzung des Himmels-Zeigers. Der Bedeutung des ungemeinen Cometen*, Jena, 1681 (item 198). *(item 197)*

Collection of tracts on comets with many illustrations, including folding plates. There is a strong religious point of view, while astrological interpretations are dismissed as having no merit.

Zinner Collection

NUC: no copy

---

204 WEIGEL, ERHARD, 1625–99

Von der Würckung des Bemuths... des neuen Cometen

Jena: J. Bielcke, 1684

21 cm. 40 leaves. Frontispiece. Bound with item 203.

Zinner Collection

NUC: no copy

205 WERNER, JOHANNES, 1468–1528?

Canones... Complectentes Praecepta & Observationes de Mutatione Aurae

Nürnberg: J. Montanus & U. Neuber, 1546

21 cm. 19 leaves. Decorative initials. Ex Libris Gerardi Barbe Vethoris Salinensis, 1631. Contemporary parchment binding.

Nürnberg astronomer and mathematician Werner is best known for his mathematical works on the triangle and the quadrant. He also made astrolabes and sundials. Zinner gives 1522 as his death date (Zinner, *Astronomische Instrumente*, p. 584).

NUC: MH

206 WIEDEBURG, JOHANN BERNHARD, 1687–1766

An die Bürger bey Gelegenheit des Kometen

Jena: Joh. Wilhelm Hartung, 1769

18 cm. 40 leaves. Illustration of the path of a comet on title page.

Wiedeburg was professor of mathematics at the University of Jena. He wrote numerous tracts including two explaining that the Copernican system does not contradict Scripture.

Bound with Wiedeburg, J., *Astronomisches Bedenken*, 1744 (item 207).

Zinner Collection

NUC: no copy

207 WIEDEBURG, JOHANN BERNHARD, 1687–1766

Astronomisches Bedenken

Jena: Joh. Adam Melchior, 1744

18 cm. 112 leaves. Frontispiece, vignette. New and enlarged edition. Bound with this work are his *An die Bürger bey Gelegenheit des Kometen*, 1769 (item 206); Semler, C., *Vollständige Beschreibung von dem neuen Cometen*, 1742 (item 174); Bode, J., *Deutliche Abhandlung*, 1769 (item 22); and *Von den Cometen*, 1769 (item 195).

Zinner Collection

NUC: CSdS; ICU; MH-AH; NIC; NNC

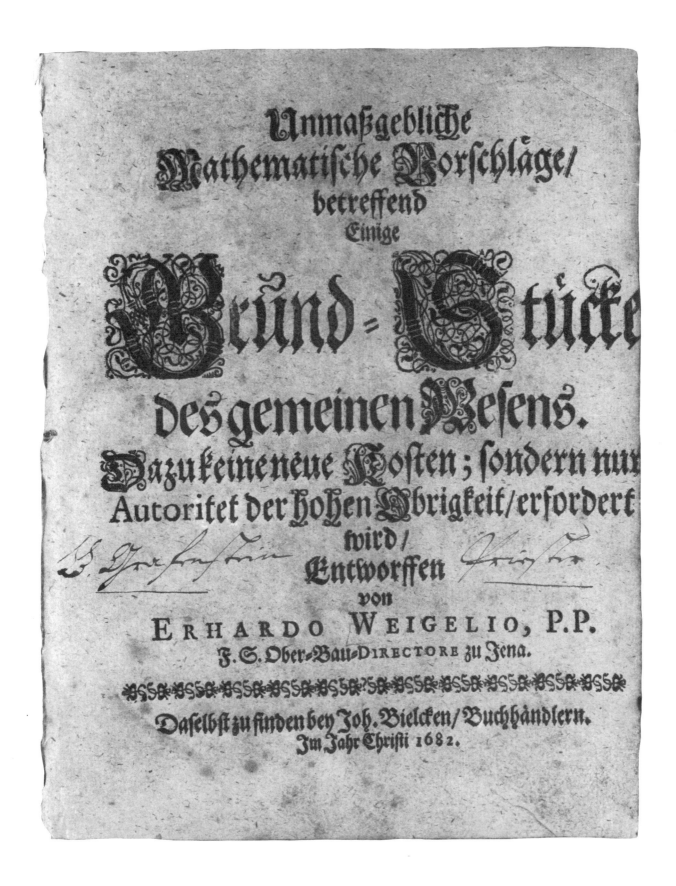

Unmaßgebliche
Mathematische Vorschläge/
betreffend
Einige

Gründ = Stücke

des gemeinen Wesens.

Dazu keine neue Kosten; sondern nur
Autoritet der hohen Obrigkeit/erfordert
wird/
Entworffen
von
ERHARDO WEIGELIO, P.P.
F. S. Ober=Bau=DIRECTORE zu Jena.

Daselbst zu finden bey Joh. Bielcken/Buchhändlern.
Im Jahr Christi 1682.

203. Weigel, *Unmassgebliche mathematische Vorschläge* [Nonprescribed mathematical propositions] (1682) title page

204. Weigel, *Von der Würckung des Bemuths...des neuen Cometen* [Concerning the effects of the influence of the new comet] (1684) fanciful depiction of the comet

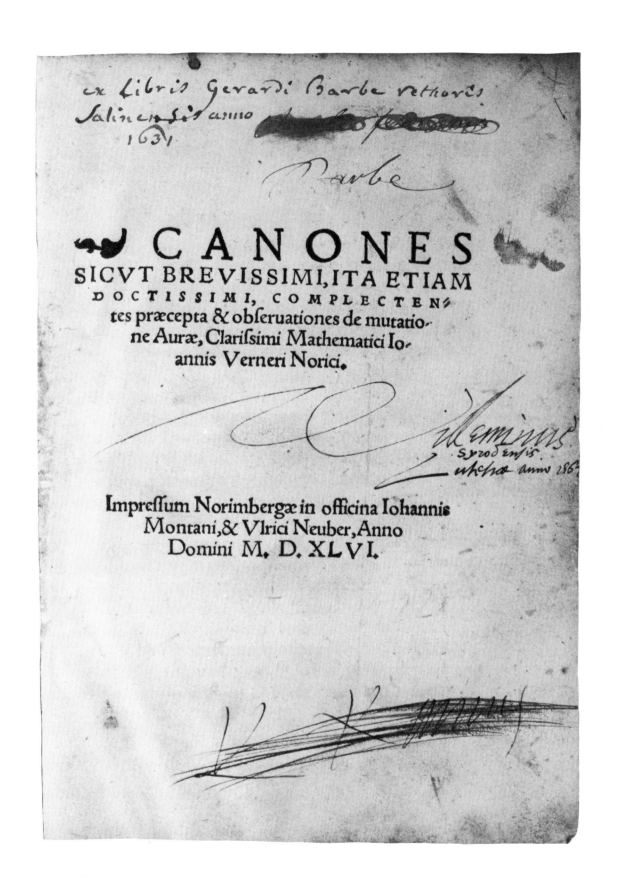

205. Werner, *Canones...Complectentes Praecepta & Observationes de Mutatione Aurae*
[Standard principles encompassing precepts and observations concerning
the changing heavens] (1546) title page

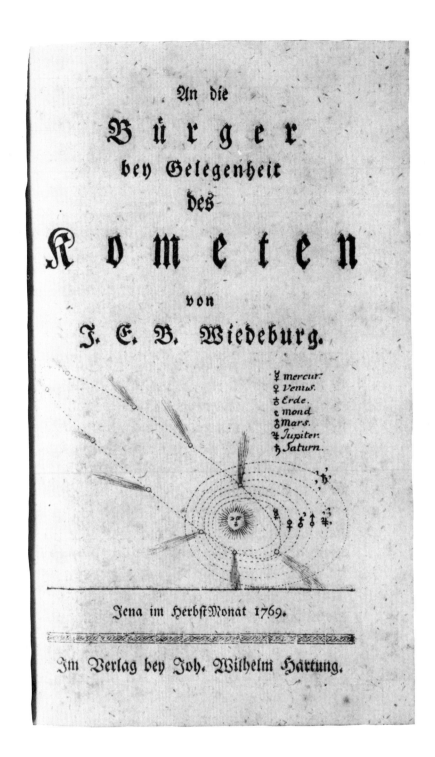

206. Wiedeburg, *An die Bürger bey Gelegenheit des Kometen*
[To the citizens upon the appearance of the comet] (1769) title page

Astronomisches
Bedenken

Ueber die Frage
Ob der bevorstehende Untergang der Welt
natürliger Weise entstehen
Ins besondere

Durch Annäherung eines

Cometen

zur Erden
werde befördert werden
Auch
binnen vier Jahren
Ein schreckliges Vorspiel desselben
zu erwarten

Nebst einer vollständigen Nachricht von dem Cometen
welcher am Ende des 1743sten und Anfang des
jeztlaufenden Jahres erschienen
entworfen
von

Joh. Bernhardt Wiedeburg.

Neue und vermehrte Auflage.

Jena, zu finden bey Joh. Adam Melchior, 1744.

207. Wiedeburg, *Astronomisches Bedenken* [Astronomical considerations] (1744)
title page and frontispiece

208 WILKINS, JOHN, BISHOP OF CHESTER, 1614–72

A Discourse Concerning a New Planet. Tending to Prove, that 'Tis Probable Our Earth Is One of the Planets

London: Printed by R. H. for John Maynard, 1640

18 cm. 130 leaves. Illustrations. First edition. Bound with his *The Discovery of a New World* (item 209).

Wilkins was a seventeenth-century theologian and writer on scientific subjects. His two books *Discovery* and *Discourse* were written for the common reader, to make known and to defend the new astronomy of Copernicus, Kepler, and Galileo.

Widely active in reconciling religion with scientific knowledge, his career included a long association with Oxford University and a shorter one with Cambridge. He took a leadership role in the Royal Society. He was committed to a policy of tolerance in an age of intolerance.

Houzeau, 1834; Lalande, p. 212

NUC: CtY; DFo; DLC; ICN; InU; MH; MWiW-C; NjP; NN; NcD; OrPR; PPL; PPT; WU

209 WILKINS, JOHN, BISHOP OF CHESTER, 1614–72

The Discovery of a New World

London: Printed by J. Norton for John Maynard, 1640

18 cm. 129 leaves. Full leather binding, gold lettering and fore edge. Frontispiece, decorative initials and borders, diagrams. Bound with item 208.

The first edition appeared in 1638.

Houzeau, 1834

NUC: CLU-C; CSmH; NN

210 WINKLER, NICOLAUS EBERHARD, ca.1529–1613

Practica und Bedencken auff das XC Jahr

Nürnberg: N. Knorr, 1590

22 cm. 8 leaves. Unbound. Almanac for the year 1590.

Nicolaus Eberhard Winkler was a doctor of medicine. Unlike his cousin Nicolaus Winkler, he opposed the intrusion of astrology into the practice of medicine.

Zinner Collection

Zinner, 3420

NUC: CSdS

211 WURZELBAU, JOHANN PHILIPP VON, 1651–1725

Uranies Noricae Basis Astronomico-Geographia

Nürnberg: Sumptibus Authoris, 1697

33 cm. 64 leaves. First edition. Two folding engraved frontispieces picturing the exterior and the interior of the astronomical observatory at Nürnberg. Decorative initials and borders, plates, tables, diagrams.

Bound with this work are his *Eclipseos Solaris quae Anno Chr. MDCLXXXIV. Die 2. Julii St. Vet. Horis Pomer. contigit.* (Nürnberg, 1685); *Eclipsis Lunae Totalis cum Mora Observata Norimbergae MDCLXXXV*; and Eimmart, G., *Ichnographia Nova Contemplationum de Sole*, 1701 (item 45).

Wurzelbau was a wealthy merchant at Nürnberg and from 1683 head of that city's Great Council. He was also elected to the Berlin Academy, the Royal Society, London, and the Royal Academy, Paris.

The author was engaged in astronomical endeavors at Nürnberg and was responsible for the construction of a fine observatory there (Lalande, p. 333).

Zinner Collection

Lalande, p. 333

NUC: CSdS; OkU

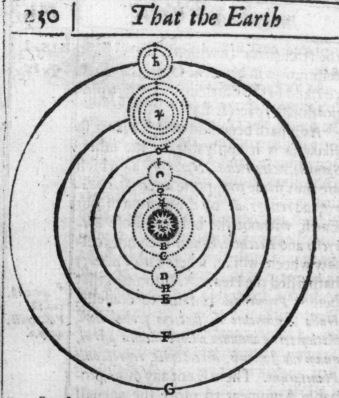

Suppose the Sunne to be scituated at **A**. Now because *Mercury* is found by experience to be alwaies very neere the Sunne, so that he do's for the most part lye hid under his Raies. As also because this Planet hath a more lively vigorous Light than any of the other ; therefore wee may inferre, that his Orbe is

is placed next unto the Sunne, as that at B.

As for *Venus*, 'tis observed, That She do's alwaies keep at a set distance from the Sunne, never going from him above forty degrees or thereabouts ; that her Body appeares through the perspective to be forty times bigger at one time than at another ; that when She seemes biggest and neerest unto us, wee then discerne her as being perfectly round. Therefore doth this Planet also move in a Circle that incompasses the Sun. Which Circle do's not containe the Earth within it ; because then, *Venus* would sometimes be in *opposition* to the Sunne ; whereas, 'tis generally granted, that She never yet came so far as to be in a *Sextile*.

Nor is this Circle below the Sun (as *Ptolomey* supposeth) because then this Planet, in † both it's Conjunctions, would appeare horned, which She do's not.

Nor is it above the Sunne, because then She would alwaies appeare in the Full, and never Horned.

Q 4 From

† *Matutina Vespertina.*

208. Wilkins, *A Discourse Concerning a New Planet* (1640) a heliocentric diagram

THE
FIRST BOOK.
THE DISCOVERY
OF A NEW
WORLD.

OR,

A Discourse tending to prove, that 'tis
probable there may be another habitable
World in the Moone.

With a Discourse concerning the possibility
of a Passage thither.

The third impression. Corrected
and enlarged.

*Quid tibi inquis ista proderunt? Si nihil aliud, hoc
certè, sciam omnia hic angusta esse. Seneca præf.
ad 1. lib. Nat. Quæst.*

LONDON:
Printed by IOHN NORTON for IOHN
MAYNARD, and are to be sold at the
George in Fleetstreet, neere St. Dunstone
Church. 1640.

209. Wilkins, *The Discovery of a New World* (1640) title page and frontispiece

URANIES NORICÆ BASIS

ASTRONOMICO-GEOGRAPHICA

sive

Inclytæ S. Rom. Imp. liberæ

CIVITATIS

NORINBERGÆ

situs Geographicus

secundùm

LATITUDINEM

istique æqualem Poli, super horizonta, (Æquatoris etiam) Elevationem, ex observationibus astronomicis deductus, cum præstitutis, Parallaxeos solaris & Refractionum, nec non Obliquitatis Eclipticæ sive maximæ Solis declinationis rationibus : ubi veterum etiam & antecessorum deducta exhibentur & deducenda

secundùm

LONGITUDINEM

ex *Lunæ eclipsium complurium aliorumque* Φαινομένων, *annis retroactis ab excellentissimis Astronomis, in variis Orbis Terrarum partibus & Regionibus, habitis observationibus, cum heic Norinbergæ sibi obtentarum collatione, & deductis inde & à Meridiano primo 40. Locorum extraneorum, distantiis Geographicis pro ulteriori operationum Uranicarum & Geographicarum promotione collectus*

vigiliis

Studio & Opera

Johannis Philippi Wurzelbaur

Civis Norinbergensis.

Sumptibus Authoris.

Anno M. DC. XCVII.

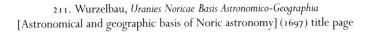

211. Wurzelbau, *Uranies Noricae Basis Astronomico-Geographia*
[Astronomical and geographic basis of Noric astronomy] (1697) title page

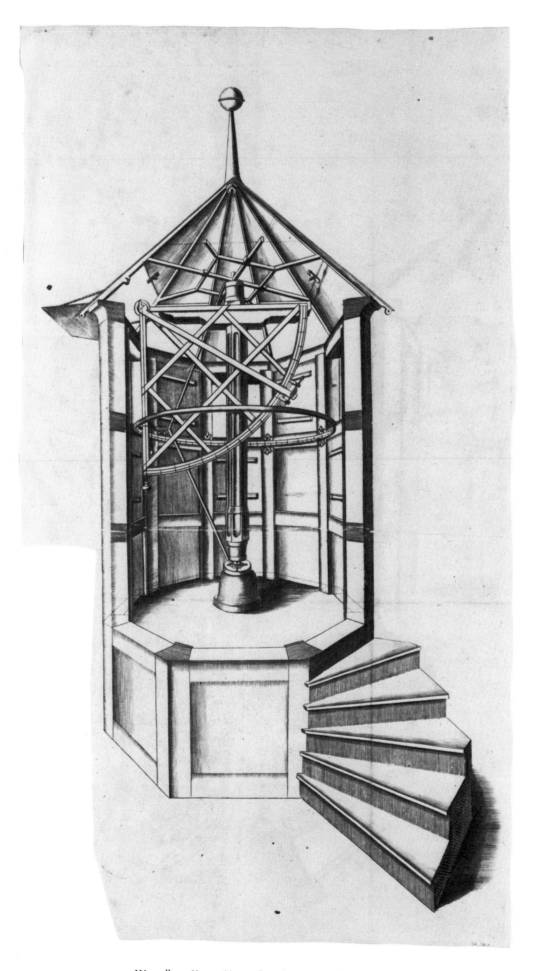

211. Wurzelbau, *Uranies Noricae Basis Astronomico-Geographia* (1697)
cross section of observatory at Nürnberg (reduced)

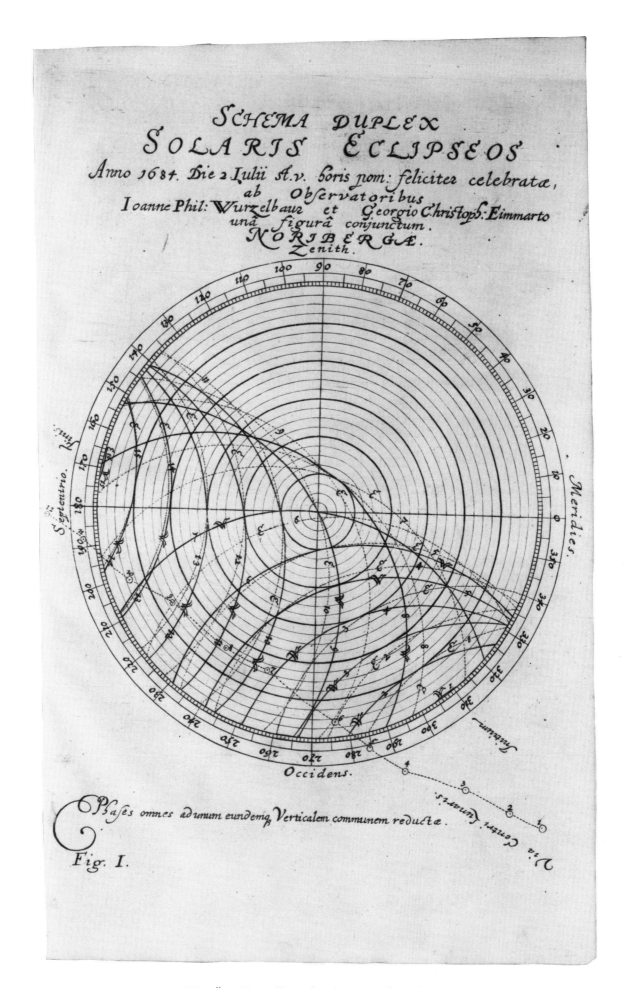

211. Wurzelbau, *Uranies Noricae Basis Astronomico-Geographia* (1697)
diagram of an eclipse (reduced)

URANIES NORICÆ BASIS
ASTRONOMICO-GEOGRAPHICA.

211. Wurzelbau, *Uranies Noricae Basis Astronomico-Geographia* (1697)
folding frontispiece showing the roof of the observatory at Nürnberg (reduced)

INDEX

The index includes the names of people and the titles of anonymous works. Page numbers in boldface refer to the authors and the titles of anonymous works listed in the catalogue.

COLOPHON
CATALOGUE OF RARE ASTRONOMICAL BOOKS
was produced for
FRIENDS OF THE MALCOLM A. LOVE LIBRARY
SAN DIEGO STATE UNIVERSITY
by PERPETUA PRESS, Los Angeles
Edited by KATHY TALLEY-JONES and LETITIA O'CONNOR
Designed by DANA LEVY
Production art by MARY BETH MACKENZIE
Typeset in PERPETUA by CONTINENTAL TYPOGRAPHICS, Chatsworth, CA
Printed by TYPECRAFT, Pasadena, CA
The edition is limited to 1,000 numbered copies

This is copy number **264**